MW01071718

"Li Ma and Jin Li have written an unusually valuable book on the recent history of Christianity in China. Unlike too many others (often speculative or ill-informed), they support their general narrative with extensive ethnographic research. The individuals they have interviewed provide fascinating insights into conversions in prison, the Christian 'harvest' from the Tiannamen Square massacres, effective evangelism at McDonald's and Starbucks, the emergence of Christian NGOs, ongoing tensions between believers and the Chinese Communist Party, the surprising emergence of self-conscious Chinese Calvinist theology, and much more. The result is extraordinary insight concerning perhaps the most important scene of Christian development in the world today."

—**MARK NOLL**
Professor of History Emeritus at the University of Notre Dame,
is the author of *The New Shape of World Christianity*

"*Surviving the State, Remaking the Church* is a truly illuminating book. Based on interviews with Chinese Christians, it provides valuable glimpses into the remarkable stories of how the Chinese churches survived during the era of the most severe repression. It also provides vivid and thoughtful accounts of the many contemporary challenges facing Chinese Christians even as their churches continue to flourish."

—**GEORGE MARSDEN**
Emeritus Professor of History, University of Notre Dame

"Readers in the West and the East alike are keen to know more about life in China, both today and in the recent past. For Christian readers, this eager curiosity extends to the churches of China, the majority of which remain officially illegal and are often hidden. What does it mean to be a Christian in China today? How do today's Chinese Christians remember the past? Why have they come to faith? What difference does Christianity make in their lives? Sociologist Li Ma and her husband, theologian Jin Li, have interviewed over 100 Chinese Christians from various parts of the nation. Their voices, so seldom heard, come through with amazing force. This book reveals the hearts and minds of Chinese Christians as never before."

—**JOEL CARPENTER**
Director, Nagel Institute for the Study of World Christianity at Calvin College

"Ma and Li have given us an invaluable set of voices from China's Christian world. Through patient combing of printed texts and many hours of interviews with people today, they allow Chinese Christians to speak for themselves and let us understand how Christianity has become China's fastest-growing and one of its most influential religions. Understanding China requires understandings its faiths and beliefs, and especially those of its youngest but most dynamic faith: Christianity."

—IAN JOHNSON
Pulitzer-Prize winning writer, Author of *The Souls of China: The Return of Religion After Mao*

Surviving the State, Remaking the Church

Studies in Chinese Christianity

G. Wright Doyle and Carol Lee Hamrin,
Series Editors
A Project of the Global China Center
www.globalchinacenter.org

Surviving the State, Remaking the Church

A Sociological Portrait of Christians in Mainland China

LI MA AND JIN LI

☙PICKWICK *Publications* · Eugene, Oregon

SURVIVING THE STATE, REMAKING THE CHURCH
A Sociological Portrait of Christians in Mainland China

Copyright © 2018 Li Ma and Jin Li. All rights reserved. Except for brief quotations in critical publications or reviews, no part of this book may be reproduced in any manner without prior written permission from the publisher. Write: Permissions. Wipf and Stock Publishers, 199 W. 8th Ave., Suite 3, Eugene, OR 97401.

Pickwick Publications
An Imprint of Wipf and Stock Publishers
199 W. 8th Ave., Suite 3
Eugene, OR 97401

www.wipfandstock.com

PAPERBACK ISBN: 978-1-5326-3460-4
HARDCOVER ISBN: 978-1-5326-3462-8
EBOOK ISBN: 978-1-5326-3461-1

Cataloging-in-Publication data:

Names: Ma, Li, author | Li, Jin, author.

Title: Surviving the state, remaking the church : a sociological portrait of Christians in mainland China / Li Ma and Jin Li.

Description: Eugene, OR: Pickwick Publications | Studies in Chinese Christianity | Includes bibliographical references and indexes.

Identifiers: ISBN: 978-1-5326-3460-4 (paperback) | ISBN: 978-1-5326-3462-8 (hardcover) | ISBN: 978-1-5326-3461-1 (ebook).

Subjects: LCSH: Christianity and culture—China | Christian sociology—China.

Classification: BR1285 M32 2018 (print) | BR1285 (ebook).

Manufactured in the U.S.A.   12/05/17

Scripture taken from the New King James Version®. Copyright © 1982 by Thomas Nelson. Used by permission. All rights reserved.

Cover photograph by Jul Medenblik.

For Calvin Li and Mercy Li

Contents

Acknowledgments | ix

Introduction | xi

1 Captives | 1

2 Worldview | 15

3 Censored | 31

4 Orphans | 50

5 Two Cities | 65

6 CCP | 82

7 Nationalism | 93

8 Charity | 106

9 Calvinism | 119

10 Marriage | 136

11 Education | 151

12 Crosses | 164

Conclusion | 176

APPENDIX 1
A Qualitative Comparative Analysis of Church-Level Data
in Two Cities | 181

APPENDIX 2
A full translation of a CCP document | 185

APPENDIX 3
Translation of an Interview with Gao Feng | 187

Bibliography | 191
Index | 203

Acknowledgments

ALTHOUGH THIS BOOK TOOK us four years to write, the intention of writing a book was not there from the beginning. While teaching in China's universities, we received a grant to conduct a study of churches, and we had intended to write only a few research articles to fulfill the requirements of this grant. With appreciation to Fenggang Yang, the leading sociologist on Chinese Christianity, we spent three years gathering data in China and discussing our relevant findings with him at Purdue University.

The first fruit of this research came out as a book chapter in *Christianity in Chinese Public Life: Religion, Society, and the Rule of Law* (Palgrave MacMillian, 2014) edited by Joel Carpenter and Kevin den Dulk. A few weeks later, in Calvin College's faculty dining room, when we conversed with distinguished historian Joel Carpenter about more stories from this project, he simply asked us, "Why don't you write a book?" This got us thinking. Thus, it was Joel Carpenter who initiated the idea of a book.

Over the next two years, alongside the busy time of having two children, we were finally able to put together two sample chapters. We sent them to Joel Carpenter and also another renowned scholar of Chinese church history, Daniel Bays. Even during his illness, Professor Bays gave us such encouraging comments that kept us motivated to write this book. Without the support and encouragement of these two distinguished scholars, the writing of this book would have been impossible and too daunting to finish.

We have presented different chapters at the Biennial Henry Symposium organized by the Henry Institute of Christianity and Public Life at Calvin College. We are thankful for these opportunities and the continued support from its director Kevin den Dulk and administrative staff Ellen Hekman. We have also benefited greatly from conversations with Professor Cordwin Smidt ever since our Purdue encounter. He has modeled for us both intellectual integrity and genuine servanthood.

A few dear friends have taken time to carefully read our chapters and then offered encouragement and helpful suggestions for improvement. We especially cherish the kindness of Emily Brink and Wayne TenHarmsel.

We are equally grateful for the many faculty and staff at Calvin Theological Seminary, where we completed the last phase of research on this project. Our thanks especially go to John Cooper, John Bolt, Ronald Feenstra, Lyle Bierma, Dean Deppe, Arie Leder, Jinny DeJong, Aaron Einfeld, Sarah Chun, Barbara Blackmore, and Jeff Sajdak. A very special thank you to Seminary President Jul Medenblik for the fine photograph he took in China which we consider such a good fit with our title.

After we finished writing the full manuscript, two other distinguished scholars, Carol Lee Hamrin and Wright Doyle from the Global China Center, further encouraged us as we prepared for publication. We especially thank Wright Doyle for his tirelessly reading and re-reading our manuscript with careful editing and enthusiastic support. We are also grateful for the friendship and conversations with Stacey Bieler, another scholar specialized in Chinese Christianity.

Our special appreciation is also extended to our long-time friends of the China Source team, including Brent Fulton, Narci Herr, and Joanne Pittman. We are deeply grateful to know Dr. Brent Fulton, whose scholarly insights, devotion to mission, and humility in service have always greatly inspired us.

We appreciate many good friends who have encouraged us along the way, including Mindong Lee and Joy Tong at Wheaton College; Jyying Kan, Yan Li, and Siyao Xing at Cornell; Professor Shining Gao and Professor Guanghu He, Wei Zhou, and Jun Wang in China; Zexi Sun and Shengjie Chen in Grand Rapids; Jerry An in Chicago; and Dr. and Mrs. Grant Chan in California. We also thank Harriette Mostert for her careful editing help.

We remember, rejoice and give thanks for the many Christians in China who shared their personal stories with us in this volume.

Above all, our deepest thanks go to the One who gave us two covenant children during the past four years of writing. It is to our children, Calvin Li and Mercy Li, that we dedicate this book from their parents' generation, as an encouragement for the spiritual journey of their own generation.

Soli Deo Gloria.
Li Ma and Jin Li
Grand Rapids, 2017

Introduction

WHEN FOUR EXCAVATORS DEMOLISHED an eight-story church building in China, the world took notice. On April 28, 2014, over 100 armed police tore down the building of Sanjiang church in Wenzhou city, a wealthy region known as the "Jerusalem of China" for being home to the largest Christian churches in China.[1] This demolition was followed by an expanding campaign against many Christian places of worship across Zhejiang province until the time of writing.[2] It is said that these actions were a result of a provincial official's frowning upon the many growing churches that seemed to him "too uncomfortably conspicuous."

Earlier in the same month came an article from *The Telegraph* with the title "China on the course to become 'world's most Christian nation' within fifteen years." It stirred up heated debates on the internet among Chinese netizens. Besides quoting the famous remark by leading sociologist Fenggang Yang regarding religion in China, the article mentions another study that showed Chinese online searches for the words "Christian congregation" (*jidu jiaohui*) and "Jesus" (*yesu*) far outnumbered those for "The Communist Party" (*gongchandang*) and the current president Xi. These recent events and news capture a dynamic and even contentious phase of development for Chinese Protestantism. So, exactly how many Christians are there in China now? Three surveys of religions in China conducted from 2005 to 2007 by the Horizon Research Consultancy Group via a disproportionately urban and suburban sampling found that Christians constituted between two and four percent of the total population.[3] However, getting a reliable estimate of

1. Philips, "China Accused of Anti-Christian," 2; France-Presse, "China Begins Demolition"; Lodge, "Mega-church Demolished"; Li, "China Denies Church Demolition"; Van Sant, "Church Demolition Highlights."

2. Philips, "Thousand Christians Forced from Church"; Johnson, "Church-State Clash in China Coalesces"; Tracy, "China Lifts High the Cross"; "List of 64 Churches Demolished in Zhejiang."

3. Pew Research Center, *Religion in China*, 13.

the Christian population is difficult because a considerable portion of local Chinese will not self-report their Christian identity and affiliation with non-state churches. Fear of harassment from political authorities may be one of the reasons for such under-reporting. Social hostility is another.

When it comes to our knowledge about the state of affairs regarding the growth of Christianity in China, we need more than just statistics and photo images. Unless we gain a sophisticated view of the social context and the dynamic processes that defy naïve generalization, a deeper and accurate understanding will be unattainable. Portraying churches in China as either persecuted or revived captures facets of truth but also obscures the complexity and fluidity of the whole picture. It is our hope that this book will acquaint readers with the real lives of Chinese Christians in their authentic context. This is also why we title this volume as a "sociological portrait," which seeks to deliver a qualitative and realistic presentation.

SOCIO-POLITICAL CONTEXT

Despite a few decades of economic liberalization, China's political regime continues to suppress civic organizations, especially Christian groups. Fear still functions as an internal control upon the minds, behavior and rule-setting of individuals. This socio-political context is key to our understanding of religious growth. As scholars term it, the Chinese still live under an "early subtype of post-totalitarian communist regime."[4] On the one hand, this regime shares features with totalitarianism in trying to maintain a suppressed civil society, where dissent is restricted. On the other hand, the regime is enjoying elite performance legitimacy through subsequent economic growth.[5] Its basis of legitimate order has shifted to the economic realm, and there is a transfer of state domination from the spiritual (or ideological) domain to the material.

Compared to a full-blown totalitarian regime, the Chinese communist regime no longer powerfully imposes a political religion with confirmed communist doctrines and devoted rituals, as it was embodied in Mao worship before 1976.[6] Since Mao's death, the deterioration of this religious aspect has created anxiety for both state actors and for the general public. As a result, the former communist value system, which dominated families, society, and life in general, has been cast aside, leading to a widespread sense of insecurity about the value of the individual and his destiny.

4. Havel, *The Power of the Powerless*; Linz, "Totalitarian and Authoritarian Regimes."

5. Thompson, "To Shoot or Not to Shoot," 63–83.

6. Leese, *Mao Cult*.

Since the 1990s, Chinese society has entered an economically thriving but spiritually depleted situation. Folk religions and different forms of spirituality have revived to fill such a void, but Christianity stands out by spreading a consistent and competing worldview against the waning official ideology of communism.[7] It is worth mentioning that the vast majority of growth happened among unregistered Protestant churches, also known as the "underground" or "house" churches.[8] In this book, we sometimes use terms like "house churches" and "unregistered churches" interchangeably. We do focus mainly on Protestantism when referring to the emerging Chinese Christianity in this volume, primarily because that is the dominant and visible part of expansion, compared to the more underground Catholic groups, to which we personally do not have much access. To document them would be another research endeavor.

A PARADOXICAL REALITY

The growth of unregistered churches is a paradoxical reality in today's China. Because of media censorship by the Party-State, all public media are under strict control; consequently, mentions of Christianity seldom appear in news media. An exception occurred in 2009 in *Southern Weekend*, an influential popular investigative newspaper, when a Christian reporter wrote an article entitled "So Unexpected to See More and More Christians Now."[9] This was the first and only time Christianity and house churches re-appeared in public media between 1949 and the present. The paradoxical reality, therefore, is that despite the growth of Protestant groups and increased mention of Christian faith on the internet, there is little publicity in most state-controlled media except a few articles commanding communist party members not to convert to religions, especially Christianity.[10] A cognitive gap exists with regard to Christianity's actual growth and the average citizen's perception of it.

The secretive existence of churches for over thirty years has also contributed to this gap. Many churches believe small and secretive

7. Aikman, *Jesus in Beijing*, 7; Bays, "Chinese Protestant," 488; Yang, "Lost in the Market," 424.

8. Although both Protestant and Catholic groups under communism have experienced suppression and underground growth, the expansion of Protestant informal networks, known as house churches or unregistered churches, make up a dominant part of the emerging Chinese Christianity. See Kindopp, "Fragmented yet Defiant," 124; Xie, "Religion and Modernity in China," 76.

9. Ying Shen, "So Unexpected."

10. Zhu, "Communist members."

home-gatherings to be the best strategy in terms of fulfilling religious duties at the same time as ensuring security and safety. Since the mid-2000s, with the legalization of private property, some churches have re-organized by using commercial space and opening their services to the public. Even these important changes are seldom documented by those researching China's social transition.[11]

Scholarly research on this topic is also strictly censored, except that which is funded by non-state sources or funding from abroad. The difficulty of doing research about the growth of unregistered Protestantism is an intriguing research topic in and of itself. When we received funding to conduct our research of unregistered churches, we were viewed with constant suspicion regarding our motives for this research project from the university leadership, since we were both working in public universities in China. There was even an attempt to discontinue research projects like ours that receive funding from overseas.

Our research also coincided with a unique phase of social change, another wave of democratization known as the Jasmine Revolution in North Africa in 2011. Social control in urban centers and internet censorship tightened. During our participation in a few international conferences regarding religion in China, a common topic was constantly raised—the sensitivity of this topic and ways that researchers use to avoid harassment from authorities. For this reason, we especially appreciate the truth-telling of the individuals we interviewed despite potential risks.

FIELD RESEARCH AND METHODS

The research we performed was difficult in a number of ways. First, due to the long-term censorship against Christianity, a researcher would not obtain much understanding if he or she relied on official media or surveys conducted by state-sponsored research programs. Secondly, many research subjects choose to block out or ignore the bleak experiences of living under a suppressive regime; and as a result, important individual-level data concerning social-psychological transformations may easily escape researchers. It takes great courage and rational prowess to look back and analyze past events when they were attended by cruelty and violence. A researcher must earn trust in order to gather personal accounts from informants. As members of the unregistered churches ourselves, we have been privileged to collect a rich pool of around 100 individual interviews using our personal networks from 2010 to 2015. The personal accounts in the chapters

11. Ma and Li, "Remaking the Civic Space."

are selected from among these interviews and are not exhaustive. We use pseudonyms (by Chinese surname) for our interviewees, unless their names have already appeared in the public domain. Apart from these in-depth interviews, we have observed approximately 40 churches and faith-based organizations in various cities.

Our interviews and observations were conducted mainly in particular Chinese cities, such as Beijing, Shanghai, Wuhan, Shenzhen, Chengdu, Nanjing and Suzhou. In each city, we first located the existing inter-church networks to gain a sense of the bigger picture in that locality, in terms of which churches are widely-known, the level of theological diversity that exists among churches, and the major milestones that mark the churches' development in that city. To obtain this type of overview, we had to find the most influential or respected leaders in each city; these connections were facilitated by our previous contacts. Then, relying on personal networks, we selected four to five "seed informants" from these networked church groups in each city for our first round of interviews. Upon completion of one individual case, we asked the respondent to refer three to four potential interview subjects that he or she knew well. Then, we selected the next few respondents from these referrals.

This method builds more credibility for future respondents and enables us to develop a more diversified sample of believers across age groups, gender, professions, education levels, and theological backgrounds. Meanwhile, we also participated in local church gatherings, including small-group Bible studies, Sunday worship services and church organizational meetings. During the three years of our study, we tried our best to stay in touch with and to follow up with each of these groups. This practice helped us to track their organizational development over a period of time.

THEME AND ORGANIZATION

As its title suggests, this book presents how Chinese Christians have coped with life in a hostile regime during different historical periods, and how Christian churches have been reshaped by ripples of social change. The social reality facing Christians in mainland China and their experiences are too complicated and dynamic to depend on quantitative measurements alone. An ethnographic analytical lens is a timely attempt to delve into the memories, convictions, changing values, and worldviews of these religious groups.

We felt obliged to write this volume after hearing so many real-life stories as well as reflecting upon them and discussing them with scholars and friends who also yearn for greater understanding about Chinese Christianity. This book captures a unique development of the Christian churches in China— diversification and the formation of group social identities. This is what we mean by the "remaking of the church." Regional variation, theological differences and socio-economic backgrounds diversify Chinese Christians into various subgroups that interact differently with social change.

Founded on this understanding, we discuss the religious involvement and social engagement that are, in the language of Tocqueville, the "ethos" of social life.[12] Our socio-historical analysis of the larger institutional environment intends to shed light on how individual lives are caught in these ripples of social change. These real-life accounts also help to fill in the details of historical complexity, especially how individual beliefs, hopes and hearts are touched and reshaped through reflections that draw out these hidden threads of Chinese history. Through this method, the lost links between theory and reality are restored, and we gain a more sophisticated and informed knowledge of this aspect of China's social fabric.

According to sociologist George Simmel, what makes social life possible is precisely the ethical relationships between individuals that mark the beginning of their communal living.[13] We claim that what makes a system of social order function (or not function) is the internal order of its individual members, an order that encompasses emotions, religious convictions, trust, love and fear. Group-level social norms evolve out of these dimensions. Social scientists tend to underestimate the importance of subjective emotions within individuals, and especially their religious convictions. By relying only on rational theorizing, they lose sight of the fascinating complexity of many human behaviors, and they fail to account for the intricacies of the social order which spring out of these emotions and tensions. These habits of the heart, according to Robert Bellah, undergird the structures of social life.[14] So in these pages you will meet real people in their unique political contexts where the Christian faith reshapes their habits of the heart. Out of these changes antithetical actions and even pioneering institutions sometimes spring up. It is our hope that you will both be amazed and touched by their humanity.

In presenting these narratives, we follow a largely chronological order, from the Three-Self campaign in the 1950s (Chapter 1) and the decade of

---

12. de Tocqueville, *Democracy in America*, 402–3.

13. Simmel, "Fundamental Problems," 3–105.

14. Bellah, *Habits of the Heart*, 3–54.

Cultural Revolution from 1966 to 1976 during with church leaders were imprisoned (Chapters 1 and 2); to a period of the emergence of secretive house fellowships after the release of church leaders in the early 1980s (Chapter 2); mass conversion and foreign Christians' re-entry in the 1990s (Chapter 3 and 4); local variation of church openness since 2000s (Chapter 5); new state-church issues and church-society issues (Chapters 6 and 7); Christians' civic engagement through charity (Chapter 8); theological developments (Chapter 9); challenges in marriage and family living for young urban Christians (Chapter 10); the emergence of a Christian education sector (Chapter 11); and recent changes among Three-Self churches (Chapter 12). Thus, the basic tension between the always-present state and local churches is traced over half a century. Given the complexity of the topic and also out of an aversion towards overgeneralization, we wrote the concluding chapter with much room for further discussion.

1

Captives

> A prison cell, in which one waits, hopes—and is completely dependent
> on the fact that the door of freedom has to be opened from the outside,
> is not a bad picture of Advent.
>
> —DIETRICH BONHOEFFER[1]

SINCE 1949, CHINA'S COMMUNIST regime has considered Christianity an opponent to its ideology. Through banning and cooptation, it has sought to eradicate this religion, as well as other faiths that rivaled communism, from Chinese society. Foreign Christians were evicted from the country, while indigenous leaders were executed or imprisoned. However, these measures did not choke out the seeds of Christianity; they led to its more resilient transformation into a fast-growing religion during the next thirty years. Although Christians believe that the way in which persecution spreads the gospel is a theme attested in the Bible and in church history, such a mystery still needs to be unfolded in China.

In his autobiography *Captive Spirits*, Xiaokai Yang narrates his first encounter with a Chinese Christian in a prison cell in the 1960s.[2] The 16-year-old Red Guard Yang was sentenced to a ten-year imprisonment after publishing a political treatise titled "Whither China?" This decade of experience in captivity turned out to be his "university education," where

---

1. Bonhoeffer, *Letters and Papers from Prison*, 416.
2. Yang and McFadden, *Captive Spirits*, 98.

1

he befriended various intellectuals imprisoned by the communist regime. Through his cellmate, a mathematics Professor Yu, Yang learned English and Calculus. Another Roman Catholic adherent Li was jailed because he refused to worship Mao. Yang was surprised to find that Li acted like a gentleman even in prison. "I marvel over the fact that anyone can be so consistently selfless," writes Yang. It was a time when prison became the only place one could meet genuine Christians.

After his release in 1978, Yang entered graduate school without a bachelor's degree due to his imprisonment. Later, he won a scholarship to study for a doctoral degree in Economics at Princeton University. Afterwards, he held a postdoctoral position at Yale University. By 2002, Yang had become a world-renowned economist who was twice nominated for the Nobel Prize. This was also the same year when Yang finally embraced the Christian faith after being diagnosed with cancer. In the last two years of his life, Yang published some important articles that campaigned for democracy from a Christian perspective.[3] For example, his treatise *My Second Testimony* centered on how his biblical worldview called into question his professional views on the value of modernization. This article was very instrumental to bring many educated Chinese into Christianity in the mid 2000s.[4] In our fieldwork, we heard many young people mentioning Yang's testimony as a contributing factor in their conversions.

Another widely spread prison cell Christian testimony that brought about many conversions is the story of Zhao Lin, a famous female activist and martyr. Like Yang, she was also born into a family of the privileged "revolutionary" political elite. Nineteen-year-old Lin was a devout follower of Mao who wrote letters calling him her "father" even during her earlier years of imprisonment. The authorities intentionally put her in the same cell with a Christian, with the intent that her thoughts be straightened out when debating with her stubborn, believing cellmate. Before her execution, Lin used her own blood as ink to write letters, with words of lament from a believing heart:

> Why would I still hold a humane hope for you [China]? What is this compassion in my heart? At its root, it is nothing but mercy and conscience given by my Heavenly Father. . . . I cry for you because you are burdened with sin and evil, which are drowning you in the swamp of destruction. Sirs, you who enslave others! Know that you are not free yourselves![5]

3. Yang, "Christianity and Democracy."
4. Yang, "My Second Testimony."
5. Quoted in Hu, "Searching for Lin Zhao."

The stories of imprisoned Christians under the first two decades of China's communist regime were seldom told: they were forbidden and became forgotten. These rare stories we read today portray the amazing resilience and freeing power of the Christian faith in the most dreadful human situations. Even prison cells created by communists became a training ground for new converts.

We tried to interview some Christians who had prison experiences when starting our research, because we are convinced that a project like this would be incomplete without their stories. However, many of these people are advanced in age or have already passed away. Therefore, we can provide only one direct account of an eighty-four-year-old medical doctor, Yuan, who had spent ten years in communist prison as well as two short accounts from those whose family members suffered imprisonment. We use these narratives to show the complexity of what really happened to most Chinese Christians between the 1950s and 1970s. There is no need to further explain that Christians had a marginalized and even criminalized status in new communist China, for they belonged to the lowest social class because of their religious ideology and affiliation with the West. But how the communist regime attempted to staunch the growing church at that time is a topic worth studying. To some extent, the Communist Revolution from 1949 to 1979 was a success, because never in China's history had the country been penetrated with an ideology so absolutely as it was under communism and Maoism.

SEEDS OF FAITH BEFORE 1949

The two decades prior to 1949 in China were years of religious tolerance. They were also times of growth for home-grown Protestant movements in China. Many government and military officials were baptized Christians.[6] Evangelism and church-planting were allowed, as were the ministries of influential figures such as John Sung, Wang Mingdao and Watchman Nee, etc. Although variant in their theological backgrounds, these founders of different sects came out of missionary-run churches. Protestant missionary work in the 1920s left a comprehensive social impact on the Chinese society by establishing schools, universities and hospitals.[7] For example, by the late 1920s, various missionary groups had founded fourteen universities, while

---

6. Song, *A Recovered Diary*, 350.

7. Hunter, *The Gospel of Gentility*, 6.
Bays, "Christianity in China 1900–1950."
Bays, "From Foreign Mission to Chinese Church.

China at that time had only three state-run universities.[8] These were the primary means of expanding the influence and of training modern personnel for Christian churches. As historian Jonathan Spence notes, "Through their texts, their presses, their schools, and their hospitals, the efforts of foreign Christians affected Chinese thought and practice. The strength of that influence is impossible to calculate . . . they protested foot-binding, commiserated over opium addiction, offered religion and education as sources of solace and change, and a new perspective on social hierarchies and sexual subordination."[9]

After 1949, civil space was compressed to a minimum through the wave of violent communist revolution. The communists sought to destroy the "old China" and rebuild a new social order through the nationalization of key resources, such as land, capital and labor allocation. The *hukou* system was installed to forbid residential mobility even during famine years. Communists also eradicated free market enterprises such as commercial guilds and private businesses. In the countryside, the gentry class which used to be a pillar of its civil society was completely wiped out through violent executions. The communist rule directly penetrated into rural villages by installing the most politically loyal cadres as watchdogs for any social activity outside of their direct control. From the 1950s to the 1970s, self-governance in urban and rural communities was not permitted. Most importantly, social trust and interpersonal networks were undermined after a series of political movements. This period also nurtured a political culture that rewarded betrayal and impersonal political loyalty to the Chinese Communist Party (CCP).

The communist rulers also utilized the involvement of the US in the Korean War to propagate nationalist fervor against "imperialist infiltration." As Spence says, "Given momentum by the anger and excitement of the Korean War, a second mass campaign was directed at domestic 'counter-revolutionaries.' Millions of Chinese who had worked for KMT or foreign organizations were closely investigated. In the summer of 1951, the CCP leadership launched a series of mass rallies in large cities to publicize this new campaign against domestic subversion. This campaign later grew in brutality, intensity and thoroughness, leaving lasting trauma for almost every Chinese person.[10] Urban authorities also used this campaign of terror to attack religious groups, including the most widespread sect of Yi Guan

8. These Christian universities were set up in succession, including St. John's University in Shanghai, Hangzhou College, West China Union University in Chengdu, Huazhong University in Wuchang, Nanjing Ginling University, etc.

9. Spence, *The Search for Modern China*, 208.

10. Ibid., 535.

Dao ('Way of Basic Unity Society')."[11] Spence notes that public media were used to disintegrate the old social order: "Propaganda networks were also developed, consisting of trained experts who could work through the media and through small discussion groups to encourage compliance with the government policies. One function of these cadres and propagandists was to break down the often tight personal, emotional, and family bonds."[12] It was also during the Maoist reforms in the 1950s when Christian groups became the targets of suppression due to their connections with foreigners.

A NEVER-ARRIVING VERDICT

The son of a family of medical practice, Yuan (pseudonym) was converted in his twenties and received an excellent education in a Christian-founded medical school in Beijing in the 1920s. His parents served with foreign Christians from the China Inland Mission in the 1940s. When Yuan was twenty years old, he entered into a pre-med program at Shanghai's St John's University. It was a campus dotted with western Gothic architecture and alive with Christian evangelism. One day he saw a Christian fellowship event flyer posted on the campus bulletin board. Such flyers were seen everywhere on the university campus. During this special gathering, a student preacher passionately spoke about God's love and called people to accept that love. Yuan's new life started from that day as a true follower of Christ. His heart longed for the path of sacrifice and glory, as his favorite hymn "The Path of the Cross is Sacrifice" illustrated.

The group with which Yuan later affiliated was the "Little Flock" (*xiaoqun*), also known as the Chinese Local Assembly (*juhuichu*) founded by Watchman Nee. It is a Protestant sect whose pietist theology has left the most far-reaching impact on Chinese Protestantism to this day. It is characterized by a pessimistic and separatist view of end-time Christian living centered around the "truth of the cross."

After graduation, Yuan was appointed to a job in Beijing. Yuan recalls the way religious space in Beijing was reduced to a minimum. In the early 1950s, an effort began to nationalize Christianity, both Protestant and Catholic, under the control of communist rulers; a few pro-communist religious leaders were selected for a committee which later became the Three-Self Patriotic Movement (TSPM). Those who refused to join became targets of public denunciations (*kongsu*) and were declared enemies of the state. The imprisonment of two religious leaders marked the state's determination

11. Ibid., 534.
12. Ibid., 537.

to eradicate Christianity: Watchman Nee, leader of the Protestant "Little Flock," and Kung Pin-mei, Catholic Bishop of Shanghai. Numerous Christian leaders were imprisoned or sent for "re-education" in harsh labor camps for up to twenty years. This widespread communist campaign was assisted by a powerful propaganda machine. Christians were stigmatized as traitors. Believers were pressured to accuse one another. An active leader of the young men's fellowship, Yuan was also listed as an "internal control element" (*neikong fenzi*) whose activities should be closely monitored. He remembers:

> Although I survived the *sufan* movement (meaning "against counterrevolutionaries") in 1957 by keeping silent about most things, my documents were labeled "internal control." Later I learned that even a family I used to visit and dine with were requested to report to the Party about my reasons for meeting with them. Once I had a conversation with two brothers of the church in a park pavilion. This scene was caught and reported as one of my criminal acts. We were reported to be conspiring against the Communist Party by helping Taiwan.

Yuan recalls being spied on, reported, and even betrayed. These strategies were used by Party watchdogs from the early 1950s. Even a private wedding celebration at a public park was spied on; this surveillance was later used as a cause for accusations against many of the party-goers. Furthermore, Yuan tells:

> In 1958, we were told that college students should not go to church activities any longer, because everyone had to work. After the church merger, those who gathered there were very different people, including many liberal Christians.[13] They took turns preaching. Once someone stepped onto the pulpit and said, "Who is God? God is we the people!" We felt very upset listening to it. Then there came another command saying that children under the age of 18 should not participate in church. Before that we had children's Sunday school classes. But this was something new. Later on, they forbade us to linger in the church after Sunday worship. So we were not allowed to talk to each other in church after that.
>
> As a result, from 1958 to 1962, our brothers and sisters only met a few times. Once it was the occasion of someone's wedding.

13. The nationalization of Protestant churches into designated worship sites was a successful political ploy to arrange believers into a system under the control of the Communist Party. After their worship space was either confiscated or merged, the pulpit messages were required to propagate nationalist and Communist ideology.

Another two times they were picnicking in the suburbs. But we did not speak about spiritual matters, and only sang hymns together. I remember our last outing was in 1962, a farewell party in the park. A group of forty Christians met in the woods of a park. We didn't even sing hymns. A sister read a letter to this couple as farewell, and then a brother recited a poem. That was it. But later the Public Security Bureau found us out and interrogated many of us. They had spied on our activities. They knew who were there, even who had arrived first and who left last. All our activities were closely watched by them.

In 1968, Yuan was accused of complaining about church matters, which had happened ten years prior when he was leading the young men's fellowship. Since then, his crime changed from being "counter-revolutionary" to "leading a counter-revolutionary group." They paraded Yuan as a public denunciation ritual and sent him to the Public Security Bureau (PSB).

Although in detention, Yuan felt more at peace because this temporary jail would protect him from even more violent campaigns outside. He had seen people being tortured to the point of disfigurement. However, in the detention center he was closely watched day and night. Sleep was not allowed. He was required to show remorse for what he did and to write up a detailed confession letter to the Party.

It was May at the time when Yuan was detained in Beijing, and his wife was working in Shanghai. Every day he waited for a verdict or for a visit from his family. The wait lasted until November, but nobody showed up with a verdict or with daily necessities. Yuan wrote to his wife, asking for some winter quilts and personal items. The following May there was still no verdict. Nobody even came by to interrogate him anymore. He recounts:

> When I protested about this situation, they sent people to me saying that my case was still under investigation. But it had been two years! I had been jailed for two years without a hearing or a verdict. I am a medical doctor. What is to become my future? Can I still perform surgery? Then I started writing to my wife, asking her to consider remarriage, because I might stay in prison for a few more years. We had been married for ten years by then. And she is a strong believer too. So she replied saying that she would wait for me no matter what happened next.

Next, Yuan was transferred into a labor camp as a part of his corrective training. His job was to clean toilets and feed farm animals. Later Yuan learned that even his wife was sent into corrective training because she was the spouse of a counterrevolutionary. She was a pharmacist but was later assigned the task of gardening and cleaning.

Yuan's verdict never came, and he had been imprisoned for ten years already. He later learned that as a member of the Little Flock, his "counter-revolutionary" label would last a life time. As counter-revolutionary elements, Yuan and his wife were not been allowed the freedom to travel and visit each other for those ten years. When Yuan was telling us his story, his silver-haired wife sat silently by his side with a meditating calmness on her face.

Even in 1976 when the Cultural Revolution ended, someone from the Beijing PSB found Yuan, asking him about his reflections upon his time of correction. The Party's label on Yuan had changed from "enemy conflict" (*diwo maodun*) to "internal conflict among the people" (*renmin neibu maodun*). But as a Christian believer, Yuan was told that he had been classified as "counterrevolutionary" from the beginning. "Do you realize your problem?" asked the cadre. Yuan said, "My problem, after ten years of prison? No." That was the end of the conversation between Yang and the Party.

In the late 1970s when things started to improve, closely-knit group gatherings of believers reappeared in private homes. In limited *Danwei*-owned space, trust among in-group members was a key to keeping the community functional. But when trust in this type of environment is undermined, not only does the community lose cohesion, but a fear and distrust for each other sinks in, weakening all social relationships. Yuan recalls how spies worked around him after they resumed secretive home gatherings in 1974:

> The political environment was still very hostile. Some believers found me and asked if they could come to our home to read the Bible together. So we sometimes had a meeting of six people; then the next day somebody would be taken away, for he or she was reported. Then we had to change our meeting location for the next time. But after our next meeting, someone in our group got reported again. So I later figured out that even among the six believers, there must be someone who worked for the Party and reported on us.

Secret spying and open monitoring continued until the 1990s. The street committee even hired people to guard his doors, counting how many people went there for a worship service. Another time Yuan was told by neighbors living across the road that someone from the authorities used their balcony to spy on Yuan's home. They also wire-tapped his phone.

Since the late 1980s, a Bible study group has formed in Yuan's home and started to gather more regularly. At the same time, more and more previously imprisoned believers like Yuan were released. Such home gatherings became customary among them.

FAITH-KEEPING FAMILIES

Imprisonment and house arrest still happen to Christians in China today, though not as frequently and haphazardly. However, there has been a major change in how church networks deal with these clampdowns. Originally, the Christian faith mainly spread through kinship and closely-knit networks, but between the 1950s and the 1970s, these social relationships were undermined by betrayal and distrust. Therefore, individual Christians were placed in very isolated and vulnerable positions to cope with state violence, such as haphazard imprisonment. It was also due to such risks that even parents were afraid to talk about the Christian faith with their children. Prison cells, on the other hand, became the most public place where one's Christian faith could be revealed, and an effective diffusion channel for the faith. Again, it is hard to quantify the number of conversions due to prison experiences; however, these social connections in the most unlikely places did spark flames that transformed lives.

Forty-year-old Wang was born into a family of believers in Shanghai who were part of the Little Flock assembly. While political movements were swirling, Wang's parents never taught him any Bible knowledge. They dug holes in the backyard and hid their Bibles there. Even so, Wang learned to pray from a very young age with the help of his grandmother. In the 1950s, they were forced to worship in Three-Self churches where sermons resembled "political reports," according to Wang. They were not allowed to linger for fellowship after the sermon.

Wang's faith suffered many setbacks because of the persecution in his family, including frequent raids by communist cadres and the imprisonment of his two older brothers. His oldest brother was an excellent student, who had admired Mao greatly from an early age. Fearful of persecution, Wang's parents dared not openly teach their children about God or against Mao. As a result, their firstborn son believed the Marxism and Leninism he was taught in school. As Wang recalls about his older brother, he says, "My parents just prayed for him. After he joined the sent-down movement to a remote region of China, one day he heard God calling him, and he was converted. He prayed through all kinds of dangers."

Later the family relocated to the countryside, and their fellowship meetings secretly resumed among relatives. By the 1980s when rural churches re-gathered, Wang's older brother won first place in a rote memorization contest of the book of Romans. And it was also the occasion when his future wife fell in love with him because of his good command of Bible knowledge. This brother also became a preacher of the Word, and he has been arrested several times for distributing Christian literature and for open air preaching.

Wang's second older brother had a weak physical condition, so from childhood he was always bullied by others. In 1980, he went to study in the US through the assistance of relatives, but God called him back two years later. He wanted to preach, but even Wang's father warned him about imprisonment. However, he could not be deterred from doing it. He said that God's calling to him was too strong to deny. He was arrested three times and spent a total of ten years in prison. Wang visited him once at a labor camp. "Even after all these trials," says Wang, "I could see that he became more zealous for God. Today some communist cadres still come with threats, but he would reply, 'Arrest me if you will, but do not talk me into your plan.'"

Fifty-year-old Liu grew up in a family that had been stigmatized during the communist campaigns. His paternal grandmother had preached with foreign Christians during the 1940s. When the communist regime took control, his maternal grandfather escaped to Vietnam. Since then, their family has been classified as having two of the most severe offenses against official communist ideology: Christianity and overseas connections. During the Cultural Revolution, Liu's home was a constant target of raids by the Red Guards. They often tied up his grandmother and parents and threw them into a stable without food for a few days. Once Liu saw his grandmother being tied to a tree and whipped by Red Guards until she lost all her teeth. These violent scenes left traumatizing marks on Liu's youth. To him, Christianity seemed to be associated with a harsh existence.

On the other hand, Liu has warm memories of how faith was lived out in his family. He was close to his grandmother because he grew up under her care. Although his grandmother was illiterate, she was very brave and wise when telling people about Jesus Christ and quoting the Bible. She knew many Bible verses by memory. Liu also remembers the loud prayers of his grandmother at five o'clock every morning:

> I often felt annoyed by her loud praying voice. Once I kicked her with my little feet and asked her to stop praying. Grandma said back to me in tears: "My boy, if we stop praying, our home is no more. God is our only hope."

Liu now understands what his grandmother meant. Their daytime was often filled with labor assignments, and evenings were used for denunciation meetings and sometimes violent public beatings against those who became targets of the day. Each early morning, prayer time was a period of release for his grandmother and parents. It was also a time of regaining the conviction that God was with them.

Liu seems to have grown up in a most hostile environment, but the resilience of his family taught him something stronger, as he says with gratitude, "I have not had a doubt about God despite all these things." What these bitter memories left him is a stronger desire for justice, and it has motivated him to find answers. These life-searching questions finally grounded him deeper into the faith to which his family held so tightly. Liu later became a preacher, just like his grandmother. He said at the end of our interview: "This is also a prayer answered, I believe."

HOUSE ARREST

As we have previously mentioned, imprisonment of Christians for their faith is now rare but not nonexistent. House arrest and detention are probably more common. Since the 2000s, some prominent churches as collective groups have emerged as a form of resistance against state suppression. This posture has been a remarkable change from the past because never in China's modern history had Christianity taken on a collective face in public. Even their experiences in prison cells became a collective presence. We include the account of Xu in recent years as an example to show this change in recent years.

After spending fifteen days in one of Beijing's suburban detention centers in the summer of 2011, Xu was released only to realize that he and his family would be placed under house arrest for the next six months. Xu was not unfamiliar with the procedures—no outing is allowed except grocery shopping when the family is accompanied by "body guards" who tail them at a distance. By that time, the pastors and elders of Xu's Shouwang Church, which has gained the global media spotlight, had been under house arrest for three years.[14]

Thirty-eight-year-old Xu holds a master's degree from one of Beijing's prestigious universities. When taking a Bible Survey class in 2001 with a renowned professor at his university, Xu became interested in Christianity

14. Hsu, "Why Beijing's Largest." In 2009, Shouwang fundraised over twenty million *yuan* (around four million dollars) to purchase its own facility, but the Beijing authorities forbad the property developer to hand the key over to the church.

and often stayed longer to ask questions. The professor was a publicly-professing Christian and an elder of the Shouwang Church; he also brought Xu into their home gatherings of mostly young professionals who worked in Beijing. After graduation, Xu took a job with a state-owned publisher that offers high pay and good benefits. In 2007, Xu decided to quit his decent job in order to found a Christian publishing company with a friend from church. His pay was reduced to half of what he used to earn, and the family had to relocate to the outskirts of Beijing, where living costs were lower.

By 2009 when Shouwang's property was taken away by authorities and congregants lost their rental lease due to political pressure, members of this church decided to assemble and worship outdoors. They gathered at public parks or plazas, where authorities were always present to round up the crowd. This tug-of-war-like drama went on for months before authorities adopted harsher measures. They detained participants of outdoor worship and recorded all their information, including IDs, addresses and job contact. Then relatives, landlords and employers of these participants, who were often not believers, began receiving threatening phone calls. These associates were used to put more pressure on members of the church who were part of outdoor worship. Many young people lost their jobs. Some were told by their landlords to terminate their rental lease. Despite these measures, a dozen or two congregants still ventured outdoors for worship. Later, detention happened more frequently, from a few hours to a few days. Xu was arrested twice, spending two days and then fifteen days in jail. He published an online article entitled "My Story in the Cell" documenting how he spent the time there. An excerpt follows:

> Rules in the cell normally allow reading newspapers and books, but I was not allowed to enjoy such privileges. Sometimes I received postcards and letters from brothers and sisters which diminished my regret of not being able to read more. I shared these postcards and letters with others in our cell. All of us read them with care, once, twice even three times.
>
> Singing is allowed in the cell as long as your singing is not too loud to attract the guards. Hymns were welcomed in the cell. I sang "The Most Beautiful Blessings" and "Life and Sun above the Cloud" to my cellmates. Lines from the latter hymn— "while I lie in a valley of darkness" and "sprinkles of rain fall on my face"—resonated with the condition of the cell and our emotions.
>
> Besides drug addicts, I met a wide range of other people in prison, including those arrested for prostitution, gambling, stealing, and black market selling, those who broke traffic rules

as well as petitioners. When I was put on duty, I prayed for everybody with whom I came in contact each day. I asked God to give me opportunities to talk with them—and to give me the right words to speak. In the first ten days, God answered every single prayer on my list. So, this prison stay became a special retreat for me. It revived my prayer life, renewed my zeal for the gospel, and rekindled my love for all kinds of people in this land. During nap time on my duty days, I watched these strange and familiar faces, this sleeping group who appeared both pathetic and lovely to me. My heart went out to them in prayers, and a love surged out of me towards them. It was in these moments that I found myself falling in love with this place. I even had desires to stay in prison longer.

Xu and his Shouwang friends are a collective testimony in prison. His cellmates knew a few names in his church very well, because these Christians were detained on and off for a few years. Knowing that his time in jail was not going to be long, Xu intentionally made friendships and shared his Christian faith with everyone he met. He even gave a public farewell address before his release with these words: "I am leaving today, but I might come back again. You don't need to remember my name. Just remember that I am a Christian."

CONCLUSION

Prison cells have been the testing grounds for the Christian faith. They have been places where vitality and authenticity of the faith attracted more followers too. In a way, the harshest means of persecution under communism, such as imprisonment and martyrdom have often produced results counter-productive to the Party's intention. It is indeed a remarkable fact that even three decades of harsh communist rule in China failed to eliminate Christianity. After the eviction of foreign Christians and the imprisonment of church leaders, it actually became a miraculous period when the faith spread widely. How was it possible? Although it is hard to provide an estimate of how many conversions happened in communist prison cells, the above accounts are quite forceful in depicting how faith not only survived communism but also took on a powerful vitality against evil and despair. Biblical imageries of imprisonment and unjust persecution provided these captives of faith with a spiritual goldmine of comfort and endurance in similar situations. Accounts of vibrant prayer life show that the Chinese gulags have trained them to stand more solidly in their faith.

The personal accounts of this chapter also show how China's churches went underground. The strategies employed by the communist regime were significantly reshaping the church's social structures. Firstly, they did so by encapsulating the public space into the state machine staffed by watchful communist cadres. It was a gradual process with a series of state commands limiting church activities, but the final goal was the discontinuation of worship meetings and religious speech. Secondly, communist cleansing tactics changed social norms of trust. Betrayals were encouraged even among close-knit groups, such as kinship networks, disintegrating inter-personal trust. From public parks to private homes, all social relationships were reduced to a politicized, spied-upon battlefield.

Freedom of assembly is an inherent pursuit of Christian groups. Even in the harshest conditions, Christians had to gather and worship. Underground or secretive worship, a common storyline of believers in this era, has made Christian fellowship more formative to believers. These less than ideal conditions have screened out the comfort, ease and prosperity which often cause inertia in a Christian's faith journey. As Christians profess, once freed in Christ, being a captive in prison cell cannot annul that freedom; once having tasted the joy of heavenly release, being a captive in prison cell cannot bring about much gloom.

2

Worldview

I believe that with the loss of God, man has lost a kind of absolute
and universal system of coordinates, to which he could always
relate everything, chiefly himself.

—VACLAV HAVEL[1]

I believe in Christianity as I believe that the sun has risen:
not only because I see it, but because by it I see everything else.

—C.S. LEWIS[2]

THE COMMUNIST REGIME IN China promoted a worldview so absolute that
any deviant thoughts would bring penalty and ostracism. Socialist values
and outlook towards the world have penetrated all textbooks and curricula
from elementary schools to university classrooms—"The communist worldview, outlook and values on life is the most scientific and correct progressive
worldview."[3] Those who suffered years of violence, fear and confinement

1. Havel, *Open Letters*, 94.
2. Lewis, "Is Theology Poetry?"
3. Gong, *Cultivation of Thoughts and Morality*, 13. This is a succinct expression
found in a required college course "Cultivation of Thoughts and Morality and Basics of
Law." In 2014, China's Education Ministry reminded all schools to use socialist values

long for alternative perspectives for looking at life. Conversion accounts from our fieldwork often include a shift in worldview. Chinese Christians value the new worldview they are growing into precisely because they have tasted what it was like to live under an antagonistic one.

In 2011, we interviewed Professor Wen (pseudonym), who works at a prestigious university in Shanghai and who still recalled some bitter childhood experiences that had once impaired his self-esteem and attitudes towards Christianity. Wen's mother, who converted in the 1940s, was politically categorized as a "counter-revolutionary" during the Cultural Revolution (1966–76). As a result, the family's farm land was confiscated and their food rations reduced, leaving them in dire poverty. With almost all social ties being cut, it became very difficult for them to make a living. Moreover, Wen's whole family became a target of scorn and contempt by villagers because of the religious affiliation of his mother. Overwhelmed by these traumatic memories, Wen had always felt averse and embarrassed about his family's background as Christians. Due to fear, his mother seldom read him the Bible, which was hidden under her bed. All these circumstances left him with a grudging resistance to believe in God. Nevertheless, he was also unable to embrace the Communist ideology and worldview after witnessing its total failure. His heart hungered for something else. It was not until three decades later when he visited a Chinese church abroad that had converts with similar experiences to his own that he again embraced his mother's faith. He said that what made a critical impact on his conversion was still the power of a consistent Christian worldview.

AN IRON-CAGE WORLDVIEW

Wen's family endured the typical treatment of Christians under Communist rule. Society regressed into a closed system of exclusion and violence, ironically contrary to the progressive view held by Communist ideology. Existing ties between Chinese society and the outside world, especially the link between Christian churches, were cut.[4] The borders of China were sealed to prevent migration, and all social organizations were forced to sever their external connections. Internally, the communist regime staffed its state machine with politically loyal cadres. Through these professed Communists, the state advanced ideological control even to the village level.[5] Living

---

as their foundation and the cultivation of a socialist worldview as their goal.
China Education Ministry, "On Cultivating and Implementing."

4. Hsu, *The Rise of Modern China*, 660–670.

5. Fairbank, *The Great Chinese Revolution,* 282. Fairbank argues that "this

under this transformed regime, individuals were faced with totalitarian control, whereby all social relationships, including family, work, religion and neighborhood, became surveyed and controlled by an "Almighty Party."

The Communist worldview was strengthened by the imposition of a social system like an iron-cage. Psychological intimidation was ubiquitous, carried out through secret police and *kongsu* movements (public denunciation and shaming) that planted seeds of distrust and fear into the hearts of every individual, isolating each one from the rest of the society.[6] Organizationally, the state nationalized all work relationships into a central-planning system made up of work units, including urban *danwei* and rural communes. Individual workers and peasants earned "work-points (*gongfen*)" in order to be supplied with food rations through their work units. Thus, the work unit established an "organizational relationship" (*zuzhi guanxi*) with every individual by tracking his or her class category, political background, marriage and family information. To sum up, these arrangements deprived individuals of any non-communist ideological and organizational affiliation. Through "thought work" (*sixiang gongzuo*) and a socialist distribution system, the state transformed people into "screw spikes" (*luosiding*), a frequently used propaganda metaphors for submissive and politically loyal members.[7] Such an individual must submit his or her own will and understanding to the party-state. Under this ideological monopoly, any worldview or ideology not aligned with Communism is seen as illegal and counter-revolutionary. By mobilizing common people to spy and report on each other, an atmosphere of anxiety and distrust prevailed. Individuals who dissented faced execution, imprisonment or labor camps.[8]

Consider the ideas of Czech politician and literary critic Vaclav Havel: since people are forced to submit to such violent rule, every individual's pretense and lies feed into the habits of the society, making it impossible for most people to question the legitimacy of such ideological terror. Gradually, everyone becomes an accomplice of this system.[9] This method is how, un-

---

organization of the countryside was far more complete than anything attempted in Chinese history." According to the estimates by historical sociologist Theda Skocpol, the Chinese government during the Qing Dynasty hired around forty thousand officials, and the number increased to two million in 1948 under the Republic of China. However, by 1952, the Communist system was staffed by three million cadres, which grew to eight million in 1958 and seventeen million in 1961. Skocpol, *States and Social Revolutions*, 260.

6. Solomon, *Mao's Revolution*, 405–509.

7. Reed, "Moral political education," 99–111.

8. MacFarquhar, "*The Cambridge History of China*," 253–58.

9. Havel, *The Power of the Powerless*.

der totalitarianism, fear becomes an enslaving and alienating power. In this process of "normalization," people lived an outer conformity without inner conviction. How to survive under totalitarianism is a question facing every individual in such a society. We use the oral history of two individuals to show how their conversion to Christianity provided them with a competing worldview to endure harsh realities.

As we wrote in the preceding chapter, beginning in 1950, Protestant groups became the targets of socialist reconstruction, and believers who joined the Three-Self system later ended up with assigned labor tasks instead of religious activities. Furthermore, churches merged so that the number of church buildings decreased.[10] The hymns in Three-Self churches were unified, and all religious activities were stipulated to happen "within specific locations and times" (*dingdian dingshi*). Church leaders who did not submit to this state-sponsored organization suffered brutal persecution and long-term imprisonment.[11]

Communist regimes re-orient human society in profound ways. They do so, not primarily through altering the economic systems reflected in the reconstruction of a nationalistic state, as theorized by the Marxist materialistic-historical view; on the contrary, Communist movements seek first to change social relationships and the ethical order within the family.[12] Even family members and relatives of those so-called "counter-revolutionaries" were socially ostracized, for their "organizational profiles" (*zuzhi dangan*) included negative labels. For example, high school students applying for college were required to fill out a form with one question about religious beliefs in the family. It was used to exclude young people with this "black

10. Zhao and Zhuang, *A Contemporary History,* 136–37. For example, in 1950 Shanghai had over two hundred church buildings, which dropped to eight in 1958. The number in Guangzhou dropped from fifty-two to one, and Beijing from sixty-six to four. By 1966, when the Cultural Revolution began, even these previously approved church buildings were closed down.

11. A leading figure among the resistance group was Wang Mingdao, who published a declaration of faith "We Resist because of Our Faith" in 1955. Two months later, he was arrested. According to our fieldwork interview data, the Shanghai government arrested over 30 leaders of the Local Churches (also called Little Flock) in 1956, followed by a public trial. An interviewee Y from the Little Flock recalls that he once watched a brother Zhang being arrested while walking on a street, after an unknown woman ran up to embrace him. He was accused of sexual assault and immediately executed without trial. It is a common practice for Communist prosecutors to bring false accusations against those who did not conform.

12. Schurmann, *Ideology and Organization,* 73–104.
Solomon, *Mao's revolution,* 160–247.
Hsu, *The rise of modern China,* 658–659.

element" in their family background.[13] Because state propaganda did everything to stigmatize individuals with counter-revolutionary tendencies, and fear was so prevalent, social prejudice against dissidents was intense as well.

SECRET CONVERTS UNDER MAOIST CAMPAIGNS

During our fieldwork, we interviewed Zhang (pseudonym, male, 65) who was converted in the high tide of Maoist campaigns. What struck us in his narratives is how he attributes the cause of his conversion to a world-view change. When we became acquainted with Zhang, he had been a famous doctor of Chinese medicine in a Southwestern city. He also leads a 200-member unregistered church. Our interview with him lasted over four hours, the longest among all our taped interviews. When our digital recorder alerted us that there was no more space, Zhang still had much to say. He had driven forty minutes from the suburbs to see us. Zhang also showed an excitement in telling us all about himself. Although we are thirty years younger than Zhang, he did not hesitate to share his life with us. As he told us from the beginning, "Young people need to learn so much about the social background of that time. If this history is not passed on to you, we would be letting God down."

Shortly after Zhang was born in 1946, his father (a primary school teacher) learned about Communist thought and began to work underground for the Communist Party. He soon lost touch with his family and joined a revolt in Xi'an that ended in his imprisonment by the KMT (Nationalist Party in the Republic of China). He was quickly released for lack of evidence and found a job back in his hometown's government. After the Communists came to rule, Zhang's father was suspected of collaborating with the KMT since they had released him. He was soon classified as a Rightist (*youpai*). Since then, political prejudice had always accompanied Zhang, including his schooling and his work. He explains:

> My father was expelled from public office in 1957 for being a Rightist. The Communist Party thought him a traitor because he was released by the Kuomintang. After that time, our family became very needy, and I was only ten. On top of our economic difficulties and political discrimination, my father had tuberculosis. My mother supported our family on her own through her

13. Cheng and Selden, "The Origins and Social Consequences," 644–668. During the socialist re-education campaigns in 1956, individuals were categorized into different classes which became the basis for their career opportunities, life and welfare such as promotion, marriage, housing, schooling and food rations.

hard work and perseverance. Our condition deteriorated until
we were starving. By 1960, my father had dropsy.

When I applied to college in 1965, it was already impossible
for Rightists' children to gain entry. But since I scored the highest in my hometown, and despite belonging to the notorious
"Five Black Elements" (*heiwulei*), they made an exception for
me to enter medical school. After a year of study, the Cultural
Revolution began and classes were suspended for six years.

During this time, the Communist movements were intense
among college students. I would not participate in all the activities, for I am the son of a Rightist and a Five Black Element. At
the same time, I was not inclined to give up my studies, so I
taught myself Chinese medicine in secret. Later, when required,
I would be present in every political meeting, but since children
of Rightists were scorned and their opinions dismissed, I just
sat there and kept scrawling in my "Quotations from Mao"
book. Actually, I was writing down medical notes, but everyone
thought that I was actively absorbing Mao's thoughts.

It is important to note that by 1966, the worship of Mao had reached
its climax.[14] Although some scholars think that people worshipped Mao
out of their rational choice, it seems that that they actually projected their
self-interests into it.[15] The object of worship was actually Mao's power of
charismatic domination, using a term coined by German sociologist Max
Weber.[16] Since Mao-worship was the only legitimate form of assembly, these
actions became largely symbolic, for almost all opposition had been elimi-
nated by that time.[17]

Because of his political status, Zhang was not qualified to join the
Red Guards. This kept some distance between him and the official ideology
imposed by the Communist state. He also had an instinctive repulsion to
Communism due to his past. In Zhang's own words, what he observed during this time taught him to doubt and think:

At the beginning of the Cultural Revolution, I believed the
propaganda. But in November of that year, I recognized these
things to be a political struggle among Mao and other top leaders, by reading and analyzing the Big Posters (*dazibao*). I began
to ask serious questions: What is truth? What is wrong with
this world? If I had not grown up seeing my family mistreated,

14. Leese, *Mao Cult*, 108.

15. Wang, *Failure of Charisma*, 249.

16. Weber, *Economy and Society*, 215–216.

17. Yang and Fadden. *Captive Spirits*, 131, 138.

perhaps I would have readily believed the official ideology. But because of what we went through, I was naturally disgusted with it. I was able to see its defects. I am now able to thank God for this.

In 1970, our whole medical school was sent down to the countryside for Labor Re-education (*laodong gaizao*). Some were assigned the task of planting corn, and others were sent to the mines. I was appointed to make fermented vinegar. Those were relaxing days, and I remember writing to my family thanking the Lord of Creation (*zaohuazhu*) for such good luck, although I did not know God then.

During this time, Zhang carried on a romantic correspondence with a former female patient. This was his second time in a romantic relationship, after a relationship in high school did not end well due to his political background. That first girl's family vehemently opposed it after learning that Zhang's father was a Rightist. Zhang's second girlfriend was poor and had tuberculosis, so he expected their status to be a good match. This may be unthinkable today, but in the central planning system, one's education, work and marriage were all closely tied to one's political status. Rightists' children faced great disadvantages in all these opportunity structures.

Zhang's choice of girlfriend now met opposition from his own family, mainly because of her illness. After Zhang's grandmother passed away, he brought his girlfriend to attend the funeral in his hometown. Opposition and conflicts escalated within the family. He had never felt so helpless. Then the thought of a school teacher, Li, came to his mind. Whenever he ran into troubles, Zhang turned to teacher Li to confide his thoughts. Below is a life-changing conversation for Zhang, and he remembered it word-for-word:

> I told him about my difficulties, and we talked for a long time.
>
> Then I asked him, "Li *Laoshi* (teacher), why are you always full of joy, even after so many political movements? Why are you different from other people?"
>
> He answered with a smile, "An empty sack does not stand."
>
> I probed further, "What is in your sack then?"
>
> He replied, "I am a Christian."
>
> Hearing this, I thought to myself, "Of course you are. And that was precisely the reason why you were sent to *Jiabiangou* (a labor camp)!" His answer appeared funny and irrelevant to me.
>
> So I asked him again, "Li *Laoshi*, I am not looking down upon you in this matter, and I know that you are a Christian. But what does it have to do with my question?"

He said, "You don't understand: Christianity is a worldview."
Then he started sharing the gospel with me.
It was the year 1971.

In the 1970s, it was still a dangerous thing for a Christian believer to share his or her faith with the intent to evangelize others. If reported, such actions would invite further political suppression. By this time, even the Three-Self system had been banned and closed down. Teacher Li well knew the political consequences his evangelistic actions could bring about. He had returned from the harshest labor camp *Jiabiangou*, also called China's Gulag, a concentration camp mainly for Rightist intellectuals and "thought criminals" (*sixiangfan*).[18] According to Teacher Li's memoir, around three thousand people were registered there from 1957 to 1960, but over half died of starvation by 1960.[19] The camp was abandoned a year later, after Li was released. Li considered his survival a miracle from God.

Zhang chatted with teacher Li all night. Although he came to Li seeking advice about relationship problems, Li unfolded a deeper answer for him—the Christian faith. Their conversations covered many teachings from the Bible. Zhang's present problem receded, and his long search for questions about truth and reality of the world was rewarded. He happily embraced it:

> After he told me about God's creation, man's sin, eternal punishment and faith in Jesus, I said to myself: "This is TRUTH!" This message is not like Maoism's "Strike down this person today and that person tomorrow. . ." How could that be truth? He also showed me Matthew 5–7. Those words were so sweet and comforting to me: "Do not worry about tomorrow, for tomorrow will worry about itself. Each day has enough trouble of its own." Then, after I heard about the final judgment, I wanted to believe! With all these injustice around us, there MUST be God's final judgment!
>
> Teacher Li also gave me a mathematical formula because he is a math teacher: Eighty divided by infinity equals zero. As he explained, eighty means eighty years of joyful living in this life, and infinity refers to the existence of hell which involves eternal pain and suffering. The result of zero means that eighty years of

18. Ai Xiaoming, a professor of Zhongshan University filmed about Jiabiangou labor camp. She was detained in May of 2014. When her documentary *Jiabiangou Elegy: Life and Death of the Rightists* came out on the internet in 2017, it was well received but soon banned. And also see Yang, *Jiabiangou Memories*; Gao, *In Search of Home*.

19. Li, *A Journey of Salvation*. Li could recall this figure because he did registrar work for the camp in 1961.

bliss may end up in nothing. He also gave an alternative explanation: eighty years of suffering for the sake of God divided by
the eternal bliss of heaven equals zero too. So, in summary, it
does not matter whether you live eighty years of earthly bliss or
suffering; what matters most is the direction of infinity, heaven
or hell.

I accepted this immediately, because all the teachings of
Communism had already collapsed within me. I think of all the
difficulties and prejudice my family had gone through. How we
need judgment from a just God! Otherwise where can we find
peace? So on the one hand, judgment appealed to me greatly.
But on the other hand, I felt terrible thinking of myself under
God's judgment if I would not believe in Jesus. Where could I
go to escape God's terrible judgment? So, I repented of my sin
and believed.

A week later, I had to leave my hometown. I did not own
a Bible and did not know where to find other believers. But
teacher Li prayed for and encouraged me. He said, "Although
your girlfriend is sick, you have to know that God can work
miracles. You should keep praying." After that time, I prayed to
God wherever I went.

This first week of Zhang's conversion was the only source of knowledge
he gained about Christianity. Over the following eight years, Zhang never
had the chance to see a Bible. It was still a dangerous thing to possess one.
Actually, from 1949 to 1986, the printing and selling of Bibles was illegal.
People like Li preserved religious knowledge by memory and passed it on by
secret oral teachings. Later, whenever Zhang came across insurmountable
difficulties in life, he would write to Li for more teachings from the Bible.

I wrote to Teacher Li, saying that although I believed in the
gospel, my life had entered into a most difficult stage, including
financial need, exhaustion from overwork, persecution at my
workplace and family strife. I told him that I could not live on
any more. I wanted to keep trusting God, but it was so hard
without any spiritual support. Teacher Li wrote me back and
said, "I did not expect that you would believe so readily. God
will bless you." Then he wrote three Bible verses in the letter:

All things work together for good to those who love God,
to those who are the called according to His purpose (Romans
8:28).

For in it the righteousness of God is revealed from faith to
faith (Romans 1:17).

Not by might nor by power, but by My Spirit (Zechariah 4:6).

I returned only once to my hometown during these years. Teacher Li and I had a few days to talk together. He shared testimonies and his understanding of the Bible. I enjoyed our conversations very much. Then he lent me his personal New Testament Bible, a small pocket-size one which he brought to Jiabiangou. It was exceedingly precious, for this book kept him company in great trials there. I secretly carried this little book with me, and I even shared the gospel with two people.

Although many preachers and ministers suffered long imprisonment or died in labor camps, the Christian faith was preserved and spread by survivors or by family tradition. Although sociologists of rational choice explain the conversions following Christian martyrdom in the early church by the effects of their "moral shock," this explanation does not apply to conversions under modern totalitarianism.[20] Since the state propaganda machine had attacked religion with the most negative labels, and many religious leaders were framed by false accusations, martyrs under Communism were so misrepresented that the common people lost respect for both them and the church.

Li did not encourage Zhang to find a church nearby, for it was almost impossible. During the Cultural Revolution, the state had closed all religious sites. Religion was classified among the "Four Olds."[21] Some released church leaders started secret meetings in their homes, limited only to trustworthy friends and relatives. Because everyone lived in *danwei*-provided housing, these meetings had to be held with extreme caution so that no watchful eyes would report them. Scholars conclude that these close-knit and high trust networks, through which authentic personal testimonies circulated, were the mechanism of mass conversion during persecution.[22]

HOUSE FELLOWSHIP

In 1979, Zhang's job relocated him to another city. Through a friend, he was referred to Pastor Liu, a minister who had been working for China Inland Mission before 1949, and was imprisoned from 1958 to 1979.[23] After

20. Stark, *The Rise of Christianity*, 163–190.

21. The propaganda term "Four Olds" refers to Old Thoughts, Old Habits, Old Customs and Old Cultures.

22 Stark, *The Rise of Christianity*, 191–208.
Vala and O'Brien, "Attraction without Networks," 79–94.

23. The official journal of the state-sponsored Three-Self church, *Heavenly Wind*, published an article about a public denunciation against Liu in its October issue of

his release, this pastor's home became a meeting point for many believers. Zhang came in touch with Pastor Liu at a desperate time. His marriage was falling apart, and his unbelieving wife had reported his religious identity to the Communist Party Committee of the hospital where he worked. Pressure and controversy surrounded Zhang:

> I did not have the qualifications to join the Party, or even the Communist Youth League. But the General Secretary of the Party, the head of our hospital and other two other thought work cadres wanted to talk with me. They were quite polite because they came to my home. The first question they asked me was, "Doctor Zhang, are you a Christian?" I answered yes. Then, all of a sudden, their faces looked downcast, saying, "The Party has nurtured you for so many years. Why wouldn't you believe in the Party? But you turned to Christianity?!"
>
> I was put on the spot, so I started explaining what my faith is about, the gospel. The director of our hospital impatiently interrupted me, saying "Let me ask you this. Do you say Chairman Mao is in heaven or in hell?" It was a big challenge.
>
> I answered, "I have no knowledge to say anything about him, because I have only seen his picture and did not know him personally." Our conversation ended in a stalemate, but after that, I became a thorn in their side. They tried to push me aside whenever they could.
>
> Whistle-blowing between husband and wife happened quite often during the Cultural Revolution, at the encouragement of the Party. The Communist political culture relied on this form of betrayal to establish its domination over individuals' loyalty and trust.[24] As Christian, Zhang did not divorce his wife after this, and their marriage lasted until the 1990s, when she passed away.

With tension at his workplace growing, Zhang desired to know other believers. He was accepted into a small group at Pastor Liu's home eight years after his conversion. With loving warmth and care, this secret fellowship of believers took the place of his family in an age when loyalty to other people was shunned:

> Whenever we had a meeting, the pastor's family would prepare good food even though it was a very difficult time economically for everyone. They were so sacrificial. I observed that they were

1958 (page 8).

24. Cheng, *Life and Death in Shanghai.*
Yang, *Spider Eaters.*

frugal people, but they gave lavishly to others. On top of this, I envied the harmony and unity in that family.

It was a spiritual home where I heard many good testimonies. I still remember one of them. A believers' family became a target to be humiliated and denounced during the Cultural Revolution. They took a young woman up on the stage, and asked her mother-in-law to sit and watch her from the front row. This old woman held up her face with a smile and looked at her daughter-in-law. She later said, "I was praying and did not feel embarrassed, for my daughter-in-law was suffering persecution for the Lord's sake. It was an honorable thing." That story was such a faith boost for me.

I also remember an Uncle Long, who treated me with such love. He had many children, so they were just making ends meet. Once he noticed that I was wearing a worn-out pair of shoes. He started saving money and bought me a pair of leather shoes. He gave them to me saying that I could wear them to evangelize more people. You have to know that in 1979, those shoes cost 15 *yuan* (roughly a month's wage)! It was too precious a gift to me, so I ended up giving them as an offering to the church.

Within Zhang's vocabulary at this time, the word "church" still conveyed imperialist connotations due to the influence of Communist propaganda to which he had previously been subjected. Although he has been a persevering believer, Zhang had never wanted to belong to a church. After a few secret meetings in this warm home, however, he was overwhelmed with such enriching and encouraging experiences. He regretted his own ignorance and uttered in surprise: "So this is what's called a church! How could I have been bought into their lies about the church, after rejecting so many of their other lies?"

Pastor Liu soon became Zhang's next spiritual mentor. His background was also remarkable. Like many other non-conforming ministers, Liu suffered imprisonment because of his unwillingness to join the Three-Self system. During twenty-one years of imprisonment, Liu never renounced his faith. But interestingly, on the first Sunday after his release, Liu went into a Three-Self church building to worship there. When asked about why he would go there, Pastor Liu gave an insightful response:

I was put into jail in the 1950s because I did not join the Three-Self. The system back then was trying to brainwash you and to turn you into an atheist. But the Three-Self system today is different. It is mainly used for a united front (*tongyizhanxian*), not to convert you to atheism. So this is why I am willing to worship in a Three-Self church now, because I intend to show them that even after twenty years of so-called "socialist reconstruction," I am still a believer in Jesus Christ. I am sitting there every Sunday for no other reason than to witness my belief.

We learn from similar accounts in our fieldwork that the line between home-based Protestant believers and Three-Self attendees became blurry after China's economic reform. Since 1978, the Communist party-state has been reforming its central-planning system. Economic pragmatism was accompanied by a slow loosening of ideological control. Building a "united frontline" was recast into a principle of utilizing all social resources for hands-on economic development. In order to revive market activities, many social boundaries that had been closed were opening up.

BIBLE SMUGGLING

Even after 1979, the process of China's opening-up has been very gradual, and political control over religion remains tight. For example, the printing and selling of Bibles became legal only after 1986.[25] Before that, foreign Christians had to smuggle Bibles into mainland China, through organizations like Open Doors. House-church believers were needed to assist foreign Christians in such illegal activities. Due to this, Zhang experienced another unprecedented trial, and Pastor Liu was re-imprisoned.

In 1983, a brother from Asian Outreach shipped us a box of about ten Bibles. It was the first time I saw a complete Bible. I then contacted a sister who worked on the train and entrusted a few Bibles her to bring to Teacher Li in my hometown. Li then gave a few to a rural church there. That church had many believers, but not even one Bible. Later I learned that Pastor Liu was re-arrested because of his involvement. I was also on the state security's blacklist after that.

In 1984 there was an eight-month long Strike Hard movement (*yanda*) across China to clamp down on crimes. State security officers also interrogated me for eight months. They mainly asked me to write up reports of what we had done. I wrote every day after work such that my report was 70 pages long, with the main facts. Pastor Liu had already been arrested by that time. They wanted to know whether it was I or Liu who

25. Even today, Bibles may be distributed only through Three-Self bookstores with limited time windows. Some of these bookstores are open only for a few hours on Sundays.

handed a contact list to Westerners. They knew a lot about what we did, and I later learned that it was because my hometown location was searched and they found many letters I wrote.

Writing confession reports was a way that state security interrogated politically disloyal suspects. They often did so repeatedly to frighten and exhaust the targets. They also lured them with opportunities for promotion. Zhang recalls fear fermenting inside of him during the long eight months of constant harassment and searches. In the two years while Pastor Liu was jailed, he became paralyzed; he died soon after his release. After that, Liu's home-based church lost many members, including Zhang. He left partly because of the guilt of leaking information about Pastor Liu. According to Zhang, the next ten years marked a weak phase of his spiritual journey.

We include only a few highlights of Zhang's life due to the volume of events he shared with us. Waves of political persecution did not shape him into an apolitical person; rather, they confirmed his political views. After Zhang became a leader in his own home-based church, he emphasized church history in his teachings, including the relationship between the Three-Self, the government and house churches. As a participant of the city's Political Council, Zhang annually submits a proposal advocating for the legal rights of Christians who gather in homes. In the proposal, he also includes a detailed research reporting corruption in the Three-Self system. When asked about the prudence of such a proposal, Zhang's words left us with a strong impression: "It is not possible for me to be an atheist in politics while being a Christian in faith. My life needs to be holistic." This level of integrity is not common among non-state church members. Interestingly, we came across another church leader who happens to be on the Political Council in another city. Although he refused a formal interview, through casual conversations we learned that he avoids revealing his religious identity because it might bring "inconvenience" to his church.

Our interview with Zhang started in the food court of a shopping mall, moved to a quieter Starbucks shop, and ended in a hotel lobby for better recording quality. Each location was like a time tunnel, bringing us back to the different historical stages of his life. The Christian faith was a sacred canopy sheltering him from despair and fear under a totalitarian regime. It also marked his identity as a politically disadvantaged doctor. As the repressive regime oscillates between hostility and tolerance towards Christianity, fear comes and goes like an old friend. But even during the weakest part of his spiritual journey Zhang was taught precious lessons that later equipped him to step up boldly for his faith.

CONCLUSION

Anthropologist Arthur Kleinman (2006) wrote about a Chinese doctor, Yan, who experienced the most tumultuous and warring years in China since the 1930s.[26] It left Mr. Yan with such trauma that even when Kleinman interviewed him a few decades later in the United States, fear of the Communist regime and for his safety and that of his children continued to haunt him. Many people who have lived under the Communist regime share similar sentiments. Ideological terror and fearful persecution have sunk deep into the people's minds and hearts, thus internally orienting their ways of thinking and behaving.

Communism and Christianity clash because they exhibit two contrary worldviews and systems of ethical relationships. The former desires to embed all social relationships, including family ties, into a collective political system, while the latter allows individual initiative to seek a transcendent yet realistic meaning expressed through equal and loving social relationships. In other words, while Communism exerts control on individuals' minds and hearts through external means of violence, Christianity reforms individuals from the inside out. This is what we mean by "internal order."

The totalitarian domination of the Chinese Communist Party penetrated all spheres of society, families and communities after 1949. The Communist state propagated a worldview of secular salvation, which seeks to emancipate the masses from other forms of religious superstition.[27] A new set of social relationships was established such that individuals were directly monitored as arranged by the monopolistic party-state. Even human emotions were manipulated to produce political loyalty. A deep fear sank into the internal psychological structure of individuals, who endured the cruel political movements during the 1950s and the 1960s. Fear became the foundation that enabled the regime to govern.

We find in our fieldwork that individuals who were politically marginalized grew more distant from communist ideology and atheist education. Such a sense of deprivation makes conversions more likely to happen among this group.[28] Even among converts in the 1990s, as we will discuss in the next chapter, many experience the same deprivation and need for some alternative value system. Other socialist contexts offer similar examples, such as the conversion of Russian writer Solzhenitsyn. People who lived in

---

26. Kleinman, *What Really Matters,* 80–119
27. Smith, "Talking Toads and Chinless Ghosts," 405–27.
28. Glock, "The Role of Deprivation," 24–36

cruel Gulags could draw closer to the Christian faith than those who lived in comfortable Moscow.

When the Communist ideal is contradicted by reality, the Christian faith provides a re-orienting worldview, which is even more precious during the darkest times of persecution. It is recognized as offering some positive "weapons of the weak."[29] Ironically, this role of religion to comfort the oppressed with an ultimate purpose of life seems to fulfill what Marx said about religion before his famous "opium of the people" remark: "Religious suffering is, at one and the same time, the expression of real suffering and a protest against real suffering. Religion is the sigh of the oppressed creature, the heart of a heartless world, and the soul of soul-less conditions."

The holistic worldview of the Christian faith gives shelter to Chinese converts as a sacred soul-sustaining canopy. For example, it offers a comprehensive understanding of all areas of life as aspects of God's creation. Such a worldview incorporates history and experience, both at the individual and cosmic level. Its emphasis on the universal principles of justice and truth shapes all areas of life, and even the injustice of an atheist Party-state is encompassed within this God-centered framework of understanding reality. This holistic Christian worldview does not escape human suffering but rather sees it through the lens of God's own incarnation and atonement in this world and divine retribution. Serving as a driving force and a re-orienting of one's purpose in God's plan for this world, it grants people hope for the future even in the midst of suffering and injustice.

---

29. Scott, *Weapons of the Weak*, 304.

3

Censored

In a time of universal deceit, telling the truth becomes a revolutionary act.

—ANONYMOUS

WHEN CHEN (PSEUDONYM) INCLUDED his cell phone number on the front advertising board of his suburban tree nursery, it was just a matter of time before the authorities would take action. The final digits of this number were "8964." In the fall of 2011, this sequence of numbers was a sufficient reason for a demolition order by the government. Later, Chen was secretly arrested.

Almost three decades after the Tiananmen crackdown on June 4 of 1989, "89" and "64" are still the most censored numbers in mainland China. Although annual memorials of this movement are well attended events in Hong Kong, inside China it remains such a sensitive topic that the slightest hint of 89 or 64 would bring government censure and even violence, as Chen's story illustrates. Journalist Louisa Lim, in her book titled *The People's Republic of Amnesia*, writes about this part of Chinese history and the futile habit that "Chinese people are practiced at not dwelling on the past," with Tiananmen being one of the "episodes of political turmoil that have been expunged from official history or simply forgotten."[1]

Chen is, in fact, one of the student activists from the summer of 1989, who has become famous as one who designs boards with this string of sensitive numbers to protest the state's attempts to erase the memory of this

1. Lim, *The People's Republic of Amnesia*, 5.

event. Chen humorously calls himself "a performing artist." One of his daring ventures was very well known. On June 4 of 2007, he sent an obituary request to the local Newspaper: "Salute the mothers of 64 victims!" This small item hid itself in the midst of numerous other rental ads, commercial information and obituaries, but the Propaganda Department of the Chinese Communist Party (CCP) eventually found it. This local newspaper came under an intense investigation, which led to the dismissal of a few staff members. It turned out that a newly-hired editor of the advertising page, a 24-year-old college female graduate who had no idea about the 1989 Tiananmen democracy movement, unwittingly approved it. Chen had told her that 64 stood for some natural disaster.

The sensitive numbers 89 and 64 in today's China are reminders of the democracy movement that marked a turning point in Chinese society. This violent crackdown against initially peaceful demonstrators severely challenged the Communist ideology, and it was followed by widespread disillusionment and demoralization. Despite the state's attempt to censor references to this event, the crackdown has nonetheless turned into a powerful symbol of protest, followed by an aftermath of religious conversions.

CRACKDOWN AND MASS CONVERSION

The most profound consequence of the Tiananmen crackdown was a widespread spiritual and moral crisis as the CCP's moral authority collapsed. The decade after the Tiananmen killings encompassed a deep spiritual crisis for China, accompanied by an astonishing growth of all kinds of pseudo-religions, including Qi Gong (literally "Life Energy Cultivation") and the rise of Falun Gong groups.[2] It was also a time of mass conversion of mainland Chinese to Protestantism.

The term "mass conversion" refers to the social phenomenon whereby the adoption of a new religion or faith happens on a large scale within a relatively concentrated time frame. As testimonies, memoirs and journalistic accounts suggest, the 1989 crackdown and these conversions are both temporally and causally related.[3] During our fieldwork, we often heard individual accounts about the significant role that the Tiananmen crackdown played in one's spiritual journey. Not only did Tiananmen-affected

---

2. Chan, "The Falun Gong in China," 665–683.

3. Chai, "Tiananmen 10 Years On," 25–26.
Chai, *A Heart for Freedom.*
Fu and French, *God's Double Agent.*
Yuan, "The 'June 4th' Generation Today," 192–95.

conversions happen on a large scale, but common emotions, reflections and discourses also emerged from individual accounts.

These narratives present striking similarities. First, they all began with strong patriotic love of their country and high hopes for real reform and improvement after the excesses of the Cultural Revolution. After the crackdown, the collapse of a nationalistic ideology that propagated a Messianic quest was acutely felt. Traumatic disillusionment was so widespread that the expression of strong sentiments, such as "Life is meaningless" or "There is no hope to live on" often appear in narratives.

Secondly, the Communist party-state engaged in a total repression of the democracy movement through not only the violent crackdown but also the subsequent set of cleansing measures and censorship against collective commemoration. Despite liberal policies for economic enterprises to develop, pro-active social groups that have to do with democracy in general experienced continuous suppression. Individuals, out of a deep fear and disillusionment either preferred not to mention the events of June 1989, adopted a form of self-censorship and turning their devotions elsewhere (e.g. materialism), or embarking on a faith quest.

We also find that post-1989 conversion took place across different cohorts, age groups, education levels and occupations. This chapter is based on the first-hand accounts of those who say that the Tiananmen events were the cause for their conversion to the Christian faith.

Disenchanted Devotee of the Party

In conversion narratives of believers who are 50 years old and above, they often place the 1989 Tiananmen crackdown into a series of historical events, including the Communist movements since the 1950s, which gradually disintegrated their Communist beliefs. Maoism sponsored a non-theistic ideology that displayed distinctly religious characteristics.[4] The state demanded the unconditional subservience of citizens, and an absolutist ideology became China's ultimate condition for forty decades. To many new believers who went through waves of political persecution and violence, their conversion to the Christian faith was preceded by a gradual detachment from the official Communist dogma, which finally disintegrated after 1989. In our field interviews, we found striking similarities in the accounts—all began with strong love for their country and high hopes for real improvement after the Cultural Revolution, followed by the Tiananmen events being the final straw to crush both their loyalty to and hope in the regime. Many also

4. Yang, *Religion in Chinese Society*.

mentioned a sense of betrayal and distrust of their earlier faith in the CCP as the Savior of the Chinese people. Thus, the disillusionment after Tiananmen did not form suddenly, but resulted from a gradual disenchantment with a state-enforced pseudo-religious value system.

Having lived through the major Maoist movements, sixty-year-old Huang (pseudonym) was once a zealous believer in Maoism. Motivated by a strong devotion to give his life to the country and the Party, Huang joined the Red Guards' march in Beijing at the age of only thirteen. He wrote numerous poems expressing his loyalty and love for the CCP, as well as his hatred towards class enemies:

> We blindly worshipped Mao because all we knew was a closed propaganda system, and we could not distinguish what is true from lies. I had such a passion for the Communist ideal that the Party led by Mao appeared to be the only Savior. So when the Cultural Revolution started, I followed Mao; and when the Party called the youth to go to the countryside, I was eager to go.

The legitimacy of Communist leadership was built upon a type of charismatic authority, which peaked during the Cultural Revolution. Although the state warred against all forms of religion, the deification of Mao won millions of devotees so that a Maoist pseudo-religion profoundly transformed Chinese spirituality.[5] For example, families began their day with a form of worship called "Morning Inquiry and Evening Report" (zaoqingshi wanhuibao), when family members stood before Mao's picture before breakfast asking for blessings and instructions for the day; in the evening, a similar ritual was performed by a quiet confession of the wrongs during the day. Some schools and workplaces also practiced such rituals.[6]

Huang's enthusiasm for Mao cooled after he joined the "sent-down youth movement" (zhiqing xiaxiang) to rural China, where he saw Chinese peasants living in stark poverty and learned about the internal strife among the Communist leaders, such as the rebellion and death of Lin Biao in 1972.[7]

---

5. Slogans like "Long Live Chairman Mao," "the Red Sun," "the Messiah of the Working People," and songs like "We think of you every minute, Respected Chairman Mao" show that Mao was deified and widely worshipped. Mao's public appearances were like religious revival meetings to the worshippers. During economic slowdown, Mao worship even boosted the industry of icon-making and metal was diverted from other industries so that icons and badges of Mao could be made for everyone to wear. Not only were Mao's writings distributed nationwide, artists put on stage plays narrating Mao as the Messiah of China. Mao was also said to have supernatural power to heal the blind and make the dumb speak.

6. Zuo, "Political Religion," 99–110.

7. Lin once enjoyed high prestige as a second-tier leader under Mao, and he was

Before Lin Biao was denounced as a traitor and class enemy, Lin once criticized the youth sent-down movement as "an exile in disguised form." Huang and his friends secretly agreed with this opinion. Life in rural communities, including sleepless nights spent reading and discussing the social reality with other sent-down youths gradually led to Huang's disenchantment. By the end of the violent Cultural Revolution, Huang had become disillusioned with Communist ideology:

> Since my teenage years, I have been exposed to the political conflicts and struggles between subgroups within the Communist Party. Oftentimes, after the Party commended someone as good and loyal, the next day the opposite was taught and this person was labeled a class enemy. The whole thing was terrible, and people turned against each other all the time. This political culture carried on into workplaces.

Huang's conversion from a zealous, party-state devotee to Christianity was a gradual process. Discord within the Communist Party, such as the Lin Biao incident, once caused many intellectuals to doubt, and these dissenting voices later led to the Xidan Democracy Wall movement in 1978.[8] Over two decades later, the 1989 Tiananmen crackdown served as a wake-up call to the general public. At the beginning, the democracy movement seemed to have produced unprecedented public civility, which we term the "Tiananmen ethos"—a positive moral impact of peaceful student demonstrators on the wider society—and which has become a distinguishing moral sentiment for other groups to voluntarily embrace.[9] The aspiring sentiments, enthusiasm and nationwide support of this movement is unprecedented in post-1949 Chinese history.[10] Furthermore, the nonviolent strategies adopted by students, such as hunger strikes, showed their strong moral grounding.

During the summer months of 1989, Huang hoarded major newspapers that favorably covered the movement. Even the state media also predicted that the student movement would end in victory. He also witnessed inspiring scenes on the streets when people from all occupations, including some elderly, marched on the street and called for anti-corruption reforms. Nameless volunteers prepared water and food for the demonstrators.

---

the most likely successor to Mao.

8. Jin, *The Culture of Power.*

9. Strand, "Protest in Beijing," 1–19.

10. Miles, *The Legacy of Tiananmen.* According to Miles, the Beijing authorities once mapped out the sites of demonstrations exhibited at Beijing's Military History Museum, and it showed more than 80 cities. Taking under-reporting into account, the actual number of cities might be higher.

According to what he heard and saw, even thieves in the city were so inspired by the students on a hunger strike that most of them stopped stealing. Huang went to see the crowd and parked his bike randomly without worrying about it being stolen. Nobel Peace Prize winner and imprisoned dissent writer Liu Xiaobo also wrote about the swelling compassion of the general public:

> I helped raise funds on the afternoons of May 15 and 16 by walking around the Tiananmen Square with a donation box. I talked to them with tears. After two rounds, my tears dried up and my throat cracked. Donations of over four thousand yuan came from workers, private-business owners, peasants, cadres, intellectuals, policemen, the elderly and children. I recall that a young woman asked her child to put a fifty-yuan bill into the box, and the little boy came up with sobbing words, "Thank you big brothers and sisters. I hope to join your hunger strike when I grow up." A poorly-clothed elderly peasant came up and donated one hundred yuan. On the west side of the monument, a group of journalists from People's Daily held up two banners saying, "The Student Movement is Not a Mob!" and "We Did Not Write the April 26 Editorial!" They applauded during my speech, and almost all of them made donations.[11]

But things changed overnight. Huang heard from a radio broadcast of the Voice of America that there were shootings against students in Tiananmen Square. After the unexpected military action, the whole nation recoiled in shock and fear. Nobody previously believed that the army, which prided itself in being a "people's army," would actually shoot students. Media reports state that most soldiers did support the students; however, the shootings did happen, and tanks crushed young lives. Such unforeseen and savage violence left a deep wound in millions of Chinese. What was crushed overnight included not only a lively and burgeoning civil society, but also the sentiments and emotions linked to this movement. No public space was given to mourn the loss of those courageous lives. The contrast between the civil ethos before and after the crackdown could not have been sharper. As observer and journalist James Miles recalls, "those tumultuous seven weeks generated more heartfelt, sustained emotion in China than any other event since the Cultural Revolution."[12] The event served as an awakening to how ruthless the regime truly was. The last beam holding up the idol of a Savior

---

11. Liu, "The Nobility of the Common." We quote this from the Internet because Liu's writings were banned. It is important to note that the average monthly wage of an urban worker is around fifty *yuan*.

12. Miles, *The Legacy of Tiananmen*.

party-state collapsed inside millions of Chinese like Huang. When Huang recounted his memories of June of 1989 during our interview, tears came to his eyes:

> We used to have some hope for this government after the open-ing-up policy in 1978. But the crackdown crushed all there was left. It was like a final crash of the stock market—hopeless. All we wanted was to live like good citizens, but would the state not allow this? I was sorrowful unto death. It was painful to bear. A few of my neighbors secretly discussed among ourselves and agreed that, with such violence, the Communist Party wouldn't last very long.

After the crackdown, Huang made up his mind to "find a religion." He read Buddhist texts and befriended Christians. Since he had always enjoyed singing, Huang joined a Three-Self church choir in late 1989 and was bap-tized there five months later. Looking back, he comments on politics from a Christian perspective: "The Communist Party sees itself as the Savior of all, and that is why it never repents. Its culture and doctrines do not have a provision for repentance. So I think the biggest problem with the Chinese society comes from people's belief." Like Huang, many converted individu-als found that the Christian theology of sin helped them make sense of the violence that rose against a peaceful movement.[13]

Rediscovering the Covered-up Truth Overseas

Some scholars claim that among the hundreds of political dissidents who fled to the U.S. after 1989, over half of them converted to Protestantism, a percentage much higher than among Chinese immigrants in general.[14] These earlier cohorts of refugee-converts later contributed to the conver-sion of many mainland Chinese students and visiting scholars who studied abroad during the late 1990s, by reaching out to them and explaining the hidden truth about Tiananmen.

As a college sophomore, Li (pseudonym) was among the student demonstrators in 1989. Although not one of the most enthusiastic ones, Li reckoned that China needed political reform. She was following some senior students to a street protest, but her mother found her and prevented her from going. The younger generation's political activism brought fear

---

13. The Communist state first resorted to an ideologically normalized account of the use of violence in Tiananmen, which was later replaced by an official account that denied any violent crackdown.

14. Wright and Zimmerman-Liu, "Atheist Political Activists Turned Protestants."

and worry to their parents, who had experienced the Cultural Revolution. From then on, Li had to rely on television reports for information about the movement's progress. She watched as the news reports turned from favorable coverage of peaceful demonstrators to branding the movement as "counter-revolutionary." The change was so dramatic that it left a haunting impression in her memory:

> I still remember watching how the two news broadcast hosts, Du Xian and Luo Jing, looked uneasy after the crackdown. They looked as if they knew something but could not tell the truth. We could not see on the news what really happened, but I sensed their facial expressions and the strange atmosphere around me. Something was seriously wrong. My parents were terrified, and they would not speak a word about it. I began to realize that many images presented in this country are distorted. Many incidents of injustice were hidden and buried. I quit watching the CCTV, for I no longer trusted its propaganda.[15] After that, I wanted to seek something that is beyond what was happening around us, something eternal. I eagerly sought for this ideal in college through reading.

Before Li became acquainted with churches in Singapore as a graduate student, she had already experienced a spiritual pilgrimage that started with distrust and disillusionment, and intensified into a strong desire for justice and truth. During her studies in Singapore, she watched some news recaps of the crackdown and discovered the truth.

Another individual whose quest for truth led him outside of China was Liu (pseudonym, male, 48), a political science student in college during the democracy movement. After the crackdown, he spent days and nights poring over the writings of Marx, trying to find out what was wrong with the path China was taking and to release pressure and despair. After graduation, all of his peers directly or indirectly suffered penalties for their involvement in the movement. They were dispatched to remote areas as middle school teachers and became targets of further "thought education" in their workplaces. He told us the following:

> Rounds of meetings were held against us, and report after report was required documenting our errors. I was in deep despair. I lost all my ideals. I picked up my old hobby of calligraphy. But once I found that my fine art works of calligraphy were taken away to be used as toilet paper, I felt slain and humiliated. All I

---

15. CCTV stands for China Central TV, the main state-run TV channel strictly controlled by the State Propaganda Department.

could do was to read whatever western literature I found in the library, for I thought there was hope in the West.

Liu eagerly read all major western philosophy texts, and he applied to graduate school in 1993 for further study. Instead of finding a place to explore ideas, Liu found the university preoccupied with the marketplace and ways to start business enterprises. Graduate school became another phase of disillusionment for Liu, although he reckons that western philosophical ideas did help to break down the Communist ideology that he had been taught for so long. In 1998, Liu graduated with a doctorate and joined the philosophy department at this school. One year later, Professor Liu traveled to Canada as a visiting scholar and connected with its Chinese churches. He met Christian converts who had participated in the democracy movement. The pastor who baptized him was also a famous activist-turned-convert. Liu recounts:

> I asked the pastor, "Weren't you also very enthusiastic then? Was it wrong to seek justice, the rule of law, and democracy?" He answered that those goals were not wrong, but the goal of our life was something greater, something ultimate. I was struck by this answer. I wanted to think about this ultimate question. So I borrowed many Christian journals from church and spent days and nights reading them. I wondered why they found God but I had not. Why did my philosophical studies not help me to find God? It was only after I prayed to God for the first time when I started to experience one thing—God is love. Nothing in this world, not philosophy, not any government will love you in this way. God is a personal, relational God. And only God has justice and righteousness.

A common thread emerges from the spiritual development of these converts, from student activism, post-crackdown disillusionment, seeking alternative ideological sources, getting in touch with overseas Chinese converts who had witnessed and experienced the crackdown differently, and their own conversions. Li and Liu both had a short stay overseas that exposed them to a free speech environment. There they could reflect on the Tiananmen movement, its truth and its impact.[16] The overseas experiences renewed their outlook on Chinese society and confirmed their faith. They both returned to China as committed Christians in their local house churches. Such overseas experiences or connections were crucial in

16. In the early 1990s, a mass conversion also took place among overseas Chinese immigrants from mainland China. These new converts actively reached out to cohorts of Chinese who later visited or emigrated in the late 1990s.

explaining the occurrence of mass conversion among the Chinese who are impacted by the Tiananmen crackdown.

The Conversion of Justice

The impact of disillusionment after the Tiananmen crackdown and the subsequent political cleansing against activists affected all age cohorts and layers of society. Fang (pseudonym) was in high school when the Tiananmen movement happened. As the student editor of his school's literature society, Fang researched a column by interviewing teachers and students about their opinions on the widely-supported student demonstrations. When Fang's father learned about his project, a familiar political sentiment of fear (*pa* in Chinese) re-emerged from the shadow of the Cultural Revolution. He urged Fang to abandon this survey project. Unable to convince him of the political risks, Fang's father even locked away all his printing tools. Fang resented his father's reaction, but looking back a few decades later, he felt gratitude. He realized that had he finished that article, it would have brought harm to him and all his family members.

Due to his curious and persistent personality, Fang always wondered why such a favored peaceful democracy movement received a unanimous "hush" from adults around him overnight. All of a sudden, the unprecedented hope for this country was gone. Fear and despair were in everyone's eyes, but nobody spoke about the movement anymore. Fang's uncle, a photographer, took many pictures of the violent crackdown. When the authorities began the post-Tiananmen cleansing campaign, his uncle asked Fang and his cousin to burn these pictures for fear of being found out.[17] At the time of the cleansing campaign, every family had already destroyed any evidence that proved their sympathy or support for the democracy movement. People who had gone through earlier Communist revolutions from the 1950s to 1970s are familiar with the sentiments of *pa*, which sums up all stages of anxiety after the loss of a political utopia.

One month after the Tiananmen crackdown, major changes were made to the National College Entrance Examination and admissions process. National enrollment of college students dropped from six hundred thousand to four hundred thousand, and examinations for arts and humanities were

---

17. Most public *danwei* work units launched a witch-hunt investigation of officials and cadres to assess their participation in the movement as well as their political reliability. According to Miles, more than 30,000 party officials were deployed to carry out the investigation, and more than one million people were subjected to such an investigation. Miles, *The Legacy of Tiananmen*, 165.

cancelled. The state attributed the 1989 political crisis to activism among college students, especially those in arts and humanities that taught critical thinking and exposed them to western thought. Changing the opportunity structure of college entrance would prevent similar student activism, the regime deduced. In addition to such entrance limitations, the new college student cohort in 1990 across China was required to start its college years with a prolonged period of on-campus military training. Universities in Beijing and in other cities where student movements were most enthusiastic, were ordered to have *twelve months* of military training. As part of the patriotic education campaigns, Communist political discourse prevailed in such sessions, with the clearly-stated purpose being to "prevent capitalistic liberal thought" and to cultivate patriotism. After 1989, university campuses also underwent a spatial re-planning to avoid over-concentration of student dorms in one location, and many campuses relocated to suburban areas that posed less of a threat to the political center. Such geographical re-designs also served to discourage connections and conversations between university faculty and young students. These deliberate institutional changes affected the life trajectories of millions, including Fang.

In the fall of 1989, Fang began the final and most intense preparatory year of his high school studies. After the summer of 1989, however, schooling became mentally torturous for him. Although he was only seventeen, he felt as if he were living in a stifling world, a world that no longer had truth, ideals or love. What is more, students were required to recite central decrees from the Communist Party in their Thought and Virtue (*sixiang pinde*) classes. Fang recalls:

> It was very painful for me to recite those creeds again and again in class. When parents and teachers started to lie to our faces about what happened that summer, I started to despise the authority all the adults around me had. They all appeared like hypocrites, because I remembered how they had acted a few months before. But after the crackdown, they all gave false testimonies. So my contempt for authority grew stronger.
>
> And because the arts and humanities exam was cancelled in 1989, the senior cohort in our school had to join our class in order to prepare for the national exam the following year. This made our situation more competitive. Although I ranked number seven in my class before that, I did not score high enough in the 1990 national exam to get into a good university. That was a blow to me, but I blamed the environment and the government, because I knew their policies were made to suppress college students. My resentment against the Communist Party intensified.

After Fang entered a third-tier college, the first month of compulsory military training was another strain on him. Intense, repetitive training and the hierarchical culture of obedience delivered by these sessions only aggravated his negative sentiments towards political authorities. Fang disliked the classes as well. He spent most of his time reading in the library or hunting for books in second-hand bookstores:

> I read many books by what they called the "insurgents." I had a passion to seek out banned books. I felt like someone who had boarded a wrong bus, and I wanted so much to return to the spring of 1989, a time that belonged to those older brothers and sisters. I sang their songs and read their books, including writings by the exiled and the imprisoned. These documents shaped my thinking.

The introduction of Western liberal thoughts and literature in the 1980s was the only legal channel for alternative ideologies to be available to the Chinese. Preceding the 1989 movement, there was a revived interest in academia in what makes the Western civilizations based on Judeo-Christian traditions different than Chinese society. Western literary classics were allowed to be published; Western movies and music were suddenly popular, and Christian images and religious expressions occasionally appeared. These and many banned books filled up Fang's library, and he found himself writing poems alluding to God or eternity. But it was not until 2003 when he watched a documentary telling stories of China's house churches, *The Cross: Jesus in China*, that he came to know about the secretive existence of Protestant churches and their strong resistance against the Communist state. Fang realized that a significant part of Chinese history of liberty had been missing from his mental schema. Later, he also befriended some house church believers who explained their faith to him. More importantly, the Christian belief in God's justice appealed to Fang. A long-held resentment and hatred towards an oppressive regime was washed away when he first prayed to God for justice:

> I thought myself to be a very righteous person, with all the high ideals for democracy and freedom. However, when I was approached by desperate petitioners outside of a local court, I (then a human rights lawyer) pushed them off and ran away. I realized that I had no true righteousness in myself. All I harbored was hatred out of self-righteousness. So I prayed to God for the first time, and I was all tears, crying out aloud, flat on the floor. God turned the earlier pages of my life to show me what I had gone through—all my resentment against parents, teachers

and authorities. What kept me alive was not love, but hatred. That experience was a great relief to me spiritually. I laid down my pride and sense of justice as an intellectual before God. He gave me great comfort.

Justice-seeking was at the core of Fang's conversion. The state's false accusation against student activists, its denial of the violent crackdown, the required false testimonies and the institutionalized brainwashing of revisionist history in college were all unjust activities with lasting influence on Fang's heart and mind. On an individual level, justice-seeking created tension for Fang within an increasingly disillusioned and demoralized society. Why did the Christian faith or Fang's spiritual encounter with God provide an outlet for such justice-seeking sentiments? In his own words, Fang's concept of justice was renewed by the Christian theology of God's sovereignty:

> After I became a Christian, I started to see things differently. I learned how the Bible viewed injustice. My self-righteousness and nationalistic ideals were from the flesh, so they could help bring positive changes to this society. When I look at the Tiananmen crackdown today, I still think that the government should apologize and repent of its sins. The prime minister of West Germany made a public apology at a Holocaust memorial because he lived in a Christian culture. But when you look at non-Christian cultures, like Japan and China, there is no repentance. Why not? Because they reject the gospel. So every June 4 we have prayer meetings. I used to pray for God's righteous judgment to quickly come upon the evil-doers, but I pray differently now because God is sovereign over all and His timing is perfect. So, I now pray for the oppressor as well as the victims. History will turn its account to God, including the things that were not written in history books, for God Himself knows all history.

Such passion for justice to be done prepared converts like Fang to experience a sense of great spiritual relief. We found in our fieldwork that many post-1989 conversions contain such an experiential component. Knowing some basics of the Protestant faith and acquaintance with house church believers were preparatory conditions, but such experiential struggles in prayer or meditation were quite often the final impetus to conversion. William James defines conversion as a process whereby "the religious ideas, previously peripheral in his consciousness, now take a central place, and religious aims form the habitual centre of his energy."[18] The experi-

18. James, *The Varieties of Religious Experience*, 196.

ential processes of a new consciousness or an emotional shock all tend to accelerate the changes inside individuals' values and ideals, until a new state of balance is reached.

Like many Chinese traumatized by the betrayal of the state in 1989, Fang yearned for justice to be done. However, the denial of truth and the state's subsequent strategy of basing its regime legitimacy upon economic growth only compounded injustice. The Tiananmen crackdown was merely a prelude to further social injustices in China, such as forced abortions and unwarranted demolitions, for they resulted from the same rationale of opportunism. For many, it is only in trusting in God's justice through a coming Final Judgment that such a sense of deep frustration is relieved.

Surviving the Post-Tiananmen Opportunism

Before 1989, Weng (pseudonym) had always believed what he was taught in school: that we "the people" are the masters of this "new China." A nationalistic pride motivated him to do well in school, both academically and politically. After the Tiananmen crackdown, although still a high-schooler, Weng had serious doubts about his previous beliefs. Did this country really belong to the people? Why was an anti-corruption student movement redefined as counter-revolutionary unrest? These questions were not settled even after he entered a political academy to prepare young cadres for the Communist regime. During his first month of military training, he was greatly bewildered to see disillusioned students just like him nevertheless rushing to submit their applications for Communist Party membership. Although he tried to convince himself that such was the reality in this Communist academy, his integrity did not allow him to fake an application. Weng became the only student who did not apply for membership. He recalls:

> Some senior students even came to persuade me by saying, "Why do you take it so seriously? Party membership is just a food coupon (*fanpiao*)! You've got to eat and live, no matter if you believe it or not!" Our political thought advisor approached me in the same way, but I answered him, "Belief is a major decision in my life, and I cannot write a sincere application without reading more works by Marx and Engels." He was polite but his face showed contempt for my remark. I later learned that he left this comment on my profile: "Politically immature."

What Weng experienced in this academy of Communist thought was a disorientation of values after the Tiananmen crackdown. As Bauman notes in his book *Modernity and the Holocaust*, after a large-scale massacre people

tend to replace their moral values by a survival-centered goal, which produces seemingly rational behavior of self-protection or apoliticization. But
once they are placed under extreme conditions, such rationalization and
moral indifference result in a moral disintegration.[19] Exiled Chinese scholar
and commentator for Radio Free Asia Hu Ping wrote a similar analysis concerning such value disintegration. He thinks that opening up the market
economy after 1992 has relieved the pressure on China's political regime,
yet the epidemic of nihilism and cynicism since 1989 is the most important
reason for social conformity.[20]

Weng decided to change his career, so he entered graduate school to
study Western philosophy. At the same time, some of his friends had been
visiting temples and religious sites in search of something meaningful. He
joined them for a retreat at a Buddhist temple for a few days. The serenity
of the mountains and rhythmic chanting of the monks was sublime to him,
but Weng considered it a man-made scheme, rather than an internal state of
peace which he longed for. Besides, nobody there seemed to offer a definite
answer to the source of life's meaning. After he returned to school, Weng
registered for a course on the history of Western political thoughts, and
the first book on the reading list was the Bible. Interestingly, the instructor himself was a non-Christian, but he lent Weng a leather-covered Bible.
Weng recalls:

> That was the first time I ever saw the Bible, a famous item of
> "poisonous grass" (*daducao*) to the Communists.[21] I was very
> excited and started to read from the Old Testament, but my
> interest soon faded in the endless lists of tribes and names. It
> looked just like any other book of Western myths to me. But
> one day after a student informant had accused me of expressing
> problematic political opinions. I felt discouraged and returned
> to my dorm. I carelessly flipped the Bible open and read in Gen-
> esis 1: "God said, Let there be light. And there was Light." To my
> amazement, this verse entered into my heart—the world needs
> light and God is the only source of all lights. I need this light
> too! So I kept on reading, and my heart was touched again and
> again. My will naturally accepted God's Word, and I was sure
> this book had the answer I had been looking for. That very day,
> I followed the prayer instructions on the back cover of the Bible
> and accepted Jesus as my Savior and Lord.

19. Bauman, *Modernity and the Holocaust.*

20. Hu, "Cynicism: A Spiritual Crisis."

21. A common Chinese expression used in the Cultural Revolution to mean texts
that do not line up with official ideology.

After this experience, Weng began to read all kinds of literature that had to do with Christianity. He even talked with many friends about Christianity being the greatest force behind human civilization. Later through an incidental acquaintance, Weng joined a Bible study group led by a foreign professor, and he was baptized in 1993. What Christianity offers seemed to answer most of his questions about human nature, the problem of evil and God as the Absolute Good. These reoriented his life to a more stable anchor.

Christian Love in the Midst of Social Distrust

Another convert we interviewed is Zhong (pseudonym, male, 50). He traces the changes in his life's outlook since 1988. As a college senior in engineering, he had never been exposed to any Western liberal ideas. All he had cared for was good grades and a well-paying job after university. When he started to befriend some active members of a literary society and experienced rock music and foreign movies in the last year of college, new thoughts, conversations and experiences opened his eyes to the higher ideals of freedom, democracy and the future of China. It was a year of enlightenment for him. Compared to his friends' enthusiastic pursuit of such ideals, he even felt ashamed of the mundane plans he had for his future.

After graduation, Zhong's university dispatched him to a township enterprise, together with a few graduates of his cohort.[22] These young engineers boasted that they were carrying out the mission of "changing the backward countryside of China," but Zhong observed that their moral character fell far short of this ideal to reform others. Most of them considered "down-to-earth" tasks to be beneath them; as a result, the factory underwent serious political conflicts. The conflict led to a public denunciation meeting, a humiliating and violent practice commonly used during the Cultural Revolution, targeting one factory leader. This person, whose face was badly wounded, fainted in front of Zhong after mental and physical exhaustion. This shocking moment awakened the conscience of 23-year-old Zhong. He remembers:

> When I looked at him lying on the ground, I felt some sympathy inside of me. But I immediately put on an indifferent look. Then my conscience started to accuse me—what kind of person are you? I realized for the first time that I have a very selfish nature, a cold-blooded heart. That was the beginning. After that I always sensed some guilt and anxiety.

22. In the 1980s, without the basic infrastructures of labor markets, universities dispatched their graduates to work units within the planned economy.

Violence awakened Zhong's conscience, although it also numbed the conscience of many during that time. Because he was a worker, Zhong did not participate in the democratic demonstrations, yet the violent Tiananmen crackdown still left a scar on him. Since he had not always been a keen advocate for those higher ideals, Zhong settled for self-fulfillment through exploring economic opportunities. He left the township factory and started his own private business.

The early 1990s was an easy time to launch a private business because few rules governed how a market economy operates. Officials could engage in business transactions, and local governments speculated in real estate. The Chinese economy was growing; it was full of uncertainty and risk, however. For small private businesses, it was difficult to survive. Zhong found himself constantly worried and anxious:

> I spent a lot of time thinking about how to manipulate other people, such as making your employees more devoted to your business, to maintain good *guanxi* with local officials, but I never knew if I did these things effectively. So, I was generally irritable. Nothing seemed to provide a sense of security.

For peace of mind, he visited temples and shrines as well as making friends with Buddhists, Taoists, *Fengshui* masters and Christians. In his own words, Zhong bowed to any god that he was able to find. Zhong's eagerness to find a faith allegiance intensified after his father became ill with cancer. During his father's illness, he increasingly realized that the Christian believers were the least opportunistic group. They visited and prayed for them voluntarily and selflessly, unlike the Buddhist monks. Within a short time, his father was converted; he was healed and even became a more loving person. These experiences brought Zhong even closer to the Protestant faith. After his conversion, he was able to look back with peace upon his past:

> In our education, we were never taught how to love others. Our Chinese history applauds those who manipulate others by crafty skills in order to get ahead. Now that I believe in God, I see history and things in the past differently—only God himself governs history, its causality and justice. It is not up to individuals to decide. Our duty is to love God and love the people around us. This thought gives me peace of mind.

In Christian love, Zhong has found a testable compass in navigating social relationships. He is not satisfied with the moralistic teachings of Confucianism or Daoism because they seem too idealistic to address real life difficulties. In comparison, the love of a Christian God lived out in Christians' real lives appear more authentic and down-to-earth to him.

THE TIANANMEN EFFECT, CONTINUED

The censored facts about the Tiananmen crackdown not only influenced individuals who lived through it, but also younger generations who were born after 1989 and were previously unaware of its happenings. Because of the ideological inertia in China's education system, the Communist ideology or its revised versions dominate a great proportion of the curriculum. As such, the teachings come into greater conflict with China's reality and the censored facts of the Tiananmen crackdown. The same type of moral disillusionment we have documented will happen to these young people, once they have the opportunity to gather the facts. With the Internet and anti-censorship software, their chances of accessing Tiananmen documents are greater now than with earlier cohorts.

Take, for example, Guan (pseudonym) who was born in 1989 had never heard of the Tiananmen crackdown until college. Although it is not the most discussed topic, images and stories about the Tiananmen movement were shared among groups of politically active college students and are considered "enlightenment documents" for one's political awareness. After gathering some basic facts about this part of history, Guan reflected on her earlier education with suspicion and regrets:

> Reading those materials was a shock to me. From early on we were taught in school that Communism is good and that when we develop into a Communist society, it will be like a paradise. But these teachings gradually lost their credibility when we grew up and experienced reality. Take human nature, for example. Although our teachers taught us moral lessons of doing good and just things, including traditional values, I found that the morality in our society did not improve with such teachings, but declined in spite of educational and technological advances. Although teachers taught us that our Communist society is superior to capitalist societies in the West, discovering truths like the Tiananmen movement gives you a terrible impression of China. What the college students in 1989 proposed was just democracy, a normal request.

Like many in her generation, Guan has long been skeptical of what she was taught in school. Learning the facts about Tiananmen broadened her tolerance for Western cultures and distanced her from the dominant political ideology in China. But apart from atheism, she was never exposed to other religious teachings. In her sophomore year, Guan met two campus evangelists who explained the basics of the faith to her. At the time, she had concerns over a family member's illness. After she prayed to God for healing, her loved one became well. This experience directly contributed to her conversion.

CONCLUSION

The Christian message empowers individuals who have experienced spiritual deprivation after the 1989 Tiananmen crackdown. First, they had to face the letting-go of a sense of grudging hatred against the regime based on the Christian theology of human sinfulness and forgiveness. Second, the message of personal salvation mattered more to them than any grandiose democracy plan, though some converts still advocate for basic political rights in China.[23] Lastly but also most importantly, to these Tiananmen-affected converts, the Christian faith appealed to them due to its transcendent understanding of justice. It is under these deep convictions that fear for the regime, lies behind propaganda, passive submission to fate and opportunism are overcome. It is also worth noting that by this time in the early 1990s, home groups had been sprouting across China, and the ethical teachings of peace-making and self-giving love represented by close-knit house church groups appealed to people who had seen too much darkness and hopelessness in society. These groups have rebuilt the true community and social trust that had been missing in China for the past two decades.

23. Wright and Zimmerman-Liu, "Atheist Political Activists."

4

Orphans

I will not leave you orphans.

—JOHN 14:18

STUART STEVEN'S BOOK *NIGHT Train to Turkistan* told stories of meeting Chinese Christians in Xi'an in the late 1980s.[1] By then, Three-Self churches had been allowed to re-open. The author met a Mr. Ling, a rural teacher who spoke some English, in one of the re-opened churches. Mr. Ling was very excited and eager to meet this friendly foreigner. During their conversation, he pulled out a worn Bible stuffed with foreign letters and postcards. Mr. Ling explained that these letters had come from many Christian tourists he had befriended over the years. Among them, many were short-term missionaries or tourists seeking opportunities to share their faith. Stuart Steven was fully aware that during the late 1980s and early 1990s foreign Christians often took on the identity of tourist or English teacher in order to evangelize while Communist China was opening up.

Mr. Ling treasured these friendships as well as the Bible he was secretly keeping. In an era with no Internet, he nonetheless managed to reply to these foreign friends, expressing the wish to visit them in America, Canada or Sweden. He even asked them to write some letters of invitation in hopes that he might someday apply for a passport and a visa to go abroad. These imaginary possibilities kept Mr. Ling's Christian identity alive yet anxious,

1. Stevens, *Night Train to Turkistan*.

shown in the way he mentioned these foreign connections whenever encountering another foreigner.

The author later comes to realize that this man is unlikely ever to visit anyone outside this remote area of inland China. However, Mr. Ling is determined as he questions him about how much money he will need to save in order to visit his foreign friends. Steven recalls the anxious words of this rural teacher: "I do not need much. I do not eat much. I think maybe in five or six years I could get a passport to travel. I have friends in America. We are brothers in Christ. Please, tell me. I can save money, but how much? How much?"[2] This poor man seemed to Steven as someone who is "out of place and out of time, trapped in China":

> This idea of coming to America, like the scraps of paper tucked in his bible, seemed to be holding him together. . . . He is very likely one of millions in China who were partially undone by some government-sponsored trauma, perhaps during the Cultural Revolution. His sources of hope for healing—the church, America, his foreign friends—have been woven together into a web of faith, part religion, part utopia, part delusion. The Christian church in China is a place where legacies of both imperialism and persecution can sometimes combine to form a middle race of unhappy creatures without the ability to realize a consistent identity.[3]

Many people were holding onto dreams similar to Mr. Ling's in China during the 1990s. Due to state surveillance, political evictions and missionary mobility, irregular short-term missionary work resulted in a generation of converts who found themselves with a new Christian identity but cut off from outside contacts that could provide continuous mentorship and accountable leadership. They are a generation of spiritual orphans left to grow up by themselves. Many have never seen a real church building, except on nice postcards sent by their Western brothers and sisters.

UNDERCOVER MISSION

Historian Daniel Bays once wrote, "In the first half of the 20th century, the foreign missionary movement in China matured, flourished, and then died."[4] The newly born Chinese church was left to survive as an infant,

2. Ibid., 57.
3. Ibid., 58.
4. Bays, "From Foreign Mission to Chinese Church."

homegrown faith. Ways to connect with the outside world were limited to almost zero. When Pastor Isaac Jen started preaching to mainland China through shortwave broadcast for Back to God International Ministries in 1974, he was not sure if any audience was listening to him. A few years later, however, he started to receive letters from listeners who were scattered across China.[5] In early 1980s, after twenty-plus years of separation from the outside world, when foreign Christians were able to enter China again as tourists with the first legal guided tours, they were surprised to find the Christian faith still alive, with the number of believers even increasing.

Before 1987, when Bibles were strictly banned in China, families that owned one copy would share it with other believers or copy some portions for memorization. Sometimes a church group would need to borrow the only Bible from another village for their whole neighborhood to use. They did this with great caution. We heard a testimony of a shared copy of the Bible being passed around during a secret home gathering, and many kissed it and shed tears on the red fringes of the pages. Before church networks become visible and teachings were widely available, these new converts mainly fed on bits and pieces of the Book that they could obtain.

Many of these early Bibles were smuggled into China by Western Christians. The most well-known project was led by Open Doors. In 1981, this organization launched Project Pearl, a plan to transport one million Bibles to the south seashore of China by tugboats and barges in one night. Believing villagers collected them with fishing nets, and then dried them up in the sun. Some copies were confiscated and burned by authorities, but the majority were placed in the hands of local believers.[6]

In the 1990s, foreign investment was welcomed into the coastal zones of China, and what became later called "business as mission" became another entry strategy for foreign Christians. Since the laws forbade open proselytizing, these foreigners had to work within legal boundaries by taking up "cover jobs," such as business investors or English teachers hired by universities. They relied largely on casual occasions and private conversations to spread their faith. Despite the progress they made, it was still hard for them to develop long-term discipleship and mentorship programs without being noticed. If they were discovered providing Christian teaching and training programs, the government would evict them from China and bar them from returning.

Ying (pseudonym) met her first foreign friend, Ben, in an informal gathering called English Corner on campus in 1989. This young American

5. Interview with Jerry An, April 8, 2017.
6. Quoted in Faries, *The "Inscrutably Chinese" Church*, 98–99.

was hired by the university as a foreign language teacher (*waijiao*) and later became Ying's first Bible teacher. When they first met at the weekly English Corner, Ying had difficulty understanding Ben's English. She was not able to follow what he was talking about, but she heard one word which struck her—love. This American teacher said that Ying did not know what love is. She started to argue with him in broken English, saying that of course she had her parents and teachers loving her. Then in response Ben said, "Because you do not know Jesus." Ying had never heard the word "Jesus" before, so that made her even more confused.

Later that night, Ben drew a few of the group aside, and he pointed at a book in his hands. He said something quite passionately while pointing at it, but nobody understood what he was saying. Ying thought that he even seemed a little crazy. Then Ben said to them in a sincere tone that this Jesus has changed him. That part Ying understood. Ying gained much confidence in speaking English that night as she argued with Ben. Upon leaving, she borrowed the book from him. It was an English Bible.

Over the next week, Ying turned a few pages in that Bible and put it down in confusion. Ben sent a friend to ask for his book back, saying that he will need it in church. Ben even asked them if they want to go to a Three-self church together with him. So Ying and a few other college friends went to church for the first time in their life along with this English teacher. She recalls a verse hanging outside the church wall: "Come to me, all you who are weary and burdened, and I will give you rest." Ying found this saying curious and unusual. The 1990s was a money-mongering age for all Chinese, and everyone had to strive relentlessly for success. Who cares about rest? And what is rest? She found these questions popping up in her mind.

The pastor who was preaching in this re-opened Three-Self church also left a warm impression on Ying. Unlike most Chinese people that Ying met during those days, he appeared very calm and gentle. The church was having communion that Sunday, and Ben cautioned them not to eat the bread when it was passed around. That again made Ying very curious.

Ben stayed with them for only one semester. He just answered some basic and curious questions from this small group of college students. When leaving, Ben connected Ying and her friends with an elderly Christian couple from Canada. Ying and her friends started to meet regularly at this couple's apartment to study the Bible together. Ying remembers keenly that this couple showed them pictures of their family in Canada, and then they said something strange when mentioning their deceased parents: "We will soon see them again." That struck Ying as curious and incomprehensible. This couple taught many traditional hymns to Ying's group. After the couple returned to Canada a year later, Ying and her friends only occasionally visited the Three-Self church. After graduation, some of them found jobs in other cities, so the group dispersed. Ying attended the Three-Self church only sporadically.

Interestingly, these re-opened Three-Self churches functioned as safe contact points for Western Christians to meet local people. By the nineties, these churches had formed a negotiation model of interaction with the government.[7] It used to be the law that no foreigners could assemble at a Three-Self church. But later these boundaries became blurry. Even for some strict Three-Self churches that tried to maintain the foreign-local boundary, they set up a segregated section for foreigners and checked their passports at entry points.

A few years later, Ying met another old couple in a Three-self church who invited her to a regular "fellowship" in their home. It was the first time that Ying heard the word "fellowship" (*tuanqi*), which piqued her interest. There was no such term of equivalence in the Chinese language. Ying later figured that such "fellowship gatherings" resembled what Communist Party members call "organizational life" (*zuzhi shenghuo*). Drawn by their sincerity, she went regularly and studied the Bible in greater depth than ever before. Two years later, this old couple had to leave too, entrusting some younger converts they knew to Ying, who was already the fellowship leader by that time. Ying started to lead and even preach in the fellowship. It was around year 1995. Looking back, Ying realized that her true conversion happened when she was beginning to teach from the Bible.

FOREIGN CHRISTIANS ON CAMPUS

By the late 1990s, mission organizations, such as the Navigators and Campus Crusade for Christ (abbreviated as CCC), sent their young workers to reach out on Chinese university campuses. These foreign Christians were either undergraduate college students or recent graduates from college who took gap years to gain some cross-cultural experience. They befriended Chinese college students and conversed with them in campus cafeterias or at McDonalds.[8] Bible studies and discipleship training happened in these locations too, as a convenient way to be both visible and safe from political surveillance. When communicating about Christian matters using emails, text messages or even in daily conversations, these new mission groups tend to use code language to avoid the watchful eyes of authorities.

---

7. Hunter and Chan, *Protestantism in Contemporary China*.
8. Yang, "Lost in the Market," 423–441.

Sun (pseudonym) joined a Christian campus fellowship group in 2007 as a student in one of the best graduate schools of economics in the country six years after his conversion. In 2001, Sun thought that he was the only Christian on his university campus. His only companion in this new spiritual journey was a red-fringed used Bible given to him by an old lady he met on a 30-hour train ride from Shanghai to Qinghai a week before. It was quite an unexpected encounter, but one that seemed orchestrated from above. Here is his story.

In 2001, a sophomore history major, 19-year-old Sun was an avid reader of Western literature. He extensively read books about Western ideas, especially political liberalism and democratic constitutionalism. From these readings, a common theme gradually emerged—the heritage of Christianity and the Bible. References to the Christian tradition and to the Bible seem to lie behind all great ideas of Western civilization. At that time, Sun had never seen a church or met a Christian in China. Book lover as he was, Sun began to search out all bookstores in Shanghai, hoping to buy a Bible. He had no clue that only government-sponsored Three-Self churches were allowed to sell Bibles and that these churches open their bookstores for only limited hours on Sundays.[9] Sun finally found an illustrated book of Bible stories for children in a book store, in the classical Western literature section. With this book in hands, Sun boarded a train to his hometown on the other side of China's landscape. As he was reading it, a lady in her fifties sitting opposite to him struck a conversation with him. She turned out to be the first Christian in Sun's life. After sharing her own life story, she gave Sun her personal Bible as a gift.

Although Sun dismissed this old woman's message about God creating the first man out of clay as scientifically incredulous, he held unto this Bible dearly and read it every day. Something did change inside of him, especially after reading the book of Romans written by someone named Paul. He found tears running down his cheeks while reading it. Later Sun began to ask around to find a church he could attend. A friend lived near a Three-Self church and brought him to a Sunday service there. It was the first time Sun experienced Christian hymns, and the serene singing of the choir left an unusual impression on him, but he found the sermon message almost incomprehensible. There was also a baptism on that Sunday. Sun heard the preacher read a verse from the Bible: "The streams of God are filled with water." Somehow that verse stayed with Sun, and he told his friend that he

9. The Chinese government approved Bible printing and publishing in 1987, but only one publishing company was allowed to do this—Amity Foundation. They now print copies and distribute only through Three-Self churches.

was willing to be "washed clean" too. That was the day when Sun started to identify himself as a Christian.

Sun's new identity as a Christian, although unbaptized and unchurched, was very important to him. He kept reading the Bible and prayed for God's forgiveness in his dorm room. Although it was a university campus of over 10,000 students, Sun was not aware of any fellow believers. He began to long for spiritual friendship. He sometimes missed the old lady on the train and the conversation they had about God and eternal things.

One day, a Korean exchange student initiated a conversation with Sun in the university cafeteria. This Korean young man appeared to be in his late twenties, a little older than Sun. He spoke enough Chinese for them to have a basic discussion. He gladly found out that Sun was reading the Bible on his own. He was very friendly and asked Sun if they could meet often in the cafeteria to study the Bible together. Sun gladly agreed. They met regularly to do Bible study for a year. Sun was required to memorize a lot of Bible verses and recited them to his mentor. By the end of this study, Sun learned that this first spiritual mentor of his actually belonged to a mission group called the Navigators.

After this Korean friend left, Sun was alone in the faith again. It took another two years for him to meet another student named Wang, who was also a new convert. Wang took him to a small group that gathered secretly in a rented apartment near campus. For a while, this group was equally reluctant to reveal the name of its organization. Three years later when Sun started graduate studies at the same school and became a leader of the group, he learned that this fellowship was called Campus Crusade for Christ.

In 2007, Sun had grown into a strong Christian in the faith, but he was still unbaptized and unchurched. Some house church groups he knew do not have qualified clergy to perform baptisms. Knowing that the Three-Self church is controlled by the Communist Party, Sun was reluctant to receive baptism there. He also increasingly realized that the CCC group offered more emotional support than biblical teachings. There was no qualified minister to perform baptisms or communion. The group had minimal rituals, if any. Foreign Christians came and left every year. Trying to maintain long-term discipleship is very difficult given the mobility of these short-term student Christian workers. The group became a little orphanage with two-year-old or three-year-old Christians trying to nurture new converts.

As a leader, Sun had become aware that their activities had been watched by the government. For example, a security camera was installed near where members used to have prayer time outdoors. When Zeng (pseudonym, male, 25), a member of the group, received his baptism, this young man confessed that he joined the group as an informant hired by the security staff of the university. Zeng candidly admitted that for the past three years, he has been pressured to report this group's activities and locations. But over time, the teachings and friendships gradually changed his heart, and when Zeng graduated and found a job, he decided to stop being an informant and to embrace the faith personally. On China's campuses, it is a commonly held belief that in every university classroom there is always a student informant (*xinxiyuan*) whose identity remains unknown. This "student information network" also extends to overseas campuses where Chinese students and visiting scholars concentrate.[10] Requested by the Cultural Protection Department (known as *Wenbao* on campus), these student informants are expected to collect and report information about political expressions of both faculty and students. Some of these students are active devotees of the Communist Party, but many are either pressured or even lured to carry out the task. Although Zeng belonged to the latter category, his testimony was still powerful to hear. Sun was more surprised at the genuine change that took place in Zeng. It took great courage for him to confess it. The campus fellowship embraced Zeng and gave glory to God for his changed heart.

DISCIPLESHIP TRAININGS AT FAST-FOOD CHAIN STORES

When Jian (pseudonym, female, 27) returned to Shanghai from the United States with a graduate degree and a new Christian identity, she sought to find a house church. The person Jian contacted picked a place to get to know her first, a form of "screening interview" to protect house church groups from receiving cult members or government spies. In a downtown McDonald's restaurant, Jian met with Chai (29), who was a female leader of a home-gathering group. Chai was first led to Christ by a Canadian female Christian named Susan after a year of study in the same McDonald's. Later, Chai introduced Jian to her group of mostly female associates and Susan herself, a professional personal trainer at a fitness club for the wealthiest class in the city. Susan has a flexible schedule and uses her spare time in doing discipleship training and evangelism, often using the few McDonald's near her apartment. Usually they would find a corner, with each table surrounded by four to five trainees.

In China's market economy, chain stores such as McDonald's and Starbucks provide a noisy yet public sheltered space for religious training and conversations to go undetected by the government, as sociologist Fenggang

10. Calabresi, "China Expands Student Spying."

Yang writes.[11] Even when police occasionally raided one place, interrogated one of Yang's interviewees and coerced the young convert to promise "to stop gathering at this McDonald's," this young man told Yang that since "there are dozens of them in this city," his group could always re-gather later. Yang also finds in his research that "most efforts of underground evangelism is by individual Christians," including "fired-up domestic evangelists and tent-making foreign missionaries."[12] These individual evangelistic efforts tend to be "random, informal and inconsistent," so it is hard for them to maintain a long-term relationship.

A sad piece of news from 2014 also relates to using McDonald's as a religious gathering space. A few members of the Eastern Lightning cult tried to recruit new converts in a McDonald's in Zhaoyuan city. When a woman named Wu refused to give her cell phone number, she was beaten to death on the spot.[13] Since then, police surveillance has tightened up even in McDonalds, in an effort to prevent any conversations or gatherings of a religious nature.

THE CHALLENGE OF RE-CHURCHING

By 2012, Bao (pseudonym) had been a Christian for ten years, and he was now a full-time preacher at an urban house church located in an office building near a medical college campus. This church does not have an official name, but they call themselves the "medical college church" since its members are mostly graduates, faculty, or students of this college,

Before becoming a full-time preacher, Bao served in CCC on this campus. Most members of this church were also converted through this ministry. CCC missionaries met with students one-on-one in college dorms or in the cafeteria on weekdays. After the number of converts increased to a dozen or so, they rented an apartment near campus and met up every Thursday evening. Members signed up to bring meals for the group; after a meal, they sang hymns and studied the Bible together. They had to remind everybody to keep the singing volume down as low as possible, because too much noise might annoy the neighbors. If noise was reported to the police, they would likely be evicted. Something like this had happened before, so they were renting an apartment in a different area.

Most college students stayed in this fellowship group for a period of three to four years, and after they graduated, they could no longer remain in

11. Yang, "Lost in the Market," 423–441.

12. Ibid., 425.

13. Hume, "Chinese Court Sentences Cult Members."

the group. This CCC group never held Sunday worship services or encouraged new converts to do so in other churches. That was not the emphasis of CCC ministry. Therefore, for the first four years of his faith journey, Bao was under the impression that Thursdays were the proper time for Christians to meet.

With the passing of time, Bao started to notice some problems in his Christian life. Some believers of his cohort initially showed a strong zeal for their newfound faith, but after graduation, they stopped professing their Christian identity. Some were even publicly testifying against the faith. In his own life, Bao also noticed that his realistic struggles were not renewed by the faith he initially embraced. Or in other words, the gospel message he was first introduced to seemed too superficial to counter real challenges in real life. After eight years, his Bible knowledge did not grow much beyond the New Testament because most CCC workers focus on these relatively easier books when teaching the students.

Around 2006, as more Christian publications become available, Bao and his leadership team started a reading group to delve into books about church history and theology. They gradually realized that a church is different from the loosely connected fellowship group of which they were a part. Since CCC tended not to encourage college graduate to stay with their ministry after graduation, Bao and another brother started a church later in that year to fill this gap for graduates who took up professional jobs in the city.

Re-churching believers who have lived their spiritual life without a church is challenging. Bao says that because most of college converts have been so trained in a ministry model like CCC that they are content with living a superficial Christian identity. Such an identity may even appear to be fashionable to some. Most people in his group knew nothing more about church life beyond their secret meetings. Bao does not deny the effectiveness of CCC on college campuses when few local churches were reaching out to college students. He sees college ministry in urban China as very important, because in Bao's words, "these are the people who are supposed to shoulder the cultural mandate of renewing the culture by the Gospel message, if they can be better equipped." To reach this group quick and effectively, CCC uses a simple booklet method, usually called "Four Spiritual Laws," to bring out the Christian gospel in ten minutes. By parachuting young Christians from the United States, who are mostly college students themselves too, CCC presents the Christian message in an accessible and friendly way to young college students in China. An American Christian student may reach out to hundreds of students on campus using this simple method. Thus, in terms of the quantitative growth brought by CCC ministry, it is considered highly effective.

On the other hand, as Bao reflects, because the model relies on foreigners as leaders and does not teach any church doctrine, including the importance and meanings of sacraments such as baptism and communion, a new convert's conceptualization of the Christian faith is only the "I accept Jesus" prayer. Also because of CCC's lack of emphasis on church life, its fellowship groups fail to establish contacts with local Chinese churches or aid transition of new converts into a local congregation. Consequently, new converts may know the "Four Spiritual Laws" by heart, but not much of the Bible itself.

Another difficult thing is that once these young converts enter the workplace, life seems compartmentalized into sections that are Christian and those that are not. They have not been taught to look at the world with a holistic Christian worldview. Such a lifestyle is easy to maintain in college, where life in general is more idealistic and simple. However, after graduation from college, these new converts are plucked from fellowship groups but are not regularly congregating with fellow believers. As a result, many lose their faith at later stages of life. Bao has seen many of his peers departing from the faith, because they have never been properly taught how to live a holistic Christian life.

The "medical college church" Bao is now serving also faces residual challenges from the CCC model. The leadership team realized that they needed church by-laws, but when making the rules of how to organize this church, many disputes arose among themselves. Should they have elections? Do preachers need to be ordained? Can women preach in Sunday pulpits? How should they use measures of church discipline? Should there be a closed table for communion? It seemed to Bao that they were trying to resolve some major theological disputes over the past two thousand years of church history with baby hands. It was impossible for them to reach a systematic profession of faith. The leadership team felt overwhelmed with theological differences and the making of by-laws was postponed again and again. The church has been growing since 2006 from two dozen members to over 200 in 2012, but their by-laws have still not been finalized.

PASTORING THROUGH CHRISTIAN PUBLISHING

Urban church leaders like Bao are avid readers of Christian literature because it is the primary way ministers develop spiritually. Many thoughtful lay believers also feed on books. Unlike the Christian literature fever in the early 1990s when Xiaofeng Liu edited a series on Christianity mainly geared to the unbelieving academic circle, this new wave of Christian readers consists mostly of committed members of urban churches. Political scientist Robert Woodberry demonstrate in his study that "conversionary Protestants" play an important role in creating conditions that are conducive to society, such as mass printing.[14] Christian bookstores now can be found in every major city of China, with some becoming intellectual hubs among Christian readers. A dozen Christian publishing companies produce titles ranging from devotionals, commentaries, church history, to theological treatises, apologetics and biographies. Most are translated works. Nevertheless, a few Chinese authors are also beginning to produce theological or literary expressions of their faith in the Chinese language. As the founder of one of the earliest Christian publishing companies Yun (pseudonym, 48, male) says, "As China's churches mature, there will be more books by native authors. Only then can it be truly called 'mainland Chinese Christian publishing.'"

When Christian publishing as an industry was taking off around 2013, however, the government also started to tighten things up through stricter censorship. A Christian editor says that lately religious bureau staff tend to put longer holds on Christian content, and demand that words such as "God," "Holy Spirit" or "resurrection" be deleted. The words that trigger their sensitivity vary from person to person, and also from time to time. To illustrate, consider Ben Xu, an English literature professor teaching in St Mary's College in California, who has authored a few books published in mainland China on the topic of education. As his name was gaining influence among Chinese intellectuals, a state newspaper invited him to write as a columnist. Working with a mainland Chinese newspaper meant following the censorship protocols, and the editor had to delete content from Xu's articles according to a list of censored words that varied from month to month. Once, Xu was told that "Moses" was included in the list of censored words, because this biblical character had led a revolution.

By 2017, the number of titles published by these Christian publishers had dropped by two thirds. State Administration for Religious Affairs (often known as SARA), the top council overseeing religious affairs under the National Council, stated again in 2017 that SARA alone is the legitimate entity for publishing Christian literature. Now Christian groups are creatively playing a cat and mouse game with the censoring authorities. Some have expanded techniques to include various new media on the Internet.

14. Woodberry, "The Missionary Roots."

SPECIALIZED PROFESSIONALS

With the growth of urban churches, the demand for pastoral resources is rising too. Churches not only need to reach out to college students and urban professionals and care for the homeless, they also face the need to pastor the urban elite group which we call specialized professionals, such as Christian economists, philosophers and artists teaching in state universities or academies.

Professor Wei (pseudonym, male, 62) is among China's top economists, teaching as faculty and academic dean at a top university. Befriending many Nobel Laureate economists in the west, Wei organizes conferences on economic policies across China. He is also part of a consultancy group for central political leadership. In his writing and talks, Wei is honest about his religious faith as a Christian. When pursuing a PhD degree in economics abroad, Wei was exposed to Christianity and was baptized. His daughter had a rare illness which was healed by a preacher through prayer, so he believes in the supernatural aspects of the Christian faith too. Since Wei returned to teach in China, he has had difficulties in finding a church to attend. He disliked the secretive style of house churches and found much of the preaching simplistic. It seems that what matters most is personal salvation, and other things like economics and politics are considered secular and meaningless. Wei would not be willing to join a Three-self church because the preaching there was not much better. After a while, Wei got used to not attending church in his city. Whenever he travels abroad for conferences, he finds a church to worship there. Although Wei remains the only Christian economist who could integrate the transcendental dimension into his academic writings within the area of economics, his Christianity is lived in private.

Professor Ying (pseudonym, male, 58) is the president of a top state art academy in an urban center. He holds international exhibits regularly and is considered a leading professional artist in China. He studied painting since his teenage years and specialized in painting human body parts. Since Ying and a few artists in his academy became Christians, they started a home-gathering group with a lay minister, Chong (pseudonym), teaching them the Bible. Although they appreciated Chong's devotion and piety, over the years, a theological gap began to grow between Chong and these artists. Chong's pietist and mission-centered theology downplayed the meaningfulness of art. When this house church gradually expanded to include other groups, including college students and neighboring residents, the loyal group of artists who helped start this church felt marginalized. There were a few times when Chong even preached that doing art is meaningless and secular when the whole world is waiting to be saved. Gradually, many artists stopped attending, including Ying. Many artists struggled with the meaning of their profession and its relationship to God's kingdom. Self doubts and frustration even dragged a few into a withered stage of artistic creation and emotional depression. Still desiring comfort from God's Word, Ying sometimes went unnoticed to attend the communion at a nearby Three-self church.

In today's urban churches, specialized professionals like Wei and Ying are a noticeable presence. They are highly prestigious in their professional circle, but in the church, they belong to a marginalized minority whose theological as well as social needs are seldom met. Not only are churches unable to pastor these Christian intellectuals, but very few churches successfully reach out to other specialized professionals who are seekers in the faith. Most evangelical Christians approach this group of sophisticated minds with a naïve if not an arrogant attitude while shrinking the Christian gospel to a few spiritual principles and reducing church history to broad stroke statements about church history and theology.

CONCLUSION

The remaking of the Chinese church in the 1990s began with a transformation of the missionary endeavor itself. During this time, re-entering Western missionaries brought some strategies and understandings of mission work that were quite different from their predecessors in the 1930s and 1940s. Their expectations and knowledge of the church in China were quite limited. For example, many foreign Christians were informed that the persecuted yet faithful "underground" churches, though growing in numbers and spiritual vitality, would be impossible to find and dangerous to visit. Indeed, many churches in China have experienced persecution to different degrees, but an overly romantic depiction of such persecution has been broadcast in the West. This quasi-myth has distorted the situation in China; missionary organizations aiming to raise funds have been responsible for some of this misinformation.[15] Because the Chinese authorities warned Western Christians not to do direct evangelism towards local believers, nor to worship with them, most missionaries capitulated. The use of cover jobs and short-term tourist visas are inevitable outcomes of missionary strategies during this time.

These truncated and disconnected efforts by foreign Christians left a mixed legacy for the Chinese churches. Although the number of new converts kept growing, in some regions at an impressive pace, these

15. Mike Falkenstine, *Chinese Puzzle*, 81, 89.

first-generation converts and their churches were not in good health. From 1979 to the 1990s, there simply were not enough Bibles to go around. Although China legalized the publication of Bibles in 1987, the distribution channels were intentionally minimized. Most importantly, capable teachers of the Bible were also lacking. Little home seminaries were formed and led by older converts, who had been released from prison. However, these training centers were small in scale and ineffective in pooling resources. For the vast number of younger converts in the 1980s and 1990s, many have walked a lonely and truncated spiritual journey, led and fed by different mentors that came along the way. They absorbed different theologies and styles of teaching. When this generation of believers became leaders of congregations, they often lacked the understanding of how to shepherd new believers or to teach from the whole Bible, and they also tended to view their own limited upbringing as the only correct model. Without having experienced continued mentorship themselves, they unconsciously adopted the traditional model of leadership that is hierarchical and authoritarian.

The problem of Christian believers whose lack of church fellowship has left them as orphans is exacerbated by the reality that most unregistered congregations in urban China stand alone and have minimal interaction with each other. Due to the lack of denominational structures, church leaders have not developed enough accountability. The traditional culture of "face-saving" comes in the way of conflict resolution and deters deeper communication between churches. Furthermore, the subculture of secrecy discourages efforts to collaborate. These factors all significantly shape the lack of connection and unity among urban congregations in China. The following chapter will address their evolving organizational structure.

5

Two Cities

A city that is set on a hill cannot be hidden.

—MATTHEW 5:14

WU (PSEUDONYM, FEMALE) IS A 60-year-old law professor and deaconess of a growing house church in Chengdu, an inland city in Southwestern China. When she received an invitation to attend an academic conference in Shanghai, a place she rarely visits, Wu thought it would be a good idea to use this trip to reconnect with many of her friends and former students. She hoped that she could bring them to church. Wu had assumed that a metropolitan city like Shanghai would have many churches with open arms for visitors.

After contacting a few house church leaders in Shanghai, however, Wu was frustrated to discover that the Sunday services of these groups did not admit visitors. They explained to her that visitors, even when they are believers, need to stay in a small home-gathering group for three months before they can attend the Sunday service. In Shanghai, this was known as the "three-month probation rule." Wu had never encountered such a rule in her own city. Her church, for example, would non-discriminatorily admit anyone who was willing to come to its Sunday service, including the local police who was ordered to keep an eye on their activities. The contrast between inland Chengdu and the international metropolitan Shanghai with its secretive church groups could not be sharper.

Before the passing of the new religious regulations in 2017, unregistered churches in every Chinese city faced a high level of uncertainty concerning how the authorities would regulate their activities. In both Shanghai and Chengdu, churches exist and operate with passive consent from the authorities most of the time. Nevertheless, our organization-level data show that churches in Shanghai develop along a different trajectory than their counterparts in Chengdu. This finding is counterintuitive because Shanghai is considered a more vibrant market place and globalized city than Chengdu.

A COUNTERINTUITIVE CONTRAST

Today, most unregistered churches began as private-home-gathering Bible study groups that were characterized by informal, secretive and underground features. Such organizational characteristics had become a normative state of existence for unofficial Protestantism from the 1950s to the 1990s. Since the mid 2000s, urban churches has experienced much organizational differentiation across China. Market liberalization and urbanization have paved the way for church organizational changes to occur. Some macro-institutional changes include relaxed control of foreign exchange, residential mobility, the collapse of the *danwei* system, the development of real estate and the growing usage of non-state media, such as the Internet. With the passing of private property legislation in 2004 as well as the real estate boom since 2005, more house churches gradually began to lease or move into commercial apartments or office buildings. Such a transition regarding physical space enabled churches to gain more visibility that, in turn, brought about a larger number of conversions.

Growing urban churches in China live with compartmentalized rights, however—as economic opportunities abound for them to open up and go public, the uncertain political environment still poses restraints on their continued development. For church groups who lease commercial space, police harassment and evictions from their leased facilities are common experiences. Consequently, many churches are continually relocating. An increase in the visibility of unregistered churches tends to invite attention from local authorities, who adopt a variety of control strategies. As a result, confrontations between churches and the state reflect local characteristics.

When we began our fieldwork in 2010, the general political environment was unfavorable towards any civic organizations. Such political controls are enacted differently in every city, however. For some church groups, memories of the years of persecution continue to shape their understanding of faith and public life. As a result, the inertia to remain secretive and informally organized remains strong, depending on the controls in each locality.

Shanghai

The city of Shanghai is known for being a test area of China's market reforms. This metropolis with 24.15 million population enjoys the fame of being "Oriental Paris," with a highly developed commercial culture and international flavor. Culturally, since Shanghai is home to China's largest population of internal migrants, social networks tend to be more transient. Like other global metropolitans, who deal with the fast pace of life and a high cost-of-living, Shanghai's residents are highly sensitive to time-efficiency.

Historically, two waves of religious movements strongly shaped Shanghai Protestantism. First, as the city that introduced the Three-Self Patriotic Movement in 1952, Shanghai was home to many resisting groups, both Catholic and Protestant, which went "underground" from the 1950s to the 1980s. Many church leaders suffered up to twenty years of imprisonment, especially those affiliated with the Little Flock.

Having been part of Shanghai's churches for more than a decade ourselves, we know that a United Prayer Fellowship (*liandaohui*) is currently the most extensive network, which regularly and secretly convenes leaders from over 30 unofficial church groups. There are a few other smaller inter-church networks as well, including one that connects churches with entrepreneurs who have migrated from Wenzhou, one that links inter-church campus ministry teams, and one bringing together rural migrant churches in suburban areas.

Chengdu

Chengdu is the capital city of Sichuan Province in southwest China with a population of 14.43 million and a moderate market economy. Culturally it boasts a carefree local lifestyle and slow pace of work, also named as a "teahouse culture." These social settings also breed an environment with more free speech. Historically, this city has a strong liberal tendency. For example, underground publications, which protest against communist propaganda, thrived here especially during the 1980s. With regard to religion, foreign Christians played an important role in shaping Chengdu Protestantism. They came from a different denominational background from the ones in Shanghai. In the 1940s, Chengdu was a hub for the China Inland Mission to enter the greater Southwestern China populated by ethnic minorities.

Since the 1950s, religious groups here have experienced similar political persecution as other cities of China. But the Sichuan earthquake in 2008 forced unofficial groups to engage publicly in disaster relief work, which greatly promoted openness of churches.

Since we also participated in some churches in Chengdu during long vacations, such familiarity helped us to locate the largest networks in this city also. Like other cities, Chengdu also has a United Prayer Meeting that regularly convenes leaders from over 20 unofficial church groups. There are a few smaller inter-church networks as well, including one connecting churches doing Yunnan mission work, and one connecting charismatic groups.

Table 1. A Summary of Contextual Factors of Two Cities

	Shanghai	Chengdu
Historical legacy	Headquarters of the Three-Self co-optation movement in the 1950s	Remote from state power center
Economy	Highly developed and urbanized coastal city; highly commercialized, fast pace	Inland developing city; laid-back lifestyle
Political regime	Strong party surveillance through street committees	Medium party surveillance; weak street committees
Civil strength	Independent organizations are either suppressed or co-opted; limited public space	Independent organizations are tolerated; teahouses as public space (more freedom of speech)
Religion	A large Three-Self system (over 20 congregations); most unregistered churches are closed to the public.	A small Three-Self system (2 congregations); Buddhism and Taoism thrive; most unregistered churches are open to the public.

Demographically, Shanghai churches reflect a more socially stratified urban context than the Chengdu groups. In a city attracting migrants from all other provinces, most of its church groups show social boundaries apparently overlapping with the city's social strata—there are churches comprised of white-collar professionals, those with local elderly residents, rural migrant churches, college student fellowships, etc. We think this is partly due to their closed organizational format. Unable to let new visitors or converts freely join their Sunday services, they rely on high-trust networks to recruit, which brings a great degree of homogeneity along age or socio-economic lines. Embedded in a transitory urban society, churches tend to recruit homogeneous groups. In addition, lack of diversity is not taken by leaders as a disadvantage. Only a handful of churches intentionally aim for diversity. Chengdu, on the other hand, is an inland capital city with less human migration; one finds people across all age groups, professions and educational levels in most churches. Diversification is a basic feature of churches that aids them in reaching out to their adjacent communities. Thus, it is more common to observe conversions happening across a few generations of a local family in a place like Chengdu.

TO HIDE OR NOT TO HIDE

Why has not a developed economy in Shanghai shaped churches towards more openness, compared to the less developed city of Chengdu? We analyze the causal processes at institutional, organizational and individual levels using the qualitative data from our fieldwork.

Local Institutional Environment

Shanghai

Despite Shanghai's well-known economic status, this city is less known for its restrictive local government, which imposes strong regulations on any social organizations. It develops a range of controls, including neighborhood surveillance, registration limitations and co-optation of social organizations (into a category ironically known as Government-NGOs).[1] Consequently, the number and vibrancy of social organizations in Shanghai are exceeded by those in many other Chinese cities. In addition, all residential communities are under the close surveillance of the Communist Party's watchdogs, the street committees. Since the 2010 international exposition in Shanghai, this city has seen a strengthened force of state security officers. Thus, even when popular acceptance of Protestant groups in Shanghai grew, churches still existed within a largely hostile political environment. Two

---

1. We do not claim that the government restricts all social organizations, because these controls vary with regard to the mission of different organizations. For example, organizations that focus on environmental protection and educational issues are least controlled but workers' rights and religiously-affiliated organizations are tightly controlled.

churches gained global publicity after experiencing government evictions in this city.[2]

State harassment frequently occurs when churches exceed a certain size, when they invite foreign speakers or if they include activists. Zhao (pseudonym, female, 34) was planning to attend a church training session given by a foreign speaker in its rented space. That week, the police put pressure on the landlord to discontinue the lease precisely when the guest speaker was scheduled to be there. The landlord then locked up the apartment, leaving a few dozen members of the church waiting outside. When asked whether this type of "conflict" helps the church to rebuild communication with the government, Zhao recalled this attempt as "a waste of time":

> Our church has changed five or six locations in the past three years. We had used that space for a relatively longer time. . . . We were even willing to let the police sit in on our training, showing that we had nothing to hide. But they would not give us the chance. They play tricks behind your back . . . It is not that we lack the courage to confront them; it just takes up too much of our time to go around in circles by negotiating with them, and then realize all efforts are in vain.

The time-efficiencies of this commercial city also make similar confrontations an unthinkable act of protest for urban professional believers; such participants could expect subsequent harassments, such as a job loss or a discontinued lease. In our fieldwork, many believers mention that the "Shanghai temperament" has an influence on people's reluctance to engage in any kind of activism. Forty-eight-year-old Peng, a university professor and scholar of Christianity in a local prestigious university, confirms this general impression:

> Shanghai churches are indeed more bourgeoisie (xiaozi), compared to the more political type in Beijing and the commercial type in Wenzhou. Local people in Shanghai are generally cautious and indifferent to politics. They do not like to attract a lot of attention. They focus more on lifestyle and private happiness, rather than engaging in public affairs. Another important reason is that, even if you engage actively in something, it won't bring any change.

In Shanghai, very few scholars and intellectuals would publicly confess their faith and affiliation with the unregistered church, as Peng has done.

---

2. "Christians Held in Shanghai."
"Christian Church Shut Down."

Through observation at a university faculty Christian fellowship, we found that most Christian professors are in the fields of science and technology, where they tend to keep a low-profile regarding their religious identity.

Chengdu

At that time of writing, the present political regime in Chengdu is more tolerant towards religion in general. Prior to the late 1990s, church groups in Chengdu were organizationally similar to their Shanghai home-gathering counterparts. The 2008 earthquake thrust the city into a state of emergency and allowed voluntary religious relief workers to flood in. Interviews show that unofficial churches had to form some type of network in their relief efforts, and this changed the general condition of churches with regard to their openness. This event unexpectedly expanded the city's tolerance for religious groups. After the earthquake, local NGO registration policies were revised to allow organizations with a religious background to have legal status in order to make long-term contributions. Since then, unofficial churches of this inland city have enjoyed more freedom than the more economically developed coastal cities.

Apart from the earthquake, another factor to consider is that the city's Bureau of Religion has been headed by a more liberal-minded official since 2005. In our fieldwork, we observed a friendlier interaction between believers and political actors than in Shanghai. Gao (pseudonym, male, 60) opens up his own home for church meetings, and his upstairs neighbor is a religious bureau official, who often sends out some "insider information" to Gao concerning the safety of their Bible study meetings:

> One day he would greet me and say, "These two days are intense. Have no more meetings in your home." So, we changed to another sister's home and then moved back. Later, our church grew from 40 to 100 members, so my home was not big enough. We rented a backyard from another party cadre, whose aunt was a believer. We had meetings there for over four years, until our number grew to 200. Our meetings are always open to anyone who is willing to come, including government officials.

As Gao later explains to us, there is genuine respect and dialogue between himself and this government official neighbor, as fellow citizens of the same city. It seems in this case that political actors prioritize their communal role over their professional role as state watchdogs. Such a scenario is unthinkable in Shanghai, where the local culture of professionalism has brought about the most scrutinizing group within this system, making the surveillance network much stronger than in other cities.

Organizational Resources

Leadership

Church leaders in Shanghai and Chengdu play a crucial role in shaping the organizational forms of these groups. From the 1980s to 1990s, most unofficial groups were directed by a leading brother or sister that had founding credentials and higher seniority. Over time, a secondary hierarchical order of co-workers emerged from the new converts. New converts may also start their own home-gathering groups, making the situation more chaotic. As Rong (pseydonym, male, 35) recalls, "It is a generally recognized norm that whoever was willing to start a group would automatically become its leader." In Shanghai, most *de facto* leaders of churches have never received formal theological training. Later, a transition towards having ordained and theologically-educated clergy emerged, but this idea was more welcomed by the younger generation of leaders than the first-generation, who were 50 years of age or older.

Leaders' opinions regarding the church-state relationship strongly influence how the group makes decisions about whether they should split into smaller groups or worship outdoors as a congregation after a government eviction. In Shanghai, we observed an apolitical attitude among church leaders, especially within the older generation. Uncle Yang (pseydonym, male, 80) makes a comparison between his younger years and "this age" when asked his thoughts about the outdoor-worship of the Shouwang Church in Beijing. In his day, said Yang, house church Christians were unable to assemble in such a size to confront the state:

> When the government demanded us to split, to keep in small numbers, we just followed these demands, as long as we could read the Bible and pursue spiritual growth. If you want to argue with them, wait and see how much time and effort you would have to put into it! Now there comes a younger generation, formally organized, who thinks it problematic to hide in living rooms, and they want to have a dialogue with the government. But personally, I do not think the same. God has entrusted us with His Word, and a life following Christ with His cross. We can just meet quietly, and when the church grows too numerous, we split. We do not keep a 1000-member church at the same place.

The splitting model is a commonly used strategy to divert attention from political authorities. We observed that Shanghai house churches commonly adopt this tactic. As 50-year-old Bian (pseudonym, male) recalls, although initial harassment from the local government disturbed their meetings, over the long run, the close-knit small group model helped his church to grow. On the other hand, splitting delays church openness, because what lies behind it is fear of the government; such fear begets further suspicion from the authorities who keep following their old measures of suppression.

Another noteworthy feature of Shanghai churches is the wide adoption of the three-month probation period for new members and member transfers. As 30-year-old church leader Dang (pseudonym, male) explains, this rule is first to keep secret police and cult members out, but it also allows for believers to "grow spiritually in small groups":

> We require a newcomer to commit first to his small group, and if he comes irregularly, we would not invite him into our Sunday worship gathering. We also ask the small-group leader to get to know his background, ask him to fill out a form, including his previous church, etc. Apart from security concerns, this is also for his own spiritual growth, because our small groups are strong, and he can first build up relationships with brothers and sisters there, to form some fellowship ties. We don't think Sunday worship can offer the same opportunity for fellowshipping with one another.

Although leaders in Shanghai offer reasons to justify the practice of conditional admission to Sunday services for Christians moving from other cities, this practice appears unwelcoming. Thirty-three-year-old Chang (pseudonym) belonged to an unofficial church in Beijing. After a job relocation to Shanghai, he had great difficulty joining a church in his new location. He explains:

> Many churches here limit the number of people who can attend Sunday worship. To me, this is unacceptable. They practically deprived you of your right to worship! They say you have to pass the 'observation period', etc. Apart from a few charismatic churches I have been to, most traditional churches here all have this rule. I don't think this is biblical. . . . In comparison with Beijing, I feel churches here have many restrictions; when you say you are from another church or another city, they look at you with suspicion.

In comparison, the city of Chengdu is seeing a group of new leaders who are using the Protestant faith to inform other areas of social life. To some extent, the post-earthquake situation has increased leaders' enthusiasm about social volunteerism in general. Some church leaders are interested in addressing believers' civil responsibilities as well. These social engagements with public life all require the church to open up in the first place. Before 38-year-old Lian (pseudonym, male) became a Christian, he was a lawer. A previous law case made him realize the importance of church openness:

> I used to provide legal aid for some persecuted churches, and I witnessed the consequences of lack of openness—when a church tries to stay 'underground' or closed; it tends to mimic the traits of secret societies in China's history. It fails to connect with the universal church for ecclesiological resources. Likewise, it also fails to respond adequately to this society by only hiding itself quietly and operating with its own re-invented wheel. . . . So the moment I believed, I was certain that our church needed to open up.

Lian's personal convictions about an open church became assets for his church's transition in 2009. At that time, they had been evicted from their rented apartments several times. After two months of outdoor worship, they purchased a property in an office building and placed their name plate amidst other companies and organizations in the lobby: Living Water Church (pseudonym, abbreviated as LWC). Its Sunday services have opened up to the public and have often been visited by local police and state security agents. Through participant observation, we found that, in addition to Scripture, teaching often emphasizes "praying for peace in this city" and cultivating civic virtue in public life. LWC has its own newsletter publications (also un-approved by the state), which are delivered to local street committees and police stations. This active and friendly outreach to government officials gradually reduces the suspicion of local regulators, with an effect that benefits all the other unregistered churches in Chengdu city. In our interviews with a few leaders of other churches that have purchased properties, LWC's pioneering step of buying a building relates to the decisions their churches are making, both temporally and causally.

Spatial Resources

We learn from our fieldwork that when churches lease commercial apartments or office building space, the landlord usually asks about the use of the space. For security concerns, not all of them reply honestly. Some claim to use the space for business personnel training or human resource development. They further caution the landlords that such activities may involve different kinds of people and produce some noise. Once the landlord finds out that the space is used for an unofficial church, then it is up to the landlord's discretion whether the group should move out. However, some church leaders prefer telling the truth from the very beginning and promise to keep the noise down. Nevertheless, relocation often happens in both cases, when the government finds out and pressures the landlord.

Owning a space is a pivotal turning point for an unofficial church to develop organizationally.[3] The budgeting, financing and other decisions regarding the purchase test the church group's organizational capacities. After the purchase, it may or may not lead to more openness, depending on the leaders' vision. In Shanghai, for example, although real estate prices are high, three out of our sample of 17 churches purchased a building, but none of them opened its Sunday services to the general public.

Inter-Group Influences

With the formation of inter-church networks in every city, unofficial church groups come into closer contact with each other. Since their individual organizational decisions may influence how local authorities regulate all churches, inter-group pressure has become an important factor affecting their organizational practices. Take the ordination of ministers, for example. We learned from our fieldwork in Shanghai that apart from a few fundamentalist churches, most church leaders are not formally ordained, nor do they wish to be. This makes them different from other cities. Church leader Zang (pseudonym, male, 55) applies a logic of "Chinese exceptionalism" to justify this reluctance:

> Ordination is a most troublesome matter in today's house churches. I dare not ask pastors from abroad to lay hands on me, for fear that this might become bring accusations from the government. Equally, I have difficulties in letting any co-worker in China to lay hands on me, because all the leaders who are senior to me are not yet ordained. This is a historical problem. House churches in China, when you look at it in terms of baptisms, are like Baptist churches; then, in terms of having no formal clergy, they are like the Church of the Brethren. In organizational structure, some follow the Presbyterian Church. And if

3. Ma and Li, "Remaking the Civic Space."

you ask, "What on earth is it?" I tell you, it is called "Chinese
house church."

Clergy ordination, purchase of church property and church openness
all involve political risks. In a city where no precedent has been set, the
risks seem higher. Hence, the Chinese idiom "Shoot the bird which takes
the lead." In Chengdu, LWC is willing to take such risks. Before its building
purchase in 2009, leaders of LWC received harsh criticism from many other
churches. Twenty-eight-year-old church leader Kang (pseudonym) from a
neighboring church recalls this controversy:

> At the time we all had the idea that LWC might bring risks to
> all churches in Chengdu. Although we knew that persecution
> is good for the church historically, we still had worries. . . . We
> prayed for LWC, and for Shouwang in Beijing. Now I am grate-
> ful to have them walking ahead of us. The [unregistered] church
> can have its voice heard now, and we can inform the govern-
> ment of our wishes and needs. . . . If we still act as we did before,
> doing nothing when caught and beaten, maybe things would
> still be the same many years later. Since we have legal scholars
> like Stephen, who knows the law and deals with authorities us-
> ing the state's own law, it is a blessing. Now churches in Chengdu
> are in a revival, and this has much to do with LWC. . . . LWC is
> a model to show the government that we are not doing political
> activism—we just worship God. You can come if you will, look
> at our newsletter, donation reports, sermons, etc. . . . The police
> came to our church meetings and listened to sermons.

Church-switching in these two cities also involves very different
inter-group processes. In Shanghai, voluntary switching from one church
to another is considered against the norm. Not only is this action taken as
a lack of religious commitment, but church leaders also have a tacit mutual
consent not to receive such members. Moreover, receiving members from
another church causes offense to the leader of their former church by causing him to "lose face." This practice poses a costly and difficult challenge for
a believer who grows dissatisfied with the quality of preaching or theological
position of his/her current church and wishes to change to another church.

Twenty-eight-year-old Lu (pseudonym) recalls that she and two room-
mates were initially members of a newly-founded church group, where the
young lay young preacher, also a new convert, had been teaching something
problematic to them. They and many young people grew concerned. These
three female members went to an elderly lay minister of another church,
asking if they could switch to his church. Surprisingly, he refused because

of concerns that it would harm the rapport between him and the young preacher. Receiving people who transfer from another church is considered "sheep-stealing." Lu and her friends had no other option, so they stopped going to church altogether. When she found another church that was willing to have her join, it was a year after posting the need for a biblical church on a Christian forum.

In Chengdu, members who switch churches also invite expressions of concerns from church leaders. But in some open churches, membership by-laws state clearly the procedures for changing to another church or for receiving people from other churches. Such routinization makes church-switching less strenuous. It is also a step towards freer mobility in the increasingly competitive religious market.

Theological Resources

We find that the theological stance also affects church organizational openness. For example, historically, Shanghai churches are greatly influenced by the Little Flock, whose pietistic theology focuses on individual spirituality and tends to disassociate faith and political activism.[4] Thus, concerns for church organization and openness are secondary. Among the fundamentalist churches in Shanghai that tend to adopt more openness to the public, a dispensational pre-millennial worldview helps to disintegrate the fear of political suppression. The emphasis of charismatic and Pentecostal churches upon spiritual gifts, renewals and revivals makes them more willing to open up Sunday services to potential converts. A mixture of charismatic and Little Flock theology also exists in some groups, however, which generally prevents them from adopting more openness.

The theologies of Chinese Protestant churches have been understudied. Daniel Bays points out that during the revivals in the 1920s, most clergy preached the old salvationist and revivalist message with some millenarian or Pentecostal characteristics.[5] But little is known about the theology of unofficial Protestant groups today. From the 1950s to mid 1980s, these groups expanded without sufficient copies of the Bible, for possessing them was illegal. Bible-smuggling was a mission strategy of foreigners. It was not until after Bible printing was legally allowed in 1986 and after most previously imprisoned clergy were also released that religious teachings actually resumed. So, these gap years contributed to a prevalent problem—most Protestant groups lacked the theological resources to deepen and defend

4. Lee, "Watchman Nee and the Little Flock," 68–96.

5. Bays, *A New History of Christianity in China*.

their faith. Our interviews with individuals who became converts before the 1980s show that they recall a similarly truncated faith journey.

The decision to open up, when backed up by these theological convictions, may relieve the fear of official harassments as well as putting more accountability on the members. The pastor of LWC mentions how the theology of LWC brings about a practical emphasis on church order and mutual responsibility:

> For the church to open up, everyone should observe the rules, including respecting the authority of church elders. We want God's Word to reshape the church, in areas of administration, sermons, faith statements, finance, etc. Rules can assist us in sanctification. So our Reformed ecclesiology is a big challenge to a privatized faith. If you would like to join and use this nice sanctuary, you have to take the corresponding responsibilities. . . . A few times I spoke against the government in sermons, as God's truth governs all spheres. So the congregation needs to face the fear inside of themselves. It takes some time. To some brothers and sisters, such speech is an encouragement, especially for those living in fear. They realized that it is not a big deal and were set free. Another effect is to let them think seriously about our society. . . . Over time, nothing happened to LWC, and the people have overcome their fear.

Many young church leaders in both Shanghai and Chengdu mentioned to us that for church organizations to develop, such a transition must find its basis in theology. As 30-year-old church leader Wang (pseudonym) says,

> It used to be that a church was modeled in a way to fit the spiritual maturity of the leader and believers. But this type of church will always be in an unstable state. I have seen too many such examples. The leader will always be in a state of anxiety. Institutions certainly have problems, but I gradually realized that, beneath these church institutions, theology is a very important foundation; it serves to underpin the institutions. If we don't even have a similar theological background or identification, it is hard to talk about church institutionalization. To me, this realization has much to do with reading Reformed literature.

Churches that open up to the general public need a re-education process, for most of them started as casual home gatherings, where rules or rituals had not been primary concerns. But once a church opens up its services, worship rituals and procedures of congregational meetings need to be in place. Members of newly opened-up churches in Chengdu observe the change—there are more open discussions and participation in debating and negotiation in church-related decision-making. These rule changes also meet with resistance, since some older members are concerned about "losing the house church tradition" because the traditional ways of house churches have gained a good spiritual reputation. When confronted with such questioning, 40-year-old pastor Lin (pseudonym, male) always replies:

> Yes, we are house churches, but you have to be a church in the first place! You have to know what a church is in the Bible. But evangelical theology does not offer a strong systematic answer to this question. Reformed theology does, and it challenges you to return every sphere of your life to the Word. Externally, believers have to interact with and impact the wider society; while internally, your church organization has to be re-formed, and we naturally adopt the Presbyterian church order.

We learned from our fieldwork that since the mid 2000s, China's urban churches have been going through a denominational or theological differentiation process (we will elaborate on this in Chapter Nine). Groups that used to fall under the general umbrella category of "house churches" now identify themselves as evangelical, Baptist, fundamentalist, Reformed, charismatic, Pentecostal, etc. This diversification plays an important role in the development of church organizational openness.

Political-cultural norms

Since organizations of a local society reflect its cultural norms and beliefs, as economic historian Avner Grief defines them, the "ideas and thoughts common to people that govern interaction, between these people, and between them, their gods, and other groups," unify, maintain and communicate that local culture.[6] Cultural beliefs include but venture beyond religious beliefs. By applying this notion to shed light on the organizational form of unregistered churches in China, we refer to an individual's socialized perception of his or her relationship to other individuals, including political actors, believers and nonbelievers; his or her relationship to church groups, government organizations and other social groups; and his or her relationship to God. Certain political attitudes and theological convictions all filter through a locally embedded perspective of understanding. Taking churches with fundamentalist theology, for example, we discover the one

---

6. Greif, "Cultural Beliefs and the Organization of Society," 913.

in Shanghai (GU) has adopted more openness than other churches, but the one in Chengdu (SL) remains semi-closed (see Appendix 1).

Different cultural processes in Shanghai and Chengdu are at work in keeping churches closed or shaping them towards openness. Churches in Shanghai live in a high level of uncertainty regarding religious regulations. As a result, church leaders adopt a conflict perspective on the church-state relationship. Since leadership structures remain arbitrary and hierarchical, members rely heavily on leaders for information. In addition, close-knit groups led by elderly church leaders share norms and perceptions shaped by state regulations and experiences of persecution. Secure and stable spatial resources are rare. Inter-group pressure against ordination and openness is strong. Their pietistic theology tends to disassociate faith and political activism.

Religious leaders play an important role in maintaining these cultural understandings. We found in our interviews that leaders of groups in a segregated space tended to consider this "half-open, half-closed" *status quo* as the breeding ground of house church activities; it was the cause for church growth, in their eyes. Church leaders tend to educate members "not to mess with politics" but to focus on individual spirituality and evangelism through close-knit networks. Small and secretive home-gatherings are believed to be the best strategy for simultaneously securing safety and fulfilling religious duties. Over time, these beliefs and norms have prevented groups in segregated space from attempting innovation.

Chengdu churches are also embedded in an uncertain political environment, but the post-quake local regime has given rise to more tolerance towards religious groups. In the local civil society, a social engagement culture is already in place. At the organizational level, the growing church groups coexist and interact with other active social organizations. Local officials have a natural neighborly rapport with these groups. Their inter-group connections have grown stronger as more churches successfully made property purchases. At the level of individual action, close-knit groups share norms and perceptions shaped both by state rules and citizens' ability to challenge, negotiate or detour around these rules. Again, leaders play an important role in promoting a more seasoned understanding of the state-church relationship. Over time, these beliefs and convictions toward openness have facilitated dialogues and interactions with officials. Meetings of open churches in Chengdu are frequented by plain-clothes police or state security agents, but the more openly they present themselves to these state actors, the more the government's suspicion seems to diminish. In this way, a positive feedback loop between these churches and the authorities is formed.

What is more, on the level of collective action, a few leading churches have triggered a chain reaction towards openness in Chengdu. These milestone activities include purchasing church property and founding Christian institutions (schools and seminaries). These eventual successes have lowered the overall political risks for churches in that locality. This, in turn, has encouraged more churches to follow suit, both in obtaining property and theological diversification.

CONCLUSION

Marketization in post-1978 China has reshaped the public space for church groups to evolve into new organizational forms. A range of important factors that shape these groups into gradually moving towards openness include a historical memory of past persecutions, reactions in the local regime after 2010, and believers' cultural understandings of how churches should relate to political actors. Apart from these factors, acquiring property also provides a strong impetus for churches to re-organize and open themselves to the public.

The contrast between Shanghai and Chengdu as two regional models is striking and counterintuitive, for it suggests that economic development does not necessarily prepare the way for social visibility of Christian groups. Although theological resources certainly play an important role in shaping believers' understanding of their relationship with the government, such understandings are still culturally configured by the norms of civil society in that particular locality.

6

CCP

Not to have a correct political point of view is like having no soul.

—Mao Zedong[1]

Twenty-year-old Xiao (pseudonym, female) is a college sophomore majoring in sociology in one of China's top universities. Last week was her baptism, which was an occasion full of new hope and joy. A week later, however, she appeared troubled and concerned. Before embracing the Christian faith through a campus fellowship, Xiao was a preparatory member of the Communist Party in her program. Now her new faith has brought trouble upon that part of her life.

In China's state-run universities, which Xi Jinping requires to be Communist Party "strongholds," every department has to have a branch of the Communist Party.[2] College students who excel in their programs are chosen to become preparatory members of the Party (*yubei dangyuan*). After two years of training, these preparatory members will make public vows to join the Chinese Communist Party (abbreviated as CCP) formally. Each preparatory member is assigned to a Party Counselor (*fudaoyuan*) who oversees the person's political attitudes.[3] Xiao has been assigned to

1. Mao, *Collected Works*, 5:385.

2. Philips, "China Universities Must."

3. See Lu, *Pragmatic Strategies and Power Relations,* 164. A *fudaoyuan* who monitors students' life, morality, and political thought in China's universities is not the same as that of a psychological counselor in the West, despite what the name may appear

a female Party Counselor who is responsible for mentoring her growth in "political thought." After all, she is the best student in her program in terms of grades and character. Xiao has always confided to her counselor as a sister does, even including her consideration for Christian baptism. She did not expect that this sister-like counselor would report it to her upper authorities. A stern "No" came to Xiao, followed by many warnings. To many, the inclination to seek Christian baptism would have led to a bad record that lowers one's chance of getting good employment after graduation. After a few weeks of struggling and praying about it, Xiao eventually went ahead with her baptism. Her heart was prepared for quitting her application into the CCP. After talking about quitting the Party with her counselor, however, Xiao was told that quitting was not a possibility. The counselor literally said to her that "It is the Party that chose you, not you the Party."

A NO-EXIT PARTY

Although the CCP constitution includes articles about resigning one's membership; in reality, quitting is not a live option. To people who work in public positions such as government, military and schools, the decision to quit normally brings tremendous pressure from political authorities in these workplaces. First, such deserters are seen as protestors against the regime.[4] Secondly, the occurrence of quitting the CCP is made into an indicator of local cadres' political performance, which affects their chances of promotion in CCP hierarchy. For example, if someone applies for withdrawal from CCP, it would register as a "political event" in that work place. Therefore, a CCP branch would try its best to persuade members not to leave. This involves hours of "counseling," which if ineffective would escalate to threats of loss of benefits or career.

After the 1989 Tiananmen crackdown, a college teaching faculty member Liu (pseudonym) submitted an application to leave the CCP. He

---

to mean. A *fudaoyuan*'s evaluation is weighty and it may affect a student's school records and awards. As required by universities, this position seeks to "help students in establishing a correct view of the world and of life, values, firmly proceed on the road of socialism with Chinese characteristics under the leadership of the CCP, achieving the great rejuvenation of the Chinese nation as a common ideal and conviction. Active guidance of students to continuously strive for higher goals, make the advanced elements among them establish the lofty ideals of Communism, and establish a firm belief in Marxism." The relationship between a *fudaoyuan* and a student is a power relation, and the former often use conversational and questioning techniques to obtain control.

4 For example, Falun Gong uses quitting CCP as one of its strategies of protest. Ostergaard, "Governance and the Political Challenge of the Falun Gong," 207–25.

also determinedly posted a public announcement about it on the bulletin. This act became a political event in his college. The general secretary of the CCP branch in his college warned Liu that these actions would bring "great political costs" to a young and promising professor like him. To contain the spread of the influence of this event, the department tried to hide the matter from becoming more public. Fifteen years later, Liu had the chance to look into his own personnel dossier (*dang'an*) kept by the college, and found that he was still listed as a CCP member.[5] "This is ridiculous! I haven't even participated in their meetings or paid the membership fees for all these years," Liu remarked.

Quitting the CCP may bring imprisonment, as shown by the case of Dai Qing, the step-daughter of Ye Jianying, a top CCP founding official. Dai worked as a journalist for *Light Daily* (*Guangmng Ribao*), a nationwide comprehensive newspaper under the direct leadership of the CCP Propaganda Department. Following the 1989 Tiananmen crackdown, Dai publicly announced her resignation from the party, and suffered a one-year imprisonment because of its negative political impact on the public.[6]

Even today after over thirty years of economic liberalization, the Chinese regime still maintains tight control over media, military and education institutions. Zhang Xuezhong, a law professor in East China Politics and Law University, announced his intent to quit the CCP in 2012. He also wrote an article supporting constitutional rights in his public announcement. Despite high appraisals from students of this college for this gifted teacher, Zhang's university revoked his teaching responsibilities in 2013 and later deposed him.[7] We had a few informal interviews with Zhang in 2012. He has been protesting the comeback of "CCP culture" which has penetrated higher education through required courses on Marxism, Leninism and Maoism. University students generally show disrespect for faculty who are teaching such courses. In order to force students into attending the classes, they assigned seating and required attendance-keeping as a large component of one's final grade. As one student complains, "they pretend to be teaching, and we pretend to be listening." In fact, universities allocate generous grants for keeping these classes taught by "devout" communist faculty members. So CCP membership not only relates to one's political viewpoint, but it also involves vested interests from state-funded courses and programs.

5. Chinese *Dang'an* under Communism is an archival system that records the political performance and attitudes of citizens. It also contains other documents that are considered private.

6. Dai, *My Imprisonment*.

7. Andew, "Chinese Professor Who Advocated."

Rong (pseudonym, male, 61) is a highly prestigious law professor in his university. He became a Christian and joined a house church in 2008 after a family crisis. By then he had been a Party member for over 30 years. Deep down, Rong knows that he had moved from being a zealous believer of Communism to a mere nominal CCP member. Rong did not feel bothered by keeping this nominal title until his dramatic conversion into the Christian faith. He decided to renounce his CCP membership, and because he has been such a well-known figure in that university, Rong thought that the best way to do it was through a public personal announcement.

Hoping to show respect to his department head and leadership, Rong met up with them and told them about this decision. They were, of course, shocked and unwilling to let this happen publicly. The meeting ended unpleasantly, and Rong felt that it was not a good time to act on his decision. A month later, Rong's church suffered harassment from local authorities. This ill treatment became another trigger for him to finally act on quitting the CCP. He had another meeting with department leadership. This time, they tried to persuade him that a CCP membership can be compatible with a Christian identity. They even said, "Couldn't you learn from our Buddhist or Muslim comrades? Don't talk about your faith in public, and we will allow that." Rong found this quite amusing. He opened up his Bible to show them how Jesus said that if believers disown him before men, they will be disowned before God. The department leadership all responded, "You Christians are such a strange breed!" After this meeting, the whole department knew about Rong's conversion.

Leaving the Communist Party is also a common difficulty facing many new Christian converts who work in state-owned enterprises or state firms. Many of them experience interrogation and pressure from their workplace authorities that have Communist Party branches. CCP membership is also one of the criteria for further promotions.

Huang (45) worked for a state-owned firm, and after years of good performance, the CCP branch leaders in his firm tried to recruit him. For more than a decade, a part of him has been hidden to his co-workers—his Christian upbringing. He worked hard and was nominated as one of the candidates for a managerial position. The CCP branch cadres asked him to join the Party first. Huang hesitated and told them that he came from a Christian family with complicated overseas connections. That served as a good excuse for not joining CCP. With this admission, the promotion opportunity also disappeared.

RISING CCP MEMBERSHIP

Quite counter-intuitively, the two decades after 1989 witnessed significant growth in CCP membership. Compared with a CCP membership of 47 million in 1988, by 2012, this figure had almost doubled to 85.1 million. This means that CCP membership had increased by 1.8 times. Why did this happen?

After the 1989 political crisis, CCP leadership accelerated market reform, which provided more opportunities for political officials to form a profitable alliance with economic elites. Although some scholars predicted that such growing opportunism would bring decline to CCP commitment,[8] the reality turned out to be more complicated. While Communism as a dominant ideology had come to its end by 1989, the organizational competence of the CCP-led regime has not declined. Rather, it transformed itself into an economically-oriented collusion between political and economic elites.[9] Therefore CCP membership has now become socio-political capital for seeking career opportunities.[10] Meanwhile, CCP does not allow disgruntled members to quit, so its membership growth actually includes this reluctant group. It is estimated that the total number of CCP membership has grown steadily from less than 40 million in 1980 to over 80 million in 2012.[11] China's National Civil Servants Exam website reports an even higher number.[12] Until recently, some scholars also found that parental and peer pressure play a pivotal role in converting young college students into CCP members, especially when one's parents work in the public sector.[13]

Simultaneous with the trend of "diving into the sea" of commerce is the rising fad for college graduates to obtain government posts. In 2013, a record 1.52 million test takers signed up for the exam.[14] Considered as the "golden rice-bowl," most civil-service jobs (*gongwuyuan*) and later promotions require CCP membership, a symbol of politically correct status and connections. These hidden benefits of CCP membership appealed to college students even before their graduation and job-search because most state-run universities grant scholarships and awards to students who are

---

8. Nee and Lian, "Sleeping with the Enemy," 256.

9. Walder, "The Party Elite," 189–209.

10. Bian, et al, "Communist Party Membership," 805–41; Lu and Tao. "Determinants of Entrepreneurial Activities," 261–73; Dickson, "Integrating Wealth and Power," 827–54.

11. Chen, "Structural Changes in CCP."

12. China's National Civil Servants Exam website.

13. Liu et al., "How Well Can Public Service," 191–211.

14. "Chinese Grads Still Eager."

CCP members. These processes all help explain the resurgent appeal of CCP membership.[15] In a word, China's economic reform has produced an opportunistic elite class who blur their identity boundaries to enjoy both political and economic benefits.

Netizens and bloggers have discussed whether CCP membership will better one's chance in the labor market. A junior college student asked, "I am not a CCP member yet, and many people told me that it will be a problem because even if your score is high, you are out during the interview. Is that true?" Another netizen replied, "It depends. Party and political posts certainly require it. For other jobs, if you pass the bottom score line, there is much room to maneuver. But no matter what, your later promotion depends on CCP membership." On another blog, one college freshman asked, "My mother is pushing me to join the CCP because it will make job-search easier. Will it?" Someone replied, "In college, your grades and scholarships are linked to CCP membership, so it is better to keep a high political awareness (*zhengzhi juewu gao*)."

Religious synergism of Christianity and socialism is not new. Many Christians who supported the founding of the Three-Self movement in the 1950s subscribed to the view that the socialist liberation of China by the Communist Party was "in accordance with God's plan for historical development,"[16] and that the chief mission of the church is to "serve the society."[17] Based on these tenets, religious doctrines that are not in line with socialism need to be "toned down" through a "theological reconstruction."[18] For example, the primary promoter of such a theology Bishop Ding Guangxun once claimed that atheism can be compatible with the work of the Cosmic Christ, for "the humanism of the atheists is actually just another way whereby the human race searches for God; it's just that they don't use the term God."[19] He later developed an ethical Christianity to resolve the contradiction between Christian ethics and unbelief; that is, whether atheists can do good or not for society should not be judged on the basis of salvation. The party-state supports it as the "mainstream" theology of the Protestant church in China, but it also warns party cadres who have been involved in religious affairs work for a long time that one should "keep a

---

15. "Civil-Service Exams."

16. Chen, "Drops of Theological Thought," 28.

17. Ding, "Looking Back," 363–64.

18. Xu, "The Key to Making a Success," 24–25.

19. Ding, "The Cosmic Christ," 2–4.
Ding, "The Church in China," 8–9.

clear head" in not stirring up conflicts between different opinions within the church.[20]

From our interviews and observation through China's emerging new media such as *weibo*, a Chinese version of Twitter, the conflict between CCP membership and one's Christian identity has become a heated debate. With Christianity becoming a fast-growing religion, especially among unregistered churches, the atheistic CCP regime considers it as an increasing threat to their albeit fading and increasingly less-accepted official ideology. Since 2000, hundreds of academic articles in China's higher education publications have mentioned the growing presence of Christianity on Chinese university campuses, all with negative connotations, such as "infiltration" and "prevention."[21] Obviously, as we document in Chapter Four regarding the sporadic growth of campus ministries and college believers, there has been a noticeable change of attitude among scholars who serve the CCP with their government-funded research projects.

COMMUNIST CHRISTIANS?

Should a newly-converted Christian believer retain his or her Communist Party membership? Or should he or she quit the Communist Party? During our interviews, different answers were given to these questions. Among those who see no conflict between the Christian identity and party membership, an economist and university professor Zhao Xiao has been most vocal in endorsing the no-quit solution.[22] To many others, being a Christian Communist Party member seems to be a false faith or at least a type of religious syncretism. Those who view Communist Party membership as a political religion are less likely to marry their Christian identity with it.

Before addressing why Chinese Communist Party membership poses a debatable issue for Chinese Christians, we need to first ask another

20. Zhou et al., "Encourage and Support Protestantism," 75.

21. Examples see Feng, "Methods and Features of Religious Infiltration," 114–16; He, "Religious Infiltration," 109–11; Kong, et al., "New Situations of Religious Infiltration," 59–61; Cai, et al., "Systems of Prevention against Religious Infiltration," 62–64.

22. Zhao is famous for publishing an article in 2002 entitled "Market Economies with Churches and Market Economies without Churches," which argued for a positive association between economic success and the spread of Christianity. He was formerly the Head of Economic Research Center, Macro Strategy Department of State-Owned Assets Supervision and Administration Commission of the China State Council. He also teaches at the University of Science and Technology in Beijing. Zhao claims to be a Christian and a CCP member on public occasions. He is also interviewed by the *Economist*. Zhao, "Sons of Heaven."

question: Can Communists become Christians? How likely is it? One has to know that the Chinese Communist Party is the largest political party in the world, with over 85 million members, and the total number is increasing by an average of one million people each year. According to Communist Party policies, any publicly-owned enterprise with three to fifty party members needs to establish a party branch (*dangzhibu*), so this CCP bureaucratic arrangement penetrates all public enterprises, including state-owned firms or enterprises, military troops, and all levels of educational institutions from primary schools to universities across the country.[23] Some foreign ventures, such as Wal-Mart were even required to set up party branches.[24] Given the fact that over 6.5 percent of mainland Chinese are members of the Chinese Communist Party (and this percentage is much higher among urban dwellers than rural ones), it is not a rare phenomenon for former-CCP-members to experience conversion within the growing Christian urban churches.[25]

This high likelihood is further confirmed by the recent public rules published by the Party to ban members from following religious beliefs. According to one article on *Qiu Shi*, the official publication of CCP, the central CCP committee required that "CCP members ought not have religious beliefs, but rather to educate CCP members and cadres in a confirmed Communist belief while being alert against religious erosion. Serious measures are to be taken against those who hold strong beliefs in religions at the expense of their membership, or who utilize their occupations to promote religious fervor."[26] The article highlights that this prohibition has always been "a consistent principle of our Party." A more elaborate explanation of these rules appeared again in 2015 by China's Central Commission for Discipline Inspection (CCDI), the highest internal-control institution of the CCP (see Appendix 2 for a full translation of this document).[27] This article states that "Chinese citizens have freedom of religion, but Communist party members are not common citizens; they are fighters in the vanguard for a Communist consciousness." This document hints that a sizeable group of rank and file party members have turned to religions.[28] In mid 2016, Xi Jinping unabashedly emphasized that CCP cadres must act as "unyielding Marxist atheists." According to China observer William Nee, this was a

23. "Guidance for Establishing a Party Branch."

24. "A Party Branch for Wal-Mart."

25. Yuen, "Communist Party Membership Is Still."

26. Zhu, "CCP Members Should Not Believe."

27. "If Party Members' Religious Conversions"; Gan, "Ban on Religion is 'Unshakeable' Principle."

28. "Warning over Religious Believers in CCP."

form of "obligatory Marxist atheism" that had disappeared from CCP decrees over the past few decades.[29]

The Party's "internal" control also extends its arm to overseas Chinese groups through the so-called United Front.[30] China has been sending visiting scholars since the 2000s, and many of these university professors found themselves exposed to Christianity through various Christian groups, such as campus fellowships and local Chinese churches. For example, most churches in the United States that are adjacent to college campuses have evangelistic projects to reach out to visiting scholars from China. Although most of these visiting scholars stay for only one year, many have converted to Christianity. For these new converts, one struggle is whether to get baptized in the United States.

Long (pseudonym, male, 48) is a department chair in one of Beijing's top universities. He and his family went to the United States on a one-year visiting scholarship funded by the Chinese government, and they quickly became interested in attending a local Chinese church. Long and his wife both felt converted but they hesitated to receive baptisms there. After some persuasion from the pastor and other church friends, Lin later confided to them that one of his visiting scholar friends who also came to church regularly is an informant hired by the CCP branch in his university. As a party member, Lin is concerned that a public baptismal ceremony in the United States would be reported directly to his university and that such a step would ruin his career.

By 2014, the toppling of hundreds of crosses on churches in Wenzhou had further testified to the growing intolerance of the CCP toward Christians. Provincial authorities stressed that a pre-screening examination for aspiring party members had been unevenly enforced, leading to a higher percentage of members in this area who openly espouse Christianity than other regions in China.[31] This purging campaign escalated into a national

29. Campbell, "China's Leader Xi Jinping Reminds."

30. "New Rules Harden Communist Party's Control over Religions." This news article on UCANews refers to the United Front as "particularly influential over religious groups because it oversees the State Administration for Religious Affairs, which in turn manages China's five recognized religions—Catholicism, Protestantism, Islam, Buddhism and Daoism."

31. Cao, "Zhejiang CPC Bans Religious Beliefs." This article also mentions that "Education focusing on establishing Marxist views of religion will be carried out among Party members in rural Zhejiang, while Party members will need to submit a written promise rejecting religion beliefs." Actually since early 1990s, the party-state has launched a nation-wide campaign of "education in patriotism," with the intention of deepening a way of thinking that prioritizes the love for the motherland under the leadership of the CCP over all other relations. The legally constituted authority of

consolidation of Communist ideology over the next two years. In the new year of 2015, China's Minister of Education vowed that "western values" are not allowed into China's university classrooms, and curricula are required to align with "patriotic education policies" and Marxist principles.[32] Multiple incidents of university professors being fired for speaking about universal values or against the comeback of Maoism took place.[33] During recent Christmas seasons, the education bureau of Wenzhou city has issued a ban on all Christmas celebrations in schools, and a few other city authorities did the same.[34]

CONCLUSION

Before the collapse of the socialist *danwei* system in the 1990s, the Chinese lived with a set of unified identities, either urban or rural residents according to socioeconomic classification, or classified politically either as CCP members or "the mass" (*qunzhong*). Yet with the accelerating growth of the private economy since the early 1990s, people have begun to embrace plural identities. Religious identity is an emerging one, as shown in a nation-wide 2007 survey; 84 percent of CCP members and 85 percent of non-members claimed to hold religious beliefs.[35] Although China has become an increasingly pluralistic society, these political, economic, social and religious identity boundaries often cross or even clash.[36] This contrast is especially evident when the number of urban Christians soared in the 2000s, while the CCP has correspondingly been efficient in its recruitment, forming the largest political party in the world. The inevitable overlap of these two groups has spawned interesting debates that reflect the nuanced dynamics of state-church relationships.

From what we have observed, it seems that the CCP has created an unsolvable and ironic dilemma through these intolerance campaigns. On the one hand, CCP leaders have expressed the lack of moral values in their political party, where corruption has run unchecked and rampant. On the

nationalism and patriotism has replaced the already collapsed official Marxist ideology. Religions, being a useful part of the spiritual civilization project, still have to play a supportive role in promoting such a patriotism for the party-state, the embodiment of the motherland. Marquand, "In 'China's Jerusalem.'"

32. Anderlini, "'Western Values' Forbidden."

33. "Chinese Professor Sacked."

34. Chin and Yang, "China Gets Its Claus Out."

35. Quoted in Yang, "Differentiating Religion." The 2007 Chinese Spiritual Life Survey was conducted by Horizon Research Group.

36. Tilly, *Identities, Boundaries, and Social Ties,* 8–12.

other hand, religion as a primary source of moral values has always been viewed with hostility. While the CCP requires party members who practice religion to rectify their thoughts, there is usually no easy way of quitting the party. When rectifying measures are implemented, CCP branch cadres have to work out ways to minimize the public influence of these believers, which often results in insistent Christians reluctantly wearing the hat of nominal CCP membership.

7

Nationalism

We should implement patriotic education through national education and spiritual civilization, using arts and new media, by means of persuasion of the rationality, enculturation of the ethos, and moving of the emotions. The spread of patriotism should be lively, and the patriotic theme song should be sung loudly, making patriotism a solid belief and spiritual reliance for every Chinese.

—Xi Jinping, Dec 30, 2015, formal address at CCP Central Committee meeting

Nationalism is the last refuge of scoundrels.

—Samuel Johnson

Historian Duara Prasenjit traces the origin of Chinese nationalism since 1900 to projects fostering a national identity through campaigning against religious and other identities, because "nationalism is often considered to override other identities within the bounds of the imagined nation—such as religious, racial, linguistic, class, gender, or even historical ones—to encompass these differences in a larger identity."[1] Modern governments in

1. Examples in history include the Boxer Movement in 1900 and the Anti-Christianity

China use their nationalistic identity to contain various "smaller others" in empire-like nation-states such as the PRC.[2] Since the 1950s, Christians have become one of the "smaller others" of socialist China.

Informed by this historical insight, we are not surprised when a senior Chinese official announced in 2014 that China will establish a Chinese theology to further nationalize Christianity.[3] Anti-Christian movements have been one of the continuities of modern Chinese history because Christianity has long been considered a form of cultural imperialism by the West.[4] Targeting this Western religion seemed to serve the state's national goals at multiple turning points. It is worth noting that even within the Christian camp, there are people who have become so deeply concerned with the national fate that they are equally enthusiastic proponents of Chinese nationalism.[5] In the 1950s, a group of Christians with such a mindset collaborated with the Communist regime in launching the Three-Self Patriotic campaign during the US-Korea War.[6] A militant form of nationalism came into being by including supporters of the ideology and excluding resistant groups. The CCP then demanded that churches sever overseas connections because theses ties may bring in imperialist infiltrations once the church loses its nationalistic identity. From then on, Christianity outside of the Three-Self Patriotic system has been considered a perilous force, and Christians have been viewed as traitors against their own nation and people.

NEW CHINESE NATIONALISM

With the collapse of the communist ideology at its core after 1989, some post-communist states have reconstructed their legitimacy on the ruins

---

intellectual movement in the 1920s. See Duara, *Rescuing History from the Nation*, 10. Pye, *The Spirit of Chinese politics*, 70. Esherick, *The origins of the Boxer Uprising*, 68–95.

2. Duara, *Rescuing History from the Nation*, 15.

3. "China Bans Establishment."
Keck, "Why Is China Nationalizing Christianity?"

4. Cohen, *China and Christianity*; Lutz, ed., *Christian Missions in China*.

5. Stanley argues that Christian missions in China "contributed substantially to the emergence of nationalism through the introduction of Western education, social reforms, and political ideas. Missionaries in both the late Qing and Republican periods saw themselves as proponents of an authentic and reforming Chinese nationalism, shorn of any anti-foreign elements, that would enable China to hold her head high as a modern nation that need not fear domination by Japan." Stanley, "Introduction: Christianity," 7.

6. In 1954, The First China Christian National Council had 232 Christian leaders participating, who formed the Three-Self Patriotic Movement Committee, with Yaozong Wu as the first chairman.

of communist regimes by resorting to nationalism.[7] In China, state-led nationalist movements often use the more positive term "patriotism" (*aiguo zhuyi*). Actually, the latter term or a hybrid word "nationalistic-patriotism" (*minzu aiguo zhuyi*) appeared in most state strategies such as the Patriotic Education Campaign (1991–1996), which represented the largest plan of political indoctrination in China since the Mao era. It became a substitute ideology for Marxism and Maoism.[8] It also addressed the communal void after the disintegration of the *danwei* system. The policies enacted during this phase are still largely in effect today. Nationalistic-patriotic themes dominate the curriculum in schools. A heightened awareness of China's past humiliations, as expressed in the national anthem, "The Chinese nation has come to a most dangerous moment," has given rise to a generation with exuberant nationalistic sentiments, sometimes described as the "angry youth" (*fenqing*).

Globalization has exposed China to new technologies and opportunities, but also to further tension with Western ideals because some universal values seem to be threatening the political legitimacy of CCP. As a result, China's nationalistic-patriotism has become more prominent at a time when China opens up to the outside world. Since 1999, a few nationalistic demonstrations have exemplified such a new wave of state-led nationalism.[9] The first was the Anti-Belgrade Demonstration, right after the Assembly and Demonstration Law was passed.[10] These social movements were encouraged and guided by the Chinese government, even though some activities ran against the new laws.

7. Schwarzmantel, "Nationalism and Fragmentation since 1989," 389.

8. Zhao, "A State-Led Nationalism," 287–302.

9. Zhao, "An Angle on Nationalism," 885–905.

10. After the Tiananmen crackdown, in order to prevent mass social movements from happening again, the Chinese government passed a law in October of 1989 stipulating that any demonstration must first obtain a permit from the local Public Security Bureau. The appendix of this law listed the various penalties for a crime termed as "Gathering and Disturbing." After this law, not a single demonstration was able to obtain such permits. Many lawyers and social movement leaders were arrested with the crime of "Gathering and Disturbing." In 2014, seventy-eight scholars and lawyers wrote a petition about how this law runs counter to the Constitution. The petition effort was fruitless. See "Public Petition."

Table 2. Nation-Wide Patriotic Demonstrations since 1999

Date	Target	Trigger	Slogans	Participants
May, 1999	US	The US bombing of the Chinese embassy in Belgrade, Yugoslavia during NATO's intervention	Strike down the US! No TOEFL, GRE tests! War with the US wholeheartedly!	College students
March to April, 2005	Japan	The approval of a Japanese history textbook and the proposal that Japan be granted a permanent seat on the UN Security Council	Anti-Japan! Boycott Japanese commodities! Patriotism is no crime!	Young people from all social classes.
April, 2008	France	France's poor reception of the Olympic torch prior to Beijing games . France's pro-Tibet attitudes	Support the Beijing Olympics! Boycott Carrefour! No Free Tibet!	Young people from all social classes.
2012	Japan	Diaoyu Islands disputes around Sept 18, the anniversary of the 1931 Japanese Invasion	Return Diaoyu Islands to us! Boycott Japanese commodities!	Young people from all social classes.

Nationalistic emotions still challenge how Christianity is received in China today—given the fact that a great proportion of the Chinese population is still fed by heavily-censored state media for information to understand the world. Although the Internet is widely used in China, censorship and control over all media made some social groups more susceptible to Communist propaganda. These include an elderly generation in their fifties or sixties who do not use the internet as often, rural residents and some occupations, such as people working in closed circles like public works and the military. Among these groups, most hold strongly onto the century-old view that Christianity is such a foreign faith that by converting to it, one is disconnecting from his or her Chinese ancestry.[11] Since Christian representation is low in media reception among these groups, they have little idea of how the Christian population is growing in other segments of society. When meeting individual Christians in real life, they are more likely to show hostility. In 2010, for example, some scholars and government officials have objected to the building of a Three-self church in Qufu city, because they consider Qufu as the hometown of Confucius and thus the

11. Cook and Pao, *After Imperialism.*

root of Chinese culture. Having a Christian church building there would mean undermining Chinese culture. As a consequence, the construction project was suspended even after legal documents were obtained. A similar petition was filed by some scholars again in 2016 calling for the complete removal of this church building.[12]

THE MEDIA GAP

The Chinese Spring Festival is a time for family reunions. Twenty-eight-year-old Huang (pseudonym) uses his annual two-week job vacation to visit his parents in rural Anhui. Around this time, Huang hears complaints from his church friends about how family relationships tend to be strained when they refuse to participate in superstitious activities. Fortunately, Huang's family are all Christians living in an area with many rural churches, so they do not perform many of the superstitious rituals that other peasant families do, such as sacrificing to ancestors and burning fake money for the dead on New Year's Eve. But Huang is troubled by another dispute in his own family: whether or not to watch the annual CCTV Spring Festival Gala.[13] An active Internet user, Huang is well aware that this media outlet is the "throat and tongue" of the Communist Party. He feels disgusted by the pretentious patriotic singing. But as rural peasants who only watch CCTV, his parents enjoy the show a lot. Although the family reads the Bible at home and worship in church together, Huang feels that there is still an insurmountable barrier between their faith and their understanding of state idolatry. The preacher in his rural church obviously buys into the CCTV language too. Once Huang heard the preacher praying, "God thank you for having blessed China to be such a strong and nation that we Chinese are enjoying such high status now. Thank you, God, for giving us Chairman Xi who is leading the anti-corruption campaign." That was shocking for Huang to hear, and it made him realize that something was not quite right there. Even Christians are not immune to the rising nationalistic propaganda.

Huang's experiences illustrate how differently rural and urban Christians respond to the state's manipulation of nationalistic emotions. Young professionals like Huang who have gained a bigger picture of state censorship have lost trust in the state-provided media networks, but many of their family and friends remain immersed in government propaganda. What

12. "Expansion of Christian Church."

13. CCTV is China's only national broadcaster which Communist leaders refer to as the "throat and tongue" of state propaganda. Its annual gala, *Chunwan*, is a variety show that boasts having over 750 million viewers.

writer Murong Xuecun writes on his *New York Times* blog resonates with many Chinese:

> Like most people in China prior to 1997 . . . I had no sources of information other than CCTV and a handful of state-owned newspapers. I trusted CCTV unconditionally. When CCTV praised the superiority of socialism, I felt blessed to live in a socialist paradise. . . . For many years, I knew nothing about the BBC, CNN or The New York Times. Even when these media outlets were mentioned, I used to believe they were anti-Chinese and controlled by hostile forces in the West. . . . The Internet changed everything.[14]

As David Aikman writes in his book *Jesus in Beijing* that despite ongoing persecution, the rural Christians he interviewed in 1998 took pride in their Chinese patriotism, as shown in their views opposing political independence for either Tibet or Taiwan.[15] Aikman recalls this in his post-script:

> In fact the house churches, all the ones I've met, have vociferously denied any political aspirations at all. They simply said, "Leave us alone. We want to preach the gospel, pray for the people, etc. We're patriotic, we don't want Taiwan to be independent, we don't want Tibet to be separatist, we're good patriotic Chinese citizens," and I'm sure that ninety-nine percent of the house churches believe that.[16]

At the time of Aikman's research, internet use had barely spread out, and urban churches were sparse. So his observation of 99 percent of the house churches being patriotic may not have been an exaggeration. Due to the continuous effect of the growing media gap by 2012, our observation is that this situation is largely unchanged in rural China. However, urban churches are a different story.

Unlike those joining Three-self churches or their rural counterparts, members of these expanding urban faith communities are a self-selected group who do not endorse most state propaganda. Such self-selection means that they show a certain homogeneity in political views that are less affected by state media. For example, most people in these groups know how to use censorship-circumventing software (*fanqiang ruanjian*) to access websites that are blocked by the state. There is a much higher likelihood that they are

---

14. Murong, "Beijing's Propaganda Crisis."

15. Aikman, *Jesus in Beijing*, 3.

16. Ibid, 357.

exposed to political opinions other than the ones propagated by the state.[17] This certainly does not mean that there are no political differences among this group.

IMPOSING NATIONALISM THROUGH TEST-TAKING

When 25-year-old Sheng (pseudonym) entered the Master's program of economics at a Shanghai university, all graduate students were given an orientation that included a paper with a few questions. One question on the test asked: "What is your view of the Falungong?"[18] Sheng realized that this was one of the political questions. People who are familiar with how China's propaganda system works know that the system implicitly requires certain rhetoric or ways of saying things to show political loyalty. Sheng knew very well that the expected politically correct answer would be something like "I object it and fully agree with the national policy." But as a young convert in an unregistered church, Sheng in his conscience disapproves of the government's interference with religious freedom, even when non-Christian groups are concerned. So, he wrote down some candid words: "I do not agree with its teachings." But after he turned in this test, the CCP branch secretary came to talk with him about this seemingly incomplete and thus unsatisfying answer. This Communist cadre told Sheng, "You cannot just write 'disagree.' Another sentence saying that you fully support the decision of CCP central committee would make you politically correct."

In China's education system, test-taking is often used as a strategy to indoctrinate people towards the correct political views about the Party and the state. The Education Ministry clearly states on its website that its role is to "direct the work of ideology and political education." These political test questions train students to unconsciously self-censor and learn to support the Party even against one's conscience. Since Chinese students are the most diligent test-takers, this strategy has proved highly effective. Therefore, it is no surprise that a question listed below might be included in the National Postgraduate Entrance Exam:

Choose which describes China's current system of government:

17. Internet use does not necessarily detoxify nationalism, as evidence shows a growing trend of "cyber nationalism." See Allen-Ebrahimian, "The Making of a Chinese Nationalist Internet User."

18. Falungong is a quasi-religious group that was suppressed by the Chinese government in 1999. It proves to be a most resilient resistance group because its leadership transferred operations to the US. Since then, Falungong has invested in programs and TV stations to criticize CCP.

The CCP's great creation of combining Marxism and China's reality;

The CCP's achievement of leading Chinese people through a long struggle;

A reflection of the common interests and aspirations of all ethnic groups in China;

The inevitable choice in the social development of modern China.

Interestingly, to the question above, the correct answer is "All of the above" because even listing incorrect answers here would be politically incorrect. In 2011, the same exam directly contained a true or false question that criticized Western democracy: "The Western political party system is like a football game. One team must defeat the other. Ours is like a singing chorus."[19] It is only when the West is concerned that one can choose the negative answers.

Such test-taking strategies are also used in Three-self churches and seminaries. Those who are applying to the state-sponsored seminaries must take an entrance test about socialist values. One must check all the "Yes" answers on this socialist confession in order to start his or her seminary training with the hope of becoming a pastor in the Three-self system.

Ironically, the Chinese government itself is hyper-conscious of what Western entrance tests implicitly teach and presuppose. With a rising number of Chinese high-schoolers taking the SAT test to prepare for college in the United States, the state media criticizes it as a new form of imperialism because students are expected to read political treatises that founded Western democracy, such as the Declaration of Independence.[20]

In post-graduate institutions, nationalist and anti-Western sentiments interfere with students' choice of thesis topics. Guo (pseudonym, female, 62), a leading social scientist recalls a shocking experience in 2017 when serving on a review committee for graduate theses in a top university. Instead of conducting objective and empirical research, students who desire to study the growth of religious groups, including Christian churches, have been encouraged to revise their theses to manifest methods to restrain religion from becoming channels of foreign infiltration. With memories of past ideological control fresh in her mind, Guo regrets that a similar wave is making a comeback among her students.

19. "2011 National Postgraduate Entrance Exam."
20. Quoted in Yang, "How the New SAT Test."

CHRISTIAN ETHICS AS AN ANTIDOTE

Most interviewees remember the anti-Japanese demonstrations in 2005, when tens of thousands of urban young people participated across the country. In the city of Shanghai, where people had not seen such a protest since the anti-American rallies in 1999, *The Guardian* reported, "police not only approved it, they actively encouraged it." Meanwhile, the municipal security office sent out text messages to millions of local people calling them to "show love for their country in a law-abiding way."[21]

Japan has long been a target for venting nationalistic hatred, and such hostility is also shown by the number of anti-Japanese TV dramas—more than 70 of them in 2012. As a result, a 2013 Pew research report found that 90 percent of Chinese people have an unfavorable view of Japan.[22]

Since 2000, the growing unregistered churches in China's urban centers have provided an alternative communal identity that transcends geographical, ethnic and nationalistic identity boundaries. We find that Christian ethics function as an antidote against pervasive nationalistic sentiments. When asked about their views regarding the anti-Japanese sentiments that are arising among the young Chinese people, we hear sober reflections from these young believers (all use pseudonyms):

> I disapprove such anti-Japan or anti-American sentiments. Rather than getting all excited about what is wrong with other countries, one should reflect on his or her own errors. In rebuking others, people easily vent out their anger and dissatisfaction, and these emotions even get amplified. As a Christian, I like to make a more rational analysis based on facts and solve conflicts in peaceful ways. Christians need self-control, and they should avoid parading their own self-righteousness as if other people deserve revenge. Another important thing is this: our greatest concern is even higher than the benefits of our own country.
> —Fang, age 32, male, IT professional, Shanghai

> I am not an "angry youth" (*fenqing*) as they call it. I don't think it is necessary. I don't want my heart to be contaminated by hatred, whether it is against another country or against another ideal. This reflection came to me after I became a Christian. I realized that patriotism may become an idol, and it requires you to give up your rationality. It is not wrong to love your country, but if people only irrationally vent their anger, then it has gone wrong.
> —Yan, age 23, female, college student, Beijing

21. Watts, "Violence Flares," 11.
22. Murong, "China's Television War."

Patriotism is like unrequited love. I would call those people 'brain-damaged' because they have been taking in biased information for such a long time that their brains do not function rationally. I think this way because I am a Christian. My religious faith has brought about a turn-around in my values. Before my conversion, I used to have heated discussions with my classmates about whether Communism can come true. Back then, what I heard and saw was narrow, and we talked like the people on CCTV. Now looking back, I can see that it resulted from the state's obfuscation (*yumin*) through controlling all the media over such a long period of time. —Wu, age 27, male, marketing consultant, Nanjing

Patriotism is a weak slogan today. Most of today's young people do not lack material goods but spiritual resources. In such a secular society, even patriotism is pretentious. They don't believe in anything and are full of dissatisfaction. So these demonstrations are their only opportunities to vent their dissatisfaction against society. —Hao, age 35, male, editor, Wuhan

Patriotism means something different than setting up an enemy in order to strike it down, as if striking it down means that you love your own country. That shows how twisted people's emotions are. The society is chaotic if it follows this logic. When I saw the college demonstrators, my heart really went out for them. I saw their need for true spiritual fellowship. I saw the emptiness of their hearts. —Wang, age 38, female, psychological counselor, Chengdu

Psychologist Joshua Searle-White argues that nationalists are those who tend to "carry strong attitudes and beliefs about their own people and about others, who feel their attachment to their nation passionately, and who even, at times, act with great cruelty against their enemies."[23] He further claims that nationalistic sentiments have two psychological roots: attachment and identity. In today's China, a growing sense of identity anxiety within a society experiencing ripples of conflict seems to fuel rising nationalistic sentiments, especially with growing ideological manipulation of Xi Jinping's leadership since 2012. Take Xi Jinping's "Chinese dream" for example. He promises that in 2049, the Communist Party will "solve all the country's problems," "realizing the great renewal of the Chinese nation" as "the greatest dream in modern history."[24] In 2013, the Education Ministry fashioned

23. Searle-White, *The Psychology of Nationalism*, 3.

24. Quoted in Carlson, "The World According to Xi," 6; also see "Potential of the Chinese Dream," and "China's Future: Xi."

decrees in accordance with this grand initiative by emphasizing the role of the education propaganda system as "bringing in the Chinese dream into textbooks, classrooms and people's minds."[25] This nationalistic rhetoric has not left the church without influence. Although many urban Christians find their faith instrumental in dissipating such nationalistic sentiments, due to information constraints, nationalism still leaves its mark on many Christian believers, especially in areas where state media predominates.

CHRISTIAN CHINA-CENTRISM

Many Chinese Christians treasure a China-centric vision of global mission. Leaders who actively promote such an understanding tend to depict the Chinese church as the fastest growing revival movement while the Western church languishes in sad decay. The Chinese church sees itself strategically positioned to bring the gospel to a variety of groups, such as Buddhists and Muslims. The "Back to Jerusalem" movement was envisioned by earlier church leaders in the 1920s, but it was later renewed by a few rural house church leaders in the 1990s. These later proponents stated that God is calling Chinese Christians to bring the gospel along the Silk Road back to the Middle East, where the gospel originated. They used maps of missionary expansions to show that this strategy will bring the gospel around the globe and end in a full circle before Christ's second-coming. Such a China-centric and eschatological vision has attracted many believers who claim that a Great Revival is starting from China and will usher in the End Time. This view that God will especially use China since it is the leading country of the twenty-first century has been treasured by many church leaders. Such grand narratives appeal to the typical aesthetics and imagination of the Chinese. They present a comprehensive explanation of historical experience that helps individuals gain a sense of mission and importance. However, it also forms an easy marriage with nationalist sentiments.

Such a China-centric revival mentality even influences some cultic theology. In 2013, China's official media broadcasted "The Almighty God Church," also known as "Eastern Lightning," as a violent and destructive cult. A review of their faith texts shows that this cult based in rural China has adapted many state propaganda phraseology in making their own oracles, such as "into the new era" (*zoujin xinshidai*). Their missional texts are full of China-centric callings. This cult even adapted the *L'Intenationale* of the Communist International (1919–1943) into one of its hymns.

25. Minster of Education Ministry, "Implementing the China Dream."

Few Chinese Christians have not heard of the name of a hymn composer Xiaomin. In the late 1990s this peasant girl, who had only an eighth-grade education in rural Henan province, composed a collection of nine hundred Chinese Christian hymns that have become popular in Chinese churches. This collection of Canaan Hymns (*jianan shige*) was considered by many Chinese Christains as "God's special gifts to the Chinese church." In 2008, Xiaomin composed a new hymn titled "Olympics 2008" with the following lyrics:

> As time reaches 2008, Olympics Beijing, Beijing Olympics
> Yellow River, Yangtze River, Five Lakes and Four Seas, they
> all sing to each other:
> Today China's strong and flourishing, beautiful and glorious;
> Five circles unite all our hearts, fifty-six ethnic groups are a
> big family
> 2008 Olympics in Beijing, Revival in China.

Rural-educated Xiaomin obviously borrows typical nationalistic symbolisms from state TV, such as the geographical endowments and fifty-six ethnic groups in China.[26] Compared to Xiaomin's earlier Christian hymns that were deeply devotional and biblical, one can observe that she later has been overwhelmed by a growing Olympic Pride. A closer review of her earlier hymns, however, reveals that a China-centric revival mentality had already been there.

While Western scholars expected the Beijing Olympics of 2008 to "trigger a similar opening of the political system" as the Seoul Games did in 1988,[27] China observers noticed that the games became a catalyst for an upsurge in nationalism.[28] Chinese citizens put on torch relays to showcase China's rising international status brought by these Olympics. Historical scars of Western humiliation were revisited, and a sense of Chinese pride was exuberantly expressed in street interviews. State propaganda successfully diverted attention away from internal social conflicts to reacting against foreign criticism of China. Such state-led nationalism has been an ongoing theme since the founding of the PRC. The leadership of the CCP has been portrayed as indispensible. What is unusual about the new wave—the 2008 Olympic Pride—is that, while the celebration of China's economic achievements reached its climax, international scrutiny of her weaknesses, such as pollution, human rights and media freedoms, also intensified. State

---

26. Regarding China's fifty-five ethnic minorities as a nationalistic construction, see Mullaney, "Seeing for the State," 325–42.

27. Wacker, "Beijing is Haunted," 1.

28. Zhao, "The Olympics and Chinese Nationalism," 48–57.

media then responded with even more fervent expressions of nationalism. "Harmonization" has become an equivalent word with silencing dissent.

CONCLUSION

State-led nationalism since the 1990s has failed to provide a Chinese identity with substantive communal ties; rather, it has given birth to either violent demonstrations or an imaginary community. The growth of Christianity offers a complete and transcendental value system that dissipates the narrowly-defined love for one's own nation. Its ethic of love and forgiveness dissolves the sentiments of hatred and resentment so widely used in state propaganda.

Christian theology has a powerful set of ethical principles to maintain the boundaries of the human heart. We see many themes at work here in the Chinese context. First, Christians are commanded to love God above all. There is an order to human love, as Augustine says. Misplaced love towards something so abstract, such as a nation, is considered irrational by Christians. Secondly, Christians are aware that patriotism or nationalism can easily turn into an idol. Nationalistic zeal runs counter to the command of loving God above all. Thirdly, the universality of the Christian church powerfully cuts short the disillusion of nationalistic boundaries. The common identity as fellow-believers dissolves prejudice against distant people groups. Fourthly, Christians are taught to love their enemies, and this nullifies the legitimacy of grudges and hatred in one's heart. Lastly, Christians believe that God delights in harmony instead of violence.

From a sociological point of view, the church networks nurture a group identity that is boundary-breaking, inclusive and universal. Also, because of the official suppression of unregistered churches, Christians in these churches tend not to embrace anti-West sentiments. As we wrote in Chapter Four, many believers experienced friendships and mentorships from Western foreign Christians, and these inter-cultural contacts allow them to be open and friendly to the West at large. As Christian dissidents in their country, they regularly access information untainted by state propaganda, such as *The Economist*. At the same time, not immune to these sentiments, Chinese Christians have also become divided along generational, educational, geographical and occupational lines.

8

Charity

The science of association is the mother science; the progress of all the others
depends on the progress of that one.

—Alexis de Tocqueville[1]

As the growth of urban churches coincided with a massive scale of urbanization in China, churches increasingly have found themselves faced with the need to respond to emerging social problems. Since the mid-2000s, we observe more and more young people entering into the charitable sector as their career; and among these professional charity workers, an increasing number identify themselves as Christians. After a few natural disasters, churches also gained visibility while engaging in charitable work. This chapter focuses on the growth of Christian charity, an important facet of Chinese Christianity during the past decade.

Two months after Liang (pseudonym, 40, female) was baptized, an 8.0 level earthquake destroyed her home city in Sichuan. Liang recalls that the church she had joined not long before organized its own relief team overnight. Over the next two days, a few other churches pooled their resources and set up a common office area in a shopping center in order to receive volunteers and donations from other provinces and to host and dispatch volunteers to rescue sites. Noting the sudden visibility of unregistered churches as they responded to the earthquake, Liang says, "I never knew

1. Tocqueville, *Democracy in America*, 118.

that there are so many house churches like ours in this city." Their response to the disaster was immediate, and government-sponsored relief efforts arrived days later.

The 2008 Sichuan earthquake, which caused nearly 90,000 deaths and left 4.8 million homeless marked a watershed for Christian volunteerism. Not only did an unprecedented number of unregistered churches responded visibly to the need for relief, but churches also saw a dramatic increase in conversions after the earthquake.[2] Many new converts started to devote their time and resources to post-quake relief work. These Christian charity efforts also favorably affected public opinion. A few subsequent natural disasters in the following years, such as the 5.7 level earthquake in Yunnan and Guizhou in 2012, also witnessed local Christians who were among the first to mobilize and help.

Despite these positive changes, some Christian charitable work was done without real compassion for the people suffering from the Sichuan disaster. As a result, in some regions, local townsmen gave Christians a strongly unfavorable rating. As one widely circulated blog article wrote, some Christian volunteers were so eager to spread the gospel that they "manipulated people by exploiting their psychological trauma and fear about death."[3] For instance, they only gave food to those who were willing to say the "I accept Jesus" prayer. Without a holistic understanding of the Christian gospel, some volunteers prioritized preaching over humbly meeting the practical needs of people. For them, the Christian mission is more about the talk than the walk. Patronizing attitudes, manipulations and favoritism were commonly observed problems of Chinese Christian volunteerism.

THE GROWING GREY SECTOR

Christian charity is a small stream within the growing sector of NGOs in China. In order to understand it, we need to start with the big picture. In 2014, it was estimated that over one million unregistered NGOs operated in China.[4] These organizations range from self-support groups for special needs children and migrant workers' legal aid to women's rights and house-church groups caring for the homeless. Unfortunately, these charitable efforts are mostly considered illegal by the government, although they are sometimes tolerated at the local level. The government has made regula-

2. Southam, "Converted after China's Earthquake."

3. An anonymous blogger, "Experiencing Chinese Christians."

4. "Enter the Chinese NGO"; Chen, "The NGO Community"; Lawrence, "The Lions in the Communist Den," 24–27.

tions since 2008, including instituting a collaborative model between local governments and NGOs called "buying or outsourcing services (*goumai fuwu*)."[5] In this way, local governments may monitor the activities of NGOs. Although NGOs are well known in many societies as social buffers that mitigate social anger and fill in policy cracks, the Communist state fears a "peaceful revolution" by some groups that have international connections.[6] Christian NGOs often fall into this category and are especially feared. However, with churches becoming increasingly visible in charitable causes, the number of Christian NGO workers has been on the steady rise.[7]

Then at the beginning of 2017, following Xi Jinping's statements against Western influences and ideas,[8] a new NGO law was put into effect mainly through police supervision, enacting all-around restrictions on foreign NGOs, including higher registration and administration costs, smaller ranges of activities in nine approved areas, policies on recruiting local staff and fund-raising, and legal risks facing foreign staff. Foreign nonprofits are now required to first find state agencies as sponsors, then to register with the police and submit regular reports on what they do. A telling sign of uncertainty is that when foreign groups tried to inquire through the hotline set up by China's Ministry of Public Security, their calls went unanswered.[9] This clampdown affected over 7000 foreign NGOs in China and further marginalized the nonprofit sector.[10] Programs that involved lawyers' training and workers' rights had to close their offices. An expat NGO worker

5. Quoted in Teets and Jagusztyn, "The Evolution of a Collaborative Governance."

6. "China to 'Regulate' Roreign NGOs"; "New Signs that China is Scrutinizing"; Bentley, "The Role of International Support," 16.

7. The development of Christian NGOs in China is relatively recent, as Christians and churches seek to express God's love through social action. Many are involved in local projects for the elderly, HIV/AIDS relief, rural development projects, and the provision of educational programs and scholarships. Jinde Charities and the Amity Foundation have also been involved in disaster relief work. Several Catholic dioceses now have Social Service Centers, which coordinate social outreach projects; the China Christian Council is also developing its own Social Service Committee. New disaster relief statistics show a dramatic increase in the number of Christians in this sector. According to Gao and He (2011), fifty percent of volunteers to Wenchuan after the 2008 earthquake were Christians, and eighty percent of them came from unregistered churches. Gao and He, "Main Problems," 44.

8. Xi's list of "Seven Don't-Mentions" includes constitutional democracy, universal values, civil society, market liberalism, media independence, criticizing errors in the history of the Party ("historical nihilism"), and questioning the policy of opening up and reforms and the socialist nature of the regime. Veg, "China's Political Spectrum under Xi Jinping."

9. Buckley, "Uncertainty Over New Chinese Law."

10. Wong, "Clampdown in China."

Jean says that it feels like a reversal to the time in the 1980s when it was difficult even to secure work visas to stay in China. For organizations that bring funds from abroad, it is definitely a game changer. Christian NGOs founded by foreigners are coming up with localized strategies, such as turning work over to local staff and acting as foreign consultants. Much relief or development work has been shifted, and discipleship for local leaders has become the new focus.

Meanwhile, appreciation for NGO work among the Chinese public has always been very low. In a society where the government controls everything, many people view anything "non-governmental" as risky. Many young people are discouraged from entering this sector. As a result, NGO workers, in general, are less professionalized than their counterparts in other sectors. Most NGOs are understaffed, under-resourced and unsustainable. Scholars find that these limitations have shaped China's NGOs, an important part of China's civil society, into an uncivil sphere—things need to get done through *guanxi* networks and exchanging personal favors.[11] This is the reality that Christian NGO workers inhabit.

We interviewed some Christian charity workers whose personal journeys allow us to understand these interconnected challenges. We organize this chapter around two main questions: How is the Christian faith related to their work? As members of unregistered churches, how do they cope with both internal and external challenges?

FROM ACTIVISM TO FAITH

Most of our informants consider the Christian faith to be closely related to their career choice. Although some of them experienced conversion while doing charitable works, others chose this career due to their growing faith convictions.

Zhao (pseudonym, male, 32) has an NGO dream that he cannot convey to his parents, nor even to most of his church friends. To his parents, working at a "non-profit" job is unthinkable and working for "non-governmental" groups that the government sees as illegal is insane. In the eyes of his unbelieving friends, this 30-year-old young man with a Master's degree in demography from a prestigious university could find better ways

11. Pye, "Civility, Social Capital, and Civil Society," 766–69. This unhealthy development of the NGO sector causes a chain effect of weakened social responsibility for other sectors too. For example, it is hard for big corporations to implement their Corporate Social Responsibility programs through collaborating with local NGOs, for the latter often work too unprofessionally.

of self-fulfillment than risking a marginalized identity as an NGO worker in China. Furthermore, many of Zhao's church friends also think his efforts are commendable but unrelated to evangelism.

Zhao knows very well that NGOs are marginalized in China because five years ago he founded one with the mission of helping rural migrant families in big cities. This NGO survived only two years before the government shut it down, through a policy update.[12] Since then, Zhao has been without a job, but not without a dream. After all, Zhao has come a long way.

Zhao came from a rural village in Hebei province. In 2002, he entered a prestigious college in Beijing, so his family enjoyed much fame because of it. To Zhao's disappointment, life in college was marked by opportunism and vicious competition rather than the ideals he expected. Professors were unenthusiastic about teaching from an outdated curriculum; nor were they bold enough to teach anything beyond what was allowed by state censorship. To fill this vacuum of learning, Zhao became active in social organizations founded by college students on campus, including a reading club and a rural education society. It was this circle of idealistic friends who became a positive influence on Zhao. They reflected on the closed-minded and self-centered attitudes of most college students. Since most of them had roots in rural China, these young people all cherished a dream to improve their hometowns.

By the 2000s, a massive rural-to-urban migration had taken place in China. With more than two hundred million prime-age peasants leaving their homes, China witnessed the disintegration of millions of rural families. Only the elderly, nursing mothers and children stayed behind in villages; they were sometimes referred to the "386199 troop."[13] Many social problems arose, including neglect of children and the elderly, sexual abuse of children,[14] and fractured marriage and family relationships. Zhao and his college association were aware of these needs, and they made a few study committee trips to rural areas, where villagers received them warmly. After these initial contacts, Zhao's association enacted some relief efforts to help these villagers. With this college organization gaining support in that region, local authorities were displeased and even detained them for twenty-four hours. They confiscated their cell phones, but one student was able to make an SOS phone call to a contact in Beijing. When pressure from a higher authority came upon village cadres, the student volunteers were

12. "Pummelling the little platoons." "Uncivil society."

13. In China, these digits refer to holidays for women, children and senior citizens respectively.

14. Wu, "The Abuse of China."

released. After this incident, student participation declined. Leaders of the association decided to engage in efforts that evaded direct confrontations with local authorities. Thus, two years later they started to teach in urban schools for migrant children.

It was through a summer camp for migrant children that Zhao met a volunteer who taught him about the Christian gospel and the Bible. She prayed for him, and Zhao found tears streaming down his face. His heart was filled with an unknown fluttering joy. After this camp, Zhao started attending a house church recommended by a Christian volunteer in the city. After graduation with a Master's degree, he joined an NGO founded by Christians, and met his future wife, an American. She had been a believer longer than Zhao, so he grew in his religious commitment through their marriage.

Looking back, Zhao remembers that many of his NGO peers were searching for religion. Some were seeking comfort from Buddhism, some from Zen, and others from Western faiths. As activists, most of them had thought through atheism and abandoned the state ideology. Experiences in this grey sector usually present a sharp contrast to the perception of Chinese society provided through state media, that so many NGO workers go through phases of disillusionment. To persist in NGO activism, one needs a religion for a source of higher moral ideals as well as for the strength to persist.

To Zhao, the Christian faith taught him that social change has to start from people's hearts. It also shined light upon his motivation in doing NGO work. "You can be sinning in God's eyes even when you are doing good," says Zhao. Before his conversion, Zhao wished to make his organization bigger and more famous so that there would be more donors and so that their work could be more effective. Zhao said, "I had thought that I could change the world and save people through outward expansion. I was hoping to be a Savior. I was playing God. But later God taught me to look inside myself." He now thinks that a Christian NGO activist should always reflect on his or her motivations—Does this honor or bring glory to God?

Zhao thinks that the biggest difference his Christian faith brings is a change from outward reflection to inward introspection. Before his conversion, Zhao considered himself a good man with good will to serve and help people. As he reflects now, he has become more sensitive to sin, both within himself and in people around him.

> I used to see myself as an experienced NGO worker, so I was often very critical of others' opinions. But then I read in the book of James about putting reins on one's tongue. That taught

me humility. I realize that the more experienced one is at something, it turns out to be an area of pride; and that prideful attitude often leads to problems. So, the more I read the Bible, the more I am brought into a virtuous circle, not a vicious one. I have a different mentality when implementing a project, even including how to face the interfering authorities. I used to hate these hypocrites, but then I thought about Jesus' time when similar things happened. There is nothing new under the sun. Then I feel less resentful towards them. Jesus taught his disciples to be as shrewd as snakes and as innocent as doves.

Zhao sees his career path as a freeing experience, because his conscience is no longer bound. His Master's degree may have brought a good job in government office, but going along with the norms of bribery and favoritism would go contradict his own deeper values.

Zhao's maturing reflections on the Christian faith also made him aware of the weakness of the church in performing charity work. The pastor in his church, with a narrow and fundamentalist theology, sometimes discourages Zhao from further pursing a charity career. He thinks that social justice is a mission secondary to evangelism. But Zhao finds confirmation from the book of James, where it says that true faith must issue good works. "Another problem with today's urban church," Zhao says, "is that their awareness of social injustice is sometimes lower than that of the average Chinese." Setting evangelism as a primary mission has truncated their lives into the secular sphere versus the sacred. According to most Chinese believers, NGO activism is dealing only with "earthly things." Although the Bible is full of commands for social justice, Zhao's church rarely teaches on this topic. He had wanted to switch to another church that emphasizes social justice more. After some research, he realized that most churches have the same problem. Being under religious suppression for too long, churches consider themselves too marginalized to do anything about the larger social context.

Zhao used to be very proud of his NGO activist identity. But now he says, "all in all, this is a path towards humility and dependence on God." It is humility which makes an NGO worker wiser when his or her plans are disrupted by local authorities. Zhao no longer shows disgust when confronted with the tricks they play, for these existed in Jesus' time and were used against the only doer of good in the world. Zhao also learns how to seek help from the Bible, not from men or higher authorities. Despite discouragement from family and church friends, Zhao has found a stronger anchor to secure this dream, which now he recognizes as a "calling" from God.

DOWNWARD-MOBILITY CAREER

Another NGO worker we interviewed is Feng (pseudonym, male, 33). He was an English major in college, and his language skills helped him land a good job working for a public relations company that plans international exhibitions in Shanghai. He had fat paychecks and long vacations, but he always wanted to start an NGO. Feng's family is quite supportive of his NGO dream, because his whole family was converted in the 1980s by the efforts of a Catholic missionary, who ran a business in their neighborhood. In fact, Feng received baptism when he was in fourth grade, on the same day as his father and grandfather. Feng became more committed in high school when he began listening to Good Friend Christian Radio (*Liangyou*), a shortwave broadcast stationed outside of mainland China. He wanted to own a personal Bible, so he wrote to their radio station. When a Bible was sent to his school address, it was confiscated by the school. Feng recalls being told that as a member of the Communist Youth League, he was not encouraged to read it.

Despite these obstacles, Feng had a school teacher who modeled Christian charity for him. This retired school teacher was re-hired as the school janitor, and he hang a cross in his custodial room. Feng often chatted with him and found out that he was a Christian. Feng often saw him looking into dumpster bins outside classrooms for recyclable materials such as scrap paper. He sold these items and donated the money to his church. Knowing that many young teachers had been students of this retired teacher, Feng appreciated his humble gestures to serve others. He even encouraged Feng to attempt the entrance examination of Jinling Seminary.

College associations provided Feng with real opportunities to serve others. Twice each week, Feng and his friends would volunteer to visit people with special needs such as cerebral palsy, and taught simple lessons to them. Feng gathered a number of Christian friends to do this together. One of these friends later started an orphanage.

When Feng worked as an international exhibition consultant, his job was highly admired among his friends. However, Feng saw the costs of maintaining a successful professional appearance:

> For a time I was in charge of managing high-end business meetings. My job was to invite many CEOs in foreign companies and plan conferences for them. Every time after a major conference, I saw the reality of these important people. They are physically and spiritually depleted. Their successful appearance came with a cost, including not being able to enjoy their family and real

friendships. Everybody, no matter how important you are, is just a small churning gear of this huge commercial machine.

One day Feng's boss asked him, "Would you like to see yourself becoming one of them in five years?" That question actually brought him reluctance rather than motivation. He knew deep in his heart that this kind of success was not what he wanted for his life. After three years at this post, Feng quit and went to work for a Christian NGO in Yunnan, a remote southwest province with many ethnic minorities. The pay was only half that of his former job, but he felt more at ease. As Feng says, "I hope to work at a job that seamlessly connects with my beliefs and values, and not be disconnected and strained as before."

Feng was fully aware that being a professional NGO worker meant giving up many things that are more decent-looking and comfortable. It involves reaching downwards to the most needy, rather than seeking upward social mobility. Since that is exactly the teaching of Jesus, Feng felt more content following that path.

Since that time Feng has worked at different jobs for international NGOs, and most of these organizations were founded by Christians from other countries. With ten years of professional NGO experiences, he can succinctly summarize the main challenges in this career:

> I find myself facing two Goliaths. One is a [political] system that does not welcome you and even stops you. The other is the massive group of people you are trying to help. I see their needs as well as their weaknesses. They are not angels. The orphans, the neglected elderly and the poor are bitter and wounded. If they gain any power or status, they would turn into people who harm others too. And in between these two giants, I see myself, a weak and broken sinner. Faith in God shows my motivations and my brokenness more clearly. So being a Christian NGO worker means that you have to dissect your environment, the people and yourself into observable pieces and really analyze them. This takes much endurance. But it proves God to be trustworthy too.

Feng put into words the common struggles of many Christian NGO workers we interviewed. The Christian faith does not provide them with a haven to which they may escape; rather, it gives them a microscope to see reality more soberly without being disheartened. Now a leading figure in the circle of locally-founded Christian NGOs, Feng often reminds himself of the danger of fame and power. Feng reflects on the future and says, "Although it is I who founded this organization, it does not belong to me. I hope to see it grow in real service to others, not necessarily in influence. If necessary in the future, I am content to wipe my name off it."

GOD'S LOVE AT THE DUMPSTER

An organization named Good Samaritan, which helps urban homeless people, employs 45-year-old Jiang (pseudonym, male). Seven years ago, when he himself had been homeless for a few years in a southern city, a female missionary from Sweden named Maria received Jiang into her shelter. He was converted, baptized and sent out to set up a branch of this Christian shelter in a southeastern city. Jiang gladly says that their mission "is to extend God's love to every dumpster of this city."

Good Samaritan rented a compound in suburban Chengdu which accommodates eight to ten male homeless people on an average day. Jiang and his co-worker brother Wang usually go into the city center three days a week to care for more homeless people. Their routine involves visiting the train station, transportation centers and some garbage collection sites on a regular basis. Bringing food, water and gospel tracts with him, Jiang distributes to any homeless people they can find. If some of the males wish to stay with him, Jiang brings them back to his suburban shelter. For the homeless females, only food, clothing and gospel tracts are distributed. Many of these women have suffered violence before and thus are reluctant to be approached, so Jiang often leaves hygiene products in a clean bag and tosses it to them.

Jiang actually had a good college education during the 1980s. The political turmoil of 1989 was a heavy blow to his idealism, and he had suffered from mental illness ever since. His family had high expectations for him, but Jiang seemed to see through all the vanities of life. That was the beginning of his self-imposed exile.

Jiang's homeless shelter has witnessed a variety of problems. Some homeless people were terminally-ill due to disease or drug abuse when Jiang found them, and a few even died in his shelter. These incidents caught the attention of local authorities, who threatened to close the shelter down. Jiang and his co-worker candidly told them about what they are doing, and even the landlord and neighbors testified to their good deeds. With these endorsements, the local cadres left, warning them not to bring "problematic" people into the neighborhood. They also told Jiang that preachers are not allowed to be in his shelter. Since then, Jiang never brought drug abusers or terminally ill people back to the shelter. Their shelter also suffered theft and robbery at the hands of some homeless guests. Once even the cooking utensils and furnace were stolen. Jiang never reported these losses to the local police for fear of their attention and disapproval. Over time, their mission did yield fruit, as a few became Christians, received job training and found employment.

Jiang recalls that once a 28-year-old homeless young man called him saying that he had been planning to jump from a high building to commit suicide. The young man then told him that before he tried to commit suicide, he thought of Jiang and what he said about Jesus. Jiang went into the city and found him. It was raining hard, but Jiang spent two hours trying to persuade him in the rain. This young man followed Jiang back to the shelter. Jiang learned that this young man had been homeless for twenty years after running away from a human trafficker when he was eight years old. Jiang taught him to read and simple task management. After a year, Jiang acted as a guarantor so that a grocery store would hire him as a cleaner and laborer. This young man returns to the shelter every weekend to have Bible study with Jiang and his staff.

MISFIT IN CHURCH

During our fieldwork we observed a tension between churches and Christian NGO workers. Although many churches have charitable programs, church leaders tend to view believers who are professional charity workers as engaging in the "social gospel," which is not direct evangelism. Because of the wide influence of a pietistic or separationist theology that tends to draw a line between the sacred and the secular, these leaders do not consider issues like social injustice and environmental pollution as high priorities for Christians. Their sermons rarely touch on social injustice, despite the escalating social conflicts due to widespread injustice in Chinese society. Thus, professional Christian charity workers find themselves in an unwelcome church environment, where their concerns with various social problems have not been addressed by the narrow gospel messages. Since they live such a different career life from other occupations, many find it hard to fit in.

Mei (pseudonym, female, 38) rarely goes to church now because she has felt disconnected for some time. She relocated to Chengdu city because of her fifth NGO position. By 2012, she had been a professional NGO worker for over a decade. Mei still remembers how she fled her first job as a commercial advertising designer and went to teach at a run-down village school which paid a meager 300 *yuan* monthly stipend to volunteers. Mei wanted to escape the world and find some tranquility by teaching children in rural Anhui province. There Mei found a group of young people just like her, disillusioned with what the society had to offer and aspiring to revive rural education. It was a mixed group with atheists, Buddhists, Taoists and Christians. Religion was not a taboo because most of these volunteers had converted out of materialism and were reflecting on the meaning and purpose of life. Occasionally they had some volunteers from other countries in their midst too. In 2006, Mei befriended a volunteer named Martha, who taught her the Christian gospel. Every morning before sunrise, they prayed together in a lush wheat field. During those moments, Mei felt a deep sense of peace settling in her heart, something she had never known before. Martha's stay at the school was short, but she left a few spiritual books for Mei to read. After that, Mei met a few more Christian friends. She regarded this religion with great favor because of the loving attitudes of these friends.

Interestingly, Mei observed that the more idealistic some local volunteers were, the more likely they would leave after only a short stay; that is, they showed lack of commitment to anything that was less than ideal. Although some friendships did form, these randomly connected volunteers came and went. Six years later, 30-year-old Mei was the only one who had not moved on, so she was elected to be principal of the school due to her teaching seniority. The job was more than Mei could handle, however, especially when office politics escalated between the founding committee and volunteers. By this time, she and a colleague had been regularly attending a rural church that was five miles away. She began to long for Christian fellowship. Some simple conversations with the rural preacher brought her much comfort. Mei decided to change her job in order to find a church as her spiritual family.

Three years later, Mei found another NGO job which is located in Chengdu, a city with many thriving churches within a relatively more tolerant government environment. For the first time in six years of her spiritual journey as a Christian, Mei had her own church membership. Still, she found it difficult to fit in since most members are either university professors or business professionals. Conversations rarely go deeper than asking about life's routines. Mei's job involves frequent travel to help rural schools build libraries, and she often misses Sunday services. After a few missed Sundays, Mei came to church and felt that nobody was interested to have conversations with her any more. The pastor counseled Mei and suggested that she find another job in order to make Sunday church meetings her priority. Comments like this made Mei feel unwelcome.

After three years of trying to fit into this urban church, Mei was disappointed to find that like any institution with people in it, the church falls short of the ideals. Mei increasingly felt that Christians can easily become self-serving. They express passion to care for children in remote Tibet, but they show indifference to neighbors' pains and struggles, Mei notes, "as if it is easier for our love to pour out towards some place faraway." Mei's dream of finding a perfect spiritual home came to an end. She still prays and reads the Bible on her own, and occasionally some same-career sisters reach out to her in meaningful ways that help her faith remain in step with her work.

CONCLUSION

Nowadays in China, doing good can be very costly. It is not just that an elderly person who collapses on the street often sues the Good Samaritans who tried to help them; society on many levels discourages people from forming voluntary organizations. External challenges continue to restrict the maturity of Christian charity too. Registration for legal status is still difficult, in effect erecting a barrier to fundraising and recruitment of trained full-time staff. Moreover, any social organization that has foreign connections, as well as advocacy and policy-oriented programs are closely monitored by the authorities.[15] In recent years, the government has launched new policies limiting NGOs that engage in helping marginalized groups such as rural migrants and women.[16]

As Christianity spreads to urban centers, more and more young people choose Christian charity as their career. They face tremendous challenges both from the larger political and social environment and from their churches. Status-sensitive Chinese society now discourages such self-giving efforts through scorn and suspicion. Some urban churches, with their theology and evangelistic priorities, are ill-equipped to provide pastoral support to the mission and needs of Christian charity workers. Despite all these obstacles, the massive needs of a broken Chinese society call out for conscientious believers to serve as their Lord Jesus once did.

15. "Uncivil society."
16. National Workers' Union, "Strictly Guard against Infiltrations."

9

Calvinism

Calvinism is an all-embracing system of principles . . . It is rooted in a form
of religion which was peculiarly its own, and from that specific religious
consciousness there was developed first a particular theology, then a special
church-order, and then a given form for political and social life.

—Abraham Kuyper[1]

It would be imperial thinking not to tolerate other parties besides the communist party. And if no factions exist within a party, strange things will happen.
(*Dang wai wu dang, di wang si xiang; dang nei wu pai, qian qi bai guai.*)

—Mao Zedong[2]

Anti-China forces have proposed to use Calvinist theology, thought and
institutions to consolidate illegal house churches in China . . . This actually
shows that illegal assemblies in China have grown to a sizeable scale.

—Gao Feng, chairman of China Christian Council[3]

1. Kuyper, *Lectures on Calvinism*, 8.

2. Mao, Closing speech at the Eleventh Plenary Session of the Eighth Central
Committee of the Chinese Communist Party on August 22 of 1966.

3. Phoenix TV, "An interview with Gao Feng." See a full translation of this interview

An undeniable fact about the theological landscape of China's protestant churches today is the emergence of Calvinism.[4] Visit any urban Christian bookstore in China, and one can find many titles bearing this theology, from classic works by John Calvin to books by contemporary Presbyterians, such as Timothy Keller. This trend has largely been an urban phenomenon in cities like Wenzhou, Beijing and Chengdu, where leaders and members are better educated and theologically savvy. In some churches, where a larger portion of the members are university educated, a Calvinist-Kuyperian public theology is a favored topic of sermons and lectures. It is interesting to note that Oxford historian Alister McGrath also highlights this urban characteristic being present even during the Reformation in Europe.[5] The growth of urban ministry creates a demand for theological developments that effectively respond to the wide spectrum of questions posed by a younger generation. In 2014, the Grace to City Convention in Hong Kong featuring Presbyterian pastor Timothy Keller gathered over two thousand pastors and leaders from mainland China. Its reformed and urban church-planting approach appealed to an even larger number of Chinese. Calvinism is generally considered as one that elevates the grace and sovereignty of God with a grander "creation-fall-redemption-consummation" framework.

We should also note that "Calvinist" and "Reformed" are not strictly synonymous terms. "Reformed" may include theology that does not adhere to strict Presbyterian teaching on the covenant of God, infant baptism, or church government, but accept the world-and-life view of Calvin and some Dutch reformed thinkers and the emphasis upon God's sovereignty and God's grace. It is a broader category than "Calvinist." This Reformed theology has come to China largely by way of the "Grace to the City" movement led by Timothy Keller of Redeemer Church in New York. Annual conferences in Hong Kong have featured Keller and others, like D.A. Carson and John Piper, who are not Presbyterians. These teachers do not emphasize either church government or the political "implications" of biblical theology. Rather, they focus on God's free grace towards sinners.

Meanwhile, across the country, many urban churches are developing a stronger quasi-denominational identity that is characterized by Calvinism or more broadly Reformed theology.[6] For example, when we interviewed

in Appendix 3.

4. Brown, "Chinese Calvinism flourishes"; Fällman, "Chinese Christianity Is More"; "Calvinism on the ground."

5. McGrath, A Life of John Calvin, 83.

6. Liu and Wang, Observing China's Urban House Churches, 45.

individuals from churches with a Wenzhou background, they mention the Calvinism-Arminianism divide as a top controversy in most churches there. Some people in Wenzhou churches hold onto a Calvinist identity as a mark of greater orthodoxy, to distinguish themselves from the general evangelical camp.

China's growing Calvinist groups did not develop in a vacuum. The earliest Protestant missionaries, including Robert Morrison and William Milne, were Calvinist in their theology. They were followed by Presbyterian missionaries in the 1840s. Although they planted churches and even founded a seminary in North China in the 1930s, that historical influence was largely lost in the 1950s when China plunged into Communism. In the absence of foreign missionaries, the dominant theology among Chinese Protestants, if any, rooted itself in fundamentalist, pietistic or even Pentecostal traditions through indigenous evangelists such as Watchman Nee and John Song.

In today's China, when asked about their theological background, most Christians will say "evangelical." Why do they identify themselves as such? It is a wide category and a safe one, both to church people and the authorities. Since many elderly church leaders were converts before the Cultural Revolution, their self-identification as evangelicals is a strategy to evade political persecution against specific Christian factions. Another reason for the generality is the influence of more recent foreign Christians who are less inclined to tout a particular denomination. Since the 1980s, churches in China have been re-introduced to Christianity in a post-denominational age. Sixty-two-year-old preacher Liang (pseudonym, male) commends this lack of denominationalism as an advantage of Chinese churches:

> We don't speak about denominations, but rather three musts: Bible, Holy Spirit and Christian living. These are the three legs of a proper Christian, no matter what background one comes from. Mention denominations and you will be viewed as someone who steals (sheep) from others. Having no denominations is a big blessing to our Chinese church. We'd better not talk about denominations.

After China's opening-up, a revived interest in Calvinism did not first begin in the church. Rather, as early as the 1980s, Calvinism had become a subject of academic interest because of the Chinese translation of Max Weber's *The Protestant Ethic and the Spirit of Capitalism*. Chinese scholars debated the role of Calvinism in shaping Western capitalism and its possible implications for China's growing economy. Swedish scholar Fredrik Fällman quotes a statistic showing that approximately 4,300 academic articles in China have referenced Calvin or Calvinism since the 1990s.[7] Another way that Reformed theological influence came to China arose from the translation of Augustine's writings in the fields of political theory and literary classics. For example, works by Augustine, such as *City of God* and *Confessions* were translated and issued by multiple publishers in different versions. Before church-attending Christians embraced Calvinism and Reformed theology, it was a group of "cultural Christians" (intellectuals and scholars who study Christianity but are not members of Christian churches) in Chinese academia who showed strong interest in these writings.

Real change in churches' theological outlook took place around 1999, when taped copies of sermons by Indonesian Chinese evangelist Stephen Tong were being widely distributed. Reformed literature translated by Dr. Charles Chao before the 1940s was reintroduced and printed underground. Dr. Chao's son Jonathan Chao and his associates also travelled in China to teach. Meanwhile, the Pentecostal movement was also growing in cities. Many churches sought in Calvinist theology a counterbalancing influence that would guard their members against the emotion-oriented tendency.

Since the 2000s, Christian publishers with Calvinist leanings have started introducing and translating more works by classic and contemporary authors. Chinese who studied in Calvinist seminaries returned to China to teach. Faculty members from these schools also travelled to China and gave lectures. More and more Chinese Calvinists are making ample use of technologies such as blogs, microblogs, and online and print magazines in recent years to engage more readers within and outside the church. Even as *Time* magazine listed New Calvinism as No. 3 in its list of "10 Ideas Changing the World Right Now" (2009), the same new tide was rising in China as well.

CALVIN RE-ENTERS CHINA

Every Friday afternoon in 2006, retired religion professor Phil Holtrop met with visiting scholar Song (pseudonym, male, age 45) for a few hours on the Calvin College campus in Grand Rapids, Michigan for a one-on-one reading of John Calvin's classic, *The Institutes of the Christian Religion*. Within a year, they read it from cover to cover. Song became a Reformed Calvinist in Michigan after having been a Christian believer for a decade in China.

Song is now a professor of philosophy at one of Beijing's most prestigious universities, and also an elder of an unregistered congregation of 1000 members, most of whom are young professionals. After his return to

7. Fällman, "Calvin, Culture and Christ?" 156.

China in 2007, Song became actively involved in the publication of Calvin's *Institutes* in Chinese within mainland China.[8] Before this time, the Three-Self churches also imported Calvin's works, but the volumes being sold in Three-self church bookstores were censored, abridged versions. Under Song's editorial efforts, Calvin's unabridged *Institutes* were published and have been sold in regular and online bookstores since 2010. Song also produced some subsequent academic publications of Calvin's thinking for the Chinese context.[9] Such was the start of Calvinist fervor among Chinese urban churches.

In the early 2000s, the places where Calvinism was spreading fastest are the elite universities, where Christian philosophers and educators are teaching, writing and translating more Calvinist works. For example, the Alvin Plantinga Center for Human Value at Beijing University was an initiative to bring Calvinist Philosophers into dialogue with Chinese intellectuals.

Since the late 2000s, a few lawyer-turned-ministers who profess to be Calvinists have arrived on the scene at the right time to help this theological influence become more widely known. Their previous legal trainings and exposure to public affairs have enabled them to write and respond to social issues in a Christian way. These leaders cultivated Calvinist theology in Chinese soil, and they pushed for an indigenous movement of Calvinist churches. A related characteristic of the growing strand of Calvinist churches is their interest in social issues, such as democratization, constitutional rights and social justice. Members of these churches tend to be a self-selected group with similar awareness. Lastly, these churches tend to have a more formal liturgy because they place much emphasis on corporate worship. Such public witnessing of their faith requires more visible presentations of who they are, so they make their by-laws and confessional statements available publicly. However, this greater visibility and order tend to attract intensified surveillance from the authorities.

ALL SPHERES OF LIFE

In the West, the mention of Calvinism may bring to mind a stereotypical controversy over the theological concept of TULIP.[10] In contrast, in the

---

8. Early Chinese versions are published in Hong Kong and Taiwan.

9. Chan and Sun, eds., *John Calvin and Sino-Christian Theology*.

10. The five points of TULIP is often used as an acronym for Calvinism: Total depravity, unconditional election, limited atonement, irresistible grace, perseverance of saints.

Chinese context, Calvinism is more about Christian worldview.[11] This common appeal of Calvinism to urban converts came up frequently in our interviews—its empowering call for Christians to live out their faith in all spheres of life. In contrast, the separationist and pietist theology that has enjoyed wider popularity among Chinese churches offers a truncated view of life made up of a secular sphere and a sacred one. Forty-year-old preacher Pan (pseudonym, male) says that an increasing number of Christians are yearning for a systematic Christian worldview that makes their outlook on the world and politics a holistic one:

> I found something striking in Abraham Kuyper's *Stone Lectures on Calvinism*. He says that a battle requires structural planning. This is true in the battle of theological ideas too. If you want to explain and defend your Christian faith, you need a theological framework to back you up. In this sense, evangelical firepower is not strong enough. Only Calvinist theology is rooted in God's sovereignty as its framework, and it covers all spheres of life. It challenges the believer to bring every part of his or her life back in line with God's Word. In doing this, one is constantly aligning oneself with the root—God.

When ministers like Pan compare reformed theology to the broader evangelical faith, the latter seems to lack piety because it is only confined to the private sphere. Most church leaders prior to the 1980s embraced a separatist view of faith and society that helped them focus on individual spirituality in the midst of severe political persecution. Piety characterizes their Christianity, but so does individualism. Often times, piety is considered equivalent to not challenging leaders of the church or the government. With the mass conversion of more educated young urbanites, however, this pietistic theology and patriarchal governance have not been able to satisfy their deeper inquiries into the Christian faith. They wonder: Why do some people leave the church after conversion? What makes a true believer? How should Christians live ethically and missionally in a capitalist urban environment? What does submission to authorities mean? To some extent, the spread of Calvinist theology disintegrated many believers' reliance on the old generation of lay clergy, who were less theologically trained.

In the above statement, Pan was speaking about his own spiritual journey. While he once majored in philosophy in Beijing University's graduate

---

11. It is worth mentioning that many Chinese Christians were exposed to Kuyperianism before reading Calvin's major work (the *Institutes*), because the first publication about Calvin's life included Abraham Kuyper's famous *Stone Lectures* from 1898 that expounded Calvinism as a life system and a worldview.

school, Pan has adhered to a series of major schools of thought for his life's compass, from Communism and Buddhism to classical liberalism and finally Christianity. It was only when he read the works of Calvin and Kuyper that Pan felt his fervent longings for a holistic Christian outlook fulfilled. In fact, becoming a Calvinist was like a second conversion for him. Pan believes that Calvinism may prove intellectually satisfying to many educated Chinese who were once classical liberals:

> As intellectual seekers, we used to find comfort in Western democratic thought and the rule of law. When we go on our spiritual journeys, we seek a holistic faith, one that connects with our expertise in law, philosophy, economics and politics. Calvinism brought a systematic renewal to my academic interests, values and sense of responsibility. It was a structural overhaul to my thinking processes. It enables me to view things more biblically, especially church and state, faith and society.

Scholar Alexander Chow confirms the general appeal of Calvinism to those who have "a strong theological interest in engaging in the public sphere around subjects like the rule of law, constitutionalism and a civil society."[12] A grander view of God's sovereignty and of the Gospel supplies these resources. But when it comes to the ecclesiology of Calvinism, that is, its high view of church order and polity, not all liberal-minded intellectuals find it appealing. They fear that in the corporate motions of worship, they might lose their much cherished individuality and freedom. As 60-year-old law professor Jing (pseudonym) who serves as a church deacon says,

> Intellectuals do not necessarily embrace Calvinist theology, because most of these educated people are very atomized and individualistic. They like academic topics, and their lifestyle is to read and write at home. They have a natural aversion to institutionalized things, such as church gatherings. Many agree with John Calvin but see Calvinism as problematic.

In China when intellectuals call themselves "liberal," that means they are admirers of classical liberalism as it connects to the free market, rule of law and human rights. This political ideology has been the leading school of thought in China for the past two decades, counterbalancing the Communist ideology. Many people in this camp were previously involved in the 1989 Tiananmen democracy movement. The disillusionment they felt afterwards forced them to find an alternative value system, that is, classical liberalism. Among these people, many embraced Christianity and joined

---

12. Chow, "Calvinist Public Theology," 158–175.

churches. However, despite the affinity of the classical liberal worldview with a Christian worldview, these converts may still cherish the influence of Enlightenment thinkers whose thought centers on humanity apart from deity.

Although Calvinism provides a grander lens by which to view state and society, many humanist Chinese converts find its emphasis on God's sovereignty and the apparent downgrading of human freedom unacceptable. Thirty-five-year-old Lin (pseudonym, male), a doctoral student in economics, expresses his approval of Arminian theology over Calvinism in this way: "As a firm believer in individual liberty and human dignity, I find it natural to say that humans have a free will that deserves respect." As a passionate new convert, Lin certainly believes in an all-sovereign God, but he cannot work out the tension between classical liberalism and Calvinist Christianity.

Indigenous Christian writer Wei Zhou (male, 39) knows this tension well. Having traveled the same road as most liberal intellectuals who converted to Christianity, Wei thinks this conflict is part of the growing pains of China's reformed churches. In his recent writing, Wei insightfully summarizes two types of Chinese Calvinists in a recent writing (Zhou 2015):

> The first is to continue to build themselves up in the faith, seeking answers for social and political ills by an in-depth theology. On certain topics, their response may be similar to that of a proponent of liberalism but is definitely gospel-oriented in essence. A second way is to use theology to justify classical liberalism, replacing the gospel message with social and political concerns. What these churches preach will eventually become a social gospel, lacking any call to salvation and repentance.[13]

By "an in-depth theology," Wei Zhou refers to churches that embrace Calvinism. He further writes that this first group of classically liberal converts can be as "happy as a fish in water (*ru yu de shui*)" within Calvinist churches. At these fellowships, they not only find systematic and empowering expressions of their God-centered Christianity to be intellectually satisfying, but their compassion for social problems also find down-to-earth solutions through various church ministries. In 2014, Calvinism even appeared in an article on China's most widely circulated investigative magazine *Caijing*.[14]

---

13. Zhou, "Liberalism and China's Churches."
14. Li and Ma, "The Belhar Confession."

"FISH IN WATER" CALVINISM

A church leader who enjoys the deep waters of Calvinism would naturally implement reforms to church governance. Historically, unregistered churches in China have one of two models of church governance: the Jesus Family tradition in northern China and the Little Flock tradition in southern China.[15] Both these traditions are pietistic in theology, such that church governance is largely informal and leader-oriented. The theology, personality and preferences of the founding leader(s) often form the building blocks of a governance style. No church has by-laws because that would make it appear too organized and attract attention from local authorities. These characteristics are in sharp contrast with what a Calvinist church should look like in terms of governance.

Many Calvinists believe that a presbyterian structure of church governance supplies biblical checks on power abuse by electing representative assemblies of elders. Chinese intellectuals with Calvinist leanings favor this set-up because the abuse of power runs rampant in Chinese culture, even within churches. Fifty-year-old Huang (pseudonym, male) has been elected as an elder of his re-structuring church of 200 members. He gladly reports to us regarding the church's progress in becoming "truly reformed" in church government:

> Our teaching elder is becoming ordained to be the main pastor this year. After that, he will be the main convener for consistory meetings. Then our plans and decisions will all be passed by the elders. This is not an easy path to take, but we think it is biblical. The Apostle Paul set up groups of elders in churches he planted so that disputes could be brought up to a higher assembly of authority. This model protects the pastor from all kinds of temptations, like money and power. His preaching is under the evaluation of elders too, and that also protects the pastor from misusing the pulpit for personal opinions.

Chinese Calvinist churches highly emphasize Christian education for both adults and children. Their signature curricula for Sunday school classes are the catechisms. New converts study the *Shorter Westminster Catechism* together. Many churches also have reading groups that survey classic texts, such as Calvin's *Institutes*. They treasure these texts as the flesh and

15. Both traditions are characterized by patriarchal governance where some elderly believers serve as the leading authority over most decisions, including spiritual, financial and organizational affairs. Anti-intellectualism is the trend as believers are not encouraged to read theological books or enter into seminaries. Only books by the old patriarchal leaders of their traditions are encouraged, such as Watchman Nee.

blood of their reformed identity. We once attended a Christmas party when a reformed congregation adapted these texts into a stage drama. A sense of finding Christianity's longstanding heritage is cherished. Twenty-four-year-old college student Zhang affirms the benefits of learning from these historic resources:

> Compared to the old days when we used materials written by some random modern teachers, I really enjoy these time-tested jewels of the Calvinist tradition. The catechisms were written a few hundred years ago, but their theology is crystal-clear and relevant. I feel that the bits and pieces of Bible knowledge I have accumulated to this point are all coming together.

In churches that receive reformed theology with open arms, we often hear confident remarks like these about their "second conversion" into a deeper heritage of the Christian faith. The "doctrines of grace," as they are called, point out the deep and ingrained sinfulness of humans, and then go on to tell how God has freely chosen to save sinners who cannot save themselves. Through preaching and the Holy Spirit, God creates repentance and faith in people's hearts, gives them a new heart to love him, and empowers them to follow Jesus. The main point, however, is not what we must do for God, but what He has done for us. Regardless of our faults, even now he forgives Christians who truly repent and trust in Christ alone, accepts them into His gracious presence, and assures them of His love. Secure in the knowledge that God loves them, believers then find the motivation to glorify God in all their conduct.

This message has come like refreshing waters to thousands of Chinese pastors, most of whom labor under a heavy burden of expectations that they place upon themselves and that others place upon them. When they hear of God's mercy and grace, which we receive daily by faith, they experience deep peace, a new joy, and fresh strength to serve God. They no longer feel compelled to "justify" themselves by how much they do and serve in the church. As American neo-Calvinist scholar James Smith writes in his *Letters to a Young Calvinist*, people who experience such a change are often accompanied by a sense of confidence that is often perceived by non-Calvinists as "pride."[16]

---

16. Smith, *Letters to a Young Calvinist*, 5–9.

THEOLOGICAL DIVERSIFICATION

As writer Wei Zhou analyses, the conversion of a significant number of liberal intellectuals has brought challenges to urban churches. Since the theology in most Chinese churches is fundamentalist and separationist, these settings are ill-equipped to teach and care for new members steeped in systematic and analytic thought. To church leaders, these people's social advocacy may be seen as liberal concerns or risky voices. As Zhou writes, "these churches adopt a policy of withdrawal in order to survive. They stay away from social interactions and focus instead on order and stability within the church. . . . Newly converted advocates of liberalism are considered disruptive and are often 'exhorted' to leave their ideological inclinations at the door."

A former participant of the 1989 Tiananmen movement, 38-year-old Shen (pseudonym, male) is a member of a house church. Every year, he commemorates June Fourth by posting Tiananmen-related articles online. Since he became a Christian and embraced Calvinism, Shen feels more motivated for this kind of advocacy. After sending out an article to his church group by email, Shen received a reply from his lay preacher Jun warning him not to bring politics into church. The next Sunday, Jun prepared a sermon that rebuked practices mixing politics with faith. The conflicts between these two people escalated after Shen openly objected to Jun's "narrow theology" and the latter accused Shen of "hyper-Calvinism."

When chasms or clashes happen, church leaders often blame Calvinism for causing the conflicts. Divisions and splits often occur because church leaders with traditional theological understandings see their authority being undermined by newly introduced Calvinist teachings. As one of the preachers in Uncle Meng's church, 29-year-old Shi (pseudonym, male) never imagined that one day he would have to leave it. Eight years ago, Shi was brought to the faith and baptized by Uncle Meng himself. Shi has great respect for Uncle Meng, as most church leaders in this city do: Uncle Meng is the eldest leader still alive after suffering persecution in the 1950s as a member of the Little Flock group. Since the 1980s, Uncle Meng has led many to Christ and baptized even more because churches without pastors would invite him to perform baptisms or wedding ceremonies. Around 2010, Shi became exposed to Calvinist theology through reading some newly published Christian books. Since then, Shi has used some of these resources . In preaching and teaching, Shi increasingly realized the value of Calvinism. Later, after reading *Letters to a Young Calvinist* translated into Chinese and widely read by thoughtful young urban Christians, Shi wrote and published a book review advocating for Calvinism. In Shi's review article, he mentions how Calvinism may help Chinese Christians to overcome problems in traditional house churches. When this review article spread among his church members, Uncle Meng also read it and felt that Shi was challenging his very authority. He decided that Shi was no longer fit for preaching. A conflict between them was inevitable.

Incidents like this are quite common among urban churches that have intergenerational leaders or theological diversity. As a recent online article "Young, Restless and Reformed in China" observes, in such theological arguments, many are "passing quick judgments on those who are not five-pointers (those who fully accept the five points of TULIP)," and more unfortunately "a number are splitting up congregations."[17] Sometimes, such splits may actually have little to do with doctrinal differences. Younger leaders are more mindful and often critical of the traditional family rule model (*jiazhang zhi*). They tend to prefer elected committees and more openness. In contrast, older leaders tend to rely more on social norms that may be unbiblical. For example, they expect unquestioned obedience to their own personal opinions. Senior preachers tend to hold top leadership roles that determine who qualifies for second-tier leadership. Entrenched in China's authoritarian political culture, even educated church leaders tend to fall prey to this "in control" mindset.

Most church leaders prior to the 1980s embraced a separatist view of faith and society that helped them focus on individual spirituality in the midst of severe political persecution. Often times, piety is considered equivalent to not challenging leaders of the church or the government.

In some places, the word "Calvinism" has become a negative label for an arrogant attitude that promotes itself as the only correct theology. Even within one church, as we find in our fieldwork, members form unhealthy opinions by rating people on their degrees of reformed-ness. Due to its systematic treatment of sophisticated theological topics, Calvinism is a rich goldmine; but to first-generation Chinese churches it is also a force that easily triggers a variety of disputes about infant baptism, election of elders, female leadership, church discipline, the doctrine of predestination, exclusive psalmody (singing only psalms in Sunday worship) and so on. Each of these issues can become an identity-marker, and a variety of Calvinist groups are formed.

Take female leadership, for example. Although one of the biggest demographic problems among the Chinese is that there are now too many men, among the Christian population the reality is quite the contrary— there are many more believing women than men.[18] It has been very com-

17. Ibid., 10.

18. David Aikman is his book estimates that the average ratio is sixty to eighty

mon for women to act as ministry founders or leaders. Some attribute this gender imbalance to such causes as the activity of foreign women missionaries, indigenous women evangelists, the absence of men in rural villages since 1978 and a privatized and problem-centered gospel that appeals more to women.[19] In most churches, a pragmatic response to the issue is most common: "Admittedly male leadership would be ideal, but nowadays we just don't have enough spiritually mature men to be preachers or teachers" or "Wouldn't you prefer a mature Christian sister than a newly converted brother to preach?" Despite China's Confucian patriarchal tradition, the Communist Party has implemented policies to promote gender equality that greatly reshaped gender norms. Just as scholar Martin Whyte observes, changes in family values and structures that would take generations to happen in most societies were compressed into a few years in China.[20] Thus, affirming exclusively male leadership is like swimming against the tide. Groups that oppose female leadership include some fundamentalists (jiyao-pai) and the newly emerging Calvinists. Calvinist groups tend to confirm male leadership formally and teach about women's auxiliary role in the church. This stance not only invites criticism from the broader Protestant churches but also creates tensions and even divisions among their own converts. Churches with varying emphases on the role of gender in leadership come with different gender expectations with regard to the signs of spiritual maturity. In Calvinist churches that endorse male leadership, spiritual maturity is defined by having advanced theological knowledge and a "rational" approach to church governance.[21]

Among the many controversial Calvinist doctrines that lead to church splits is predestination. It indirectly challenges the authority of lay clergy to define Christian piety and salvation. Fifty-two-year-old religion professor Wang (pseudonym) in a top university told us that he often met Calvinists who started conversations by debating predestination. He adds, "Predestination is a very important doctrine, but one should not marginalize other teachings of the Bible. Among the 'five solas' of Reformation, I don't see a 'sola predestination.'" Wang identifies himself as one of the many

---

percent women in churches in mainland China. Leung estimates that in the rural expansion, the ratio between male and female in rural churches is one to five, and in underground seminaries females comprise half or more of the students enrolled. Wielander also observes the predominance of women in Chinese churches. Leung, *The Rural Churches of Mainland China*, 136. Wielander, *Christian Values in Communist China*, 160.

19. Doyle, "Gender Imbalance."

20 Whyte and Parish, *Urban Life in Contemporary China*.

21. Wielander, 161.

halfway Calvinists who reserve personal deviations from classic Reformed doctrines. His hesitation partly shows the difficulty of educated Christian men to resolve the classic tension between God's sovereignty and individual choice. Since historically, individualistic choices in the area of personal salvation through Jesus Christ has been emphasized so much, and adult baptisms happen all the time, it is difficult for many believers favoring reformed theology to completely espouse doctrines such as predestination and infant baptism. So, there are more church leaders and believers who would rather call themselves "reformed Baptists."

MISREPRESENTED CALVINISM(S)

In the west, Calvinism and its historical developments are complicated stories. In Chinese soil, over-simplified expressions of Calvinism exist that sometimes turn out to be destructive to local churches. Twenty-five-year-old Yin (pseudonym, female) was part of a self-proclaimed Calvinist church for a time. Almost all its teachings centered on predestination and anti-Arminianism; members were constantly tested by leaders to see if their doctrines were correct or not. Someone who has been a Christian for many years who remained an Arminian in doctrine would be pronounced as unsaved and in need of further intense teaching. Yin recalls the birth of an overly argumentative atmosphere:

> I felt as if I was being brainwashed. Whatever I shared with someone at church, there was always someone who jumped out and argued that what I had said was wrong. Then I would argue back because I also liked to reason with logic. So the church became a place where everyone debated with everyone else, and we wounded each other with argumentative words and attitudes. . . . I felt very pained by it, primarily because I had doubts about my own salvation after being taught these harsh doctrines in that way.

Yin reached the bottom of the pit in her spiritual journey. She felt discouraged when someone counseled her to pray more, for as she says, "I don't even have a clear idea to whom I am praying!" Shortly after this, Yin left this urban church. She spent a whole year disconnected from church life. However, it was a deeper affirmation that Jesus Christ died for her sins on the cross that brought her back. Yin recalls that this lesson taught her not to be too compliant in receiving all the teachings in church. She says, "The most important thing is to know who you do believe in." Two years later, she learned that the leader himself had renounced Calvinism, and that he would meet up with leaders of other churches and question their theology, accusing them of being false prophets.

Churches wishing to avoid these controversies often do not include "Reformed" or "Presbyterian" in their church names. They also avoid drawing up confessional statements. For example, among churches in Shanghai, election of elders and ordination of pastors are frowned upon as purely Calvinist practices. However, some churches still verbally call themselves "Presbyterian" in governance.

In our fieldwork, we heard accounts of some churches that claim to be Calvinist in theology but are actually chaotic and rampant in power abuse. Their theology does not challenge them to reform their opaque financial system nor their lax liturgy. To these leaders, Calvinism is a conveniently updated term for theological orthodoxy. There are also Calvinist groups that have gone too far in their legalism. These practices have partly contributed to the ill fame of Calvinism in some regions.

Another misrepresentation is common, too. Implementers of Calvinism sometimes adopt something that is culturally conditioned rather than essential. For example, some church leaders like to associate Calvinism with the constitutional democracy or free market enterprise in the West, quoting historical literature concerning America's founding story and Max Weber. As scholar Nanlai Cao observes in Wenzhou, where Calvinism flourishes, Christianity that has the stamp of Western witness seems to be considered more authentic than indigenous Chinese Christianity.[22]

CONCLUSION

In recent years, a trend of taking on a denominational label has taken place in urban centers where Calvinist or Reformed theology is gaining momentum. Reformed theology has begun to make an even wider and deeper impact on Chinese Christians, especially in the unregistered churches. Classic Calvinist and neo-Calvinist literature is being promoted among congregations that have developed more theological study habits than the average church. Church leaders within these groups are also working closely with Christian publishers of Calvinist persuasions in order to introduce more theological literature with a similar position. As noted earlier, the appeal of Calvinism lay partly in its comprehensive world-and-life view, partly in its view of shared leadership in the church (the "Presbyterian" system of church government), and partly in the emphasis that some Calvinistic theologians placed upon what we might call the "implications" of biblical teachings.

22. Cao, *Constructing China's Jerusalem.*

These included a belief in limited government and even democracy. Sermon topics among these churches address key moral issues of society as well as prevailing social concepts, such as liberalism, secularism and relativism.

While these attempts are budding initiatives, first-generation Calvinist churches also face the tremendous internal challenges of integrating life with doctrine and love with order. An emphasis on ordered authority and submission sometimes undermines loving personal relationships. Preoccupation with getting one's doctrine right may create a polemical subculture with argumentation over theological themes. Brent Fulton insightfully observes that due to the unique educational culture of emphasizing "correctness" in the church, leaders also have the tendency to treat doctrines as an exact science.[23] Despite these challenges, the spread of Calvinist theology is seen as a hopeful catalyst for the future developments of Chinese theology.

As many have observed, and as we have pointed out in this book, Chinese Christianity tends to be highly legalistic or moralistic. Confucianism, with its emphasis upon moral self-cultivation, retains a powerful grip on the Chinese mind. Most Chinese preachers promote a form of Christianity that focuses on our duties to God: we must adhere to His moral standards, and we should follow the examples of biblical characters such as Abraham, Moses, Paul, and Jesus. Reformed theology, however, highlights God's actions, not man's. As a Chinese pastor writes, this conflicts with the culture of leadership in Chinese churches, where leaders are expected to be "extraordinary examples" or "perfect heroes."[24]

The new popularizing movement of Reformed theology in the 2010s, centered on Christ and His grace, far transcends the earlier stress on church government and potential social implications of biblical truth. It does not allow for self-righteousness on the part of those who think that they have been "chosen" by God, for they know that this election comes only from God's free grace and mercy. It is much less doctrinaire, much less legalistic, and much more oriented towards communion with God and love for others. Perhaps this "new wave" of Reformed theology will have a "softening" effect on some current expressions of Calvinism among China's churches.

23. Fulton, *China's Urban Christians*, 116–117.
24. Yang, "Dragon Leaders."

10

Marriage

Youche youfang, fumu shuangwang.
(Looking for a male who owns an apartment and a car,
but whose parents are deceased.)

—A FAMOUS RHYMING MARRIAGE MARKET AD, ANONYMOUS

I am forty-two, have never been married. I am looking for a suitable partner
who must be a committed Christian. This is the only non-negotiable standard.
I don't think it shameful to marry late or not to marry.

—A MARRIAGE MARKET AD BY A CHRISTIAN FEMALE, ANONYMOUS

WITH CHRISTIANITY SPREADING IN China, marriages are taking on new
ethical norms among the expanding groups of young Christians, although
not without challenges. For example, the two marriage ads we quote above
presents a sharp contrast between the popular consumerist values and the
unusual but emerging Christian lifestyle. In this chapter, we discuss how
different aspects of marriage and family life are restructured among young

Christians, including match-making, wedding planning, pre-marital sex, child-bearing and rearing, and bioethics such as abortion.

Observers of churches in China will notice a curious gender imbalance—there are more women than men among Christians while the country's female-male ratio has the opposite trend. Even David Aikman, author of *Jesus in Beijing*, noted in 2005 that sixty to eighty percent of congregations were women. Scholar G. Wright Doyle insightfully analyzes this peculiar phenomenon that has led to female leadership being common in churches.[1] We find similar conditions in our fieldwork: when most of these urban churches started from home-gathering Bible study groups, not only are there more women than men, but lay female leadership is often the norm. Church growth accentuated such an imbalance since women evangelized other women in their circles. Doyle views this problem as acute because it not only creates current pastoral demands but also future challenges by the lack of male leadership and Christian fatherhood. In urban churches dominated by young professionals, this gender imbalance poses many challenges for the marriage scene. In fact, finding a Christian mate and building a biblical marriage has become the most urgently needed ministry among young urban Christians. For example, many pastors of urban churches list match-making for their single female members as a top challenge. For married couples, the need for guidance in solving marital conflicts is also arising. An illustrating example is that after the publication of *The Meaning of Marriage* by Timothy Keller in its Chinese version in 2015, the book became an instant best-seller in most Christian bookstores and many churches bought it in wholesale quantities.

MARRIAGE AND SOCIAL CHANGE

China's one-child policy, established in 1979, has greatly shaped the country's gender ratio as well as marriage expectations and family culture. According to Greenhalgh, "at 120 boys per 100 girls, China's sex ratio at birth is now the highest in the world," which is likely to result in thirty million bachelors in future decades.[2] Besides this demographic change, marriage values and norms are also shifting among Chinese people. According to anthropologist Yunxiang Yan, towards the end of 1990s, even in rural China, a huge generational gap existed in the way marriage and family were viewed, since the younger generation was becoming more entrenched in consumerism and

---

1. Doyle, "Gender Imbalance in Chinese Churches."
2. Greenhalgh, *Cultivating Global Citizens*, 1.

self-fulfillment.[3] Not only did families request a much higher bride price and attach more value to material belongings, but people's views of marriage have also been influenced by trends arising from the modern sexual revolution. As a result, for example, pre-marriage sex, cohabitation and extra-marital affairs have become more common.

Twenty years after Yan's study, marriages for the Chinese have changed even more. Take qualities sought in a partner, for example. For people born in the 1950s, their primary considerations for finding a marriage partner included "political appearance" (*zhengzhi mianmao*) and the family's "class category" (*jieji chengfen*). Family members and relatives usually functioned as match-makers. *Danwei* (work unit) cadres were often involved in formally introducing the couple and chairing unadorned marriage ceremonies vowing and bowing to a picture of Mao. For the generation born after 1979, education level, income and career paths became prioritized when seeking a mate.[4] Parental involvement in match-making became less common. With the disintegration of the *danwei* system, marriage ceremonies became more personalized, to the point of being lavish. For young people born after 1990s, sights are set on potential mates who own real estate and automobiles.[5] A young man is considered unmarriageable if he does not have an apartment and lacks a good career. Among women, popular slogans like "I would rather cry inside a BMW than laugh on a bicycle" are embraced undisguisedly. These secular trends and highly materialistic mindsets are also exerting influence on Christians, especially young members of growing urban churches.

FINDING A MATE

The difficulty for a young Christian woman to find a mate lies not only in the slim chance of meeting Christian males in their churches, but also in the high standards she commonly holds regarding potential partners. Twenty-eight-year-old Xu (pseudonym, male) belongs to an urban professional church where the gender ratio is less of a problem. There are around 25 male and 45 female members, most of whom are in the marriageable age range. During the summer of 2011, this church held five weddings. However, a dozen women above the age of thirty remained single. Most of them aspire

3. Yan, *Private Life under Socialism.*

4. A few studies show the macro trends: Han, "Trends in Educational Assortative Marriage." Li, "Changes in the Dating Market." Qi, et al.,"Dating and Marriage in China."

5. Griffiths, *Consumers and Individuals in China*, 145–47

to marry a Christian male, for their preacher has placed much emphasis on this matter. But Xu has been observing how people in this church date and he sadly comments, "Unbelieving women usually look at your career and wealth, but many Christian sisters ask for even more—similar secular expectations and your spirituality!" By "secular expectations," Xu refers to the common requirements of an apartment and a high paying career in the city. "Even if the girl does not value these," says Xu, "her parents will push her in this direction."

Singlehood is not encouraged in Chinese culture; it is actually considered a dishonor to one's parents.[6] And when it comes to putting high pressure on young people's marriage choices, traditional Chinese parents are in a class by themselves.[7] Most of them grew up during the Communist era when marriages had to be approved, if not arranged, by parents and work place authorities. In those days, an ideal dating partner would be considered "both red and with specializations" (*youhong youzhuan*). Thus, they are prone to become manipulative when it comes to their children's marriages, including finding the spouse, details concerning the ceremony, and even when to have a baby. Besides such calculative preferences, they expect to preserve or even to earn "face" by showing off children who marry well to relatives and friends.

Each Spring Festival, many urban-dwelling professionals in big cities such as Beijing and Shanghai return to their small town or rural hometowns for the annual family reunion. A Chinese poem expresses the sentiments aptly as "feeling twice homesick on festival days."[8] For single females in the church, it is often the most difficult time when they again face the pressure of demanding parents who either rebuke them for their singlehood or force them to go on arranged dates with male strangers. Someone even rewrote the poem as "being twice as forced to marry on festival days." Below are a few firsthand accounts of such experiences (all names are pseudonyms):

> After the Spring Festival ended, I was waiting for the train back to Beijing. My mother pulled me aside and rebuked me for an hour. Her words were harsh: "If you don't get married this year, you'd better not come back home next year! Go spend your life in Beijing with your church!"

6. According to sociologist Yong Cai in an interview by *Salon*, while Western societies always have ten to fifteen percent of the population that remains single, whereas in China, the percentage has always been less than one percent. "All the *shengnu* (leftover) ladies."

7. "Parent Meddling."

8. A classical Chinese poem by Wang Wei, titled "Thinking of my brother on the Double Ninth Festival."

—Yun, female, 33, marketing staff

Reunions with our extended family are awkward for my parents. They see that my cousins who are much younger than I am are already married, some with children. They feel ashamed about my singlehood, and especially when they are asked by relatives about it. Year after year, they are putting more and more pressure on me.

—Gong, female, 35, accountant

My parents generally respect my choice, but they are worried that I will never marry. The point of confrontation between us is that they think my faith has much to do with my singlehood. So, they argue with me about my Christian commitment and blame me for being too fervent towards God to think about getting married.

—Hong, female, 31, investment bank consultant

My parents forced me to go on a blind date with the son of my father's friend, because my father thought this young man was quite reserved. I obeyed just to let their hearts settle for a while. But meeting this man shows me how corrupt society is today. We had a quick meal, and I wanted to catch the train back to Shanghai. Then my date suggested to me that I could spend the night with him. I asked him, "So you are the (sexually) open type?" He replied with his own question: "Aren't [all] people in Shanghai this way?" I left with disgust and never contacted him again.

—Cheng, female, 34, salesperson

It is important to note that Spring Festival days already tend to witness more friction between young Christians and their families because it is a time when ancestor worship and other superstitious rites are widely practiced. By not participating, Christians are considered unfilial or disrespectful to the elderly. Such discord easily stirs up arguments about delayed marriage choices.

Consider the story of 37-year-old Wan (pseudonym, female) who got her PhD degree in the United States and now works in China as a university professor. She became a Christian overseas and has since wanted to marry a believer. Her parents are educated intellectuals too so they have not pushed her as hard as other parents would. As Wan's age has increased, they have also become quite concerned and sometimes use her faith as a scapegoat. Having been a member of an urban church for over six years, Wan finds very few available Christian young men around her. Through some mutual contacts, she got to know a 50-year-old medical doctor in the church who had never been married. The man looks even older than his real age, but Wan appreciates his sincerity in the faith. "It is hard to talk about romantic feelings between us," says Wan, "but at least he is a Christian brother." Before they entered into a committed dating relationship, Wan thought it would be better to let her parents meet him first, for she feared that his aged appearance would be a problem to them sooner or later. The meeting was unpleasant, just as she had expected. Her parents vehemently objected to their relationship. After this, Wan discontinued personal contact with this brother. She felt that her feelings for him were not strong enough to withstand the storm from her parents.

A Christian couple, Shang (pseudonym, 29, female) and Liu (pseudonym, 31, male), had been dating for eight years. They were high school sweethearts and both became Christians in college through the Campus Crusade fellowship. Shang's parents knew about their relationship from the beginning, but because Liu came from a working family of humble means, they expressed their objections early on. After graduation, Liu became a full-time campus ministry staff. He later was diagnosed with Hepatitis B. His illness and career brought even more objections from Shang's parents. Shang's determined father refused to speak with her for six months. As their only daughter, Shang faced tremendous pressure. She and Liu broke up and then got back together several times. All their church friends prayed and supported them. Some suggested that they get married in church without their parents being present. But Shang and Liu were determined to get Shan's parents' blessings first. During one trip back to her hometown of Xinjiang, Shang's mother was persuaded by the grandmother, who reminded her that she had done the same thing by marrying Shang's father despite family disapproval. After eight years of warring against her daughter, the mother's heart softened. Shang and Liu had a big Christian wedding, a much-awaited event with over four hundred guests.

CHURCH DISCIPLINE

Dating-age believers not only face pressure from their family and friends, but also harsh discipline from the church if they cross certain boundaries, such as marrying an unbeliever or having pre-marital sex. In a social environment where cohabitation and abortions abound, many urban churches impose strict checks on these behaviors. Some even put these warnings in writing within their open statements and by-laws, explaining that such actions may incur discipline, such as being banned from communion.

One story that illustrates this situation is that of 35-year-old Ling (pseudonym, female). She had had a few unhappy experiences before. On the day before her wedding to Kong (pseudonym, male, 38), her heart ached as she thought about her decision to marry an unbeliever. Ling had been a Christian for ten years and a leader for five years. She had always desired to marry a Christian brother. A few dating experiences with different believing men ended unsuccessfully. Ling recalled the most recent one when she met a brother in a Three-self church who boasted about being an itinerant preacher. Four months of getting to know this person revealed that he has been hopping from church to church without a committed church life. His attitudes towards women were often domineering, and he often quoted Bible passages as proof for women's submission. This man told Ling that God has shown him in a dream that she was to become his wife. She was quite taken by that for a while, but after a year, she felt increasingly disturbed by the idea of marrying this man. The break-up was ugly but quick.

Just a year later, a friend introduced Ling to Kong, a refined and courteous university instructor. Kong appeared to be the ideal man for her, but the only obstacle was that he was not a believer. Actually, he was an ardent Maoist. Ling and Kong got a long very well as a couple, as long as spiritual and political conversations were put aside. Ling was hoping that Kong could grow into becoming a Christian through their dating relationship, and fortunately he was quite open to the Bible and church life. Six months after they started dating, Kong proposed. Ling had mixed feelings of joy and sadness. She was happy to think that her unbelieving parents would smile this time during Spring Festival reunion because she had found such a fine young man with a good career and safe political aspirations. At the same time, sadness engulfed her because she knew deep in her heart that this broke God's law. As a mentor to many new converts in church, she would face scornful looks and frowns from many fellow believers. This torrent of emotions made her pull back a few times after agreeing to register for a marriage certificate with Kong. But Kong was quite understanding and never became annoyed about it. In the end, they did get married. After that, Ling stepped down from leadership positions and received a notice that she would not be welcome at communion for six months. Since then, she has only occasionally showed up in church, most times without her husband.

Others to face church discipline are Rong (pseudonym, female, 26) and Shu (pseudonym, male, 27), who had been dating for three years. Their dating relationship started at a campus fellowship. Since no resistance had been encountered from family, things were quickly developing towards marriage. However, they spent a night together and Rong became pregnant. Shu immediately planned a wedding in his hometown. After a few months, they both felt convicted about their secret sin and met up with their lay preacher. According to the rules, they were banned from taking communion for six months, and the preacher made a public announcement about their committing the sin of premarital sex. He commended Shu for taking the responsibility by marrying Rong immediately afterwards and choosing to keep the baby. He also urged brothers and sisters to receive them into fellowship because they had repented.

During this gathering, another church member objected to such public discipline because he considered it inappropriate to make such a private sin publicly known. A debate took place among members of the church. Although it quieted down after a few weeks and the couple felt acceptance from fellow believers in the church, it did leave a scar on the unity of the church. Two years later, when a second-tier leader divorced his spouse, the preacher did not publicize his name when announcing church discipline. The way he dealt with this incident was in sharp contrast to the previous case. Some members then blamed the preacher for favoritism. Another debate arose and led to a split. Rong and Shu left that congregation together with half of the members.

CHRISTIAN WEDDINGS

In today's China, weddings are joyous occasions for family reunion, but they are also times to show off achievements and "earn face." Among families with social status, the planning of a wedding should always include admirable symbols of wealth, such as an extravagant banquet for guests in a four-star hotel, the parading of luxury cars, the price of the wedding gown and diamond rings, etc. At some weddings, traditional elements are also blended in, such as dressing up in traditional Chinese gowns and kowtowing to heaven and earth (*bai tiandi*). Many families use the wedding occasion to collect gift money by inviting as many guests as possible. For most young Christians, extravagance and superstitions are things they wanted to avoid at their wedding.

When Yuan (pseudonym, male, 28) phoned his parents about his wedding plan, he was given a stern "No." Yuan's parents are retirees from a military unit and as such belong to the most closed political subsystem in the Communist-led state machine. As the only son, Yuan was reared with high expectations that he would inherit his parents' status as a privileged military elite. They had tried to arrange his entrance into a military college, but he refused. Moreover, Yuan's conversion in 2001 made him determined to marry a Christian believer. Later, when attending a mission conference in

Hong Kong, he met Guo (pseudonym, female, 32) who was also a committed believer studying in the United States. On hearing about Guo's overseas study experience, the first reaction of Yuan's parents was, "Could she be a spy for the Americans?" Since Guo was three years older than Yuan, his parents also used the age difference against them. After the phone conversation about their plans to hold the wedding at a church, Yuan's parents reiterated their disapproval.

Consequently, Yuan and Guo had to delay their wedding and start a long-distance relationship after Guo returned to the United States. Although Guo's church friends tried to persuade them to have a wedding ceremony in the United States without the presence of their parents, Yuan and Guo were determined to have a church wedding in China so that their unbelieving parents could experience what church.

With a rising number of young Christian couples getting married in a religious ceremony, more and more specialized services have emerged, such as wedding planners and photographic studios. Since Christians generally avoid extravagant shows of status and wealth, these services offer basic and plain ceremonial elements. Such simple style sometimes attracts an unbelieving crowd, which comments on the Christian ceremony's "meaningfulness." Sermons related to Christian marriage present the audience with an unusual understanding of one of life's most puzzling dilemmas, and these often serve as contact points for later church outreach activities. Yuan and Guo planned a low-budget wedding, hiring a decorator, photographer and a make-up artist among their church friends for a total of 3000 *yuan* (around five hundred dollars).

When Yuan presented his parents with this church wedding plan, they objected even more strongly. To Yuan's father, his son's conversion was outrageous, and a church wedding smacked of open. Yuan's parents also considered it shameful to invite friends and relatives to a Christian wedding. Arguments went on, and the wedding was delayed again. Finally, Yuan decided to have a wedding without his parents present. "We are confirmed that God has brought us together," Yuan says, "and I just want to give my bride a wedding."

Although Yuan was part of a house church, he preferred using a public church facility for the wedding so that more guests could be invited. Yuan reserved a newly-built Three-Self church building for the wedding, but this brought unforeseen objections from an elderly church leader. He placed great emphasis upon the separation of house churches from registered Three-self churches and felt that using the facility of Three-self churches would be a compromise. He suggested other options like renting a multipurpose gym hall or a hotel ballroom adorned with some Christian elements such as the cross, a choir and a sermon. But Yuan and another younger leader had a more tolerant view, so the wedding happened as planned. Two days before their wedding date, a close relative persuaded Yuan's parents to attend. It was the first time for Yuan's parents to step inside a Christian church.

Yan (pseudonym, female, 31) and Hong (pseudonym, male, 33) had a similarly difficult wedding experience with manipulative parents who showed little respect for their adult children. Their objection to Hong's humble economic status lasted for eight years of their dating relationship. During this time, both Yan and Hong became Christians. Their common faith made their mutual commitment even stronger. Seeing their daughter Yan getting older in age, the parents eventually gave up their grasp reluctantly. A church wedding was planned, but the parents refused to take their role of giving a blessing at the rehearsal. At the actual wedding ceremony, when Yan's father led her down the aisle and give her to Hong, the pastor asked if he was willing to bless this new couple. To everybody's surprise and dismay, Yan's father shook his head and said no. The bride burst into tears, but the pastor managed to continue the ceremony. It continues to be a scar in the family relationship.

CHILDREARING BATTLES

Chinese families generally see having children as another milestone after a young couple marry, and this desire has been exacerbated by the one-child policy. For young Christian couples who are first-generation believers in their families, when they try to rear children in a Christian way, they usually face tremendous challenges from both families. In our fieldwork, we heard similar personal accounts of inter-generational conflicts in this area.

From the beginning of their dating relationship, Yue (pseudonym, female, 28) and Chao (pseudonym, male, 29) experienced some minor opposition from parents because Yue's parents were dissatisfied about Chao's height and salary. The culture of marrying a young man who is tall, rich and handsome (*gaofushuai*) dominated their expectations. But his parents soon found comfort in knowing that Chao's parents had purchased a two-bedroom urban apartment for him. They soon were married with blessings from both sides. Although both parents were unbelievers, they were quite open to the faith and a church wedding for it sounded fashionable and had the appeal of being Western.

A year later, Yue became pregnant, but the blessings from both sides soon reversed when her first ultrasound at five months showed a major birth defect. Doctors informed them that if they decided to continue the pregnancy, the baby would need to undergo a major surgery right after birth, and then a few surgeries within the first year. Both sets of parents encouraged the couple to abort the baby. The doctor also told them that since they were both still young, they had a good chance of having a healthy baby in the future.

For over three decades, the one-child policy has significantly reshaped people's biological ethics, especially with regard to abortion. The basic idea of this policy was to encourage every married couple, by coercion if necessary, to limit family size to one child, and abortion has become a convenient way to help them comply. Because a married woman is expected to give birth successfully once, many families optimize this once-in-a-lifetime opportunity to bear and raise the best child. Prenatal screens are widely used to detect birth defects, and couples can discontinue pregnancies if they are not satisfied with the health (or gender) of the fetus. Since cohabitation is so common among dating young couples, many hospitals advertise abortions near college campuses. Some billboards glamorize their content using romantic imagery and words such as, "Painless abortion, giving love the safest guarantee." Our acquaintances in China shared two examples that help illustrate how abortions happen routinely with little ethical struggles involved: 1) a newly married woman aborted her first pregnancy because she had taken cold medicines when she was unaware of her own pregnancy; 2) a female migrant worker aborted her twins during the second trimester because she thought having twins would bring too much of an economic burden to the family. With at least 13 million abortions per year, China has the highest abortion rate in the world, not including statistics from private clinics.[9] In recent years, Christians have started to advocate against abortion. A church in Chengdu started advocacy against abortion by putting up campaign boards in front of hospitals and clinics on the first day of June since 2012. When most Chinese families celebrate this as National Children's Day, they have renamed it "No Abortion on Children's Day."[10]

When Yue told her parents-in-law that as Christians they cannot abort the baby, they howled their anger at her. It was like a tornado. Every day the couple was bombarded with rebukes from their parents and relatives. They took turns arguing with the couple. After a week, Chao could not take it any longer. He left the home and disappeared for two days. Despite Yue's

9. "Painless Abortion Advertisements."
10. Allen-Ebrahimian, "Meet China's Pro-Life Christians."

objections, Chao's parents and relatives took her to the hospital for an abortion. The pastor and members of her church rushed to the hospital just in time to stop them. The pastor spent three hours trying to explain to them why abortion is wrong in God's eyes and why keeping the baby would not be a financial disaster because the church promised to establish a fund to help them. In the end, Chao's parents asked the pastor to sign a written agreement that since the church insisted on keeping the baby, then the church will take full responsibility for this, including paying the medical bills. The pastor did accordingly, and Yue was brought back home safely.

The next few months of Yue's pregnancy were not without storms, however. Despite their agreement with the pastor, Chao's parents still ask Yue to consider abortion from time to time. But when the fetus grew to seven months, the doctor told them that an abortion at this point would damage Yue so much that she would not be able to have children again. After hearing this, Chao's parents stopped mentioning abortion. They had hoped that after birthing this baby, Yue and Chao could still get pregnant with another healthy baby. Since Chao is the only child in the family, they considered having no grandchildren too high a cost. After their change of mind, the stress of abortion was taken away.

In the meantime, Yue and Chao's church had set up a benevolence fund for the baby's future surgeries. By the time of the baby's birth, the church has received four hundred thousand *yuan* (around eighty thousand dollars) in donations. Costs for the first surgery were covered immediately, and it went well for the baby. Yue and Chao felt that they had experienced a miracle after brothers and sisters' prayers for them. These donations and care did appear moving to Chao's parents, but they still could not tolerate the idea that the baby could die any minute.

The next argument in the family centered around who would help Yue care for the newborn after birth. In China, the month after giving birth is considered a golden time for the mother to recuperate from the birthing experience. Usually grandparents stay to help with the newborn for a few more months because the mother would need to return to work after four months of maternity leave. The family had arguments about who stay to help because Chao's parents put themselves into a great dilemma: they insisted on caring for Yue after she gave birth because they considered her recovery important for a future pregnancy; at the same time, however, they refused to look at the newborn, for they feared that it would make them too attached to the baby when he inevitably dies. At the time of our writing, this miracle baby has survived two more major surgeries, and the benevolence fund has been growing.

In urban churches, many believers' marriages are between older women and younger men. A woman aged thirty or more is likely to invite worries from the in-laws about her chance of bearing a healthy baby, and multiple prenatal tests are encouraged. We have met many Christian couples who have finally decided not to take any prenatal screening tests because they are determined to have the baby no matter what the tests may say. Such a decision can once for all resolve all anxiety, although it is often a tough battle by itself.

Qing is a third-generation Christian who married at the age of twenty-seven. Her husband Zhai became a Christian in college after his mother was healed of a severe sickness and converted. Qing's parents had a good impression of Zhai, a refined and courteous young man. After they were married and when Qing was five months pregnant, a prenatal test showed a major birth defect. Zhai's parents urged her to abort the baby, but Qing insisted not to. The child was born prematurely and required major surgery. When Qing and the baby were in hospital, Zhai never visited them; instead, he had a big fight with Qing's parents, blaming them for encouraging their daughter's decision. Zhai himself accused Qing of not respecting his own decision in the matter and "destroying his beautiful life." It was not until then that Qing realized Zhai's Christian faith did not get him farther than health and wealth. Zhai's whole family opposed further surgeries on the child. A few months later, Qing and her newborn baby moved back to her parents' home. Their church started praying for the baby until he got better. When the child reached one year old, Zhai asked for a divorce. After the divorce, Zhai refused to pay anything towards the child's living costs. Qing and her parents reared this child until he was five years old. Then Zhai felt regretful and asked Qing for remarriage on the condition that she leave the child with Qing's parents. Qing and her parents did not take this attitude as true repentance, and Qing refused Zhai's proposal. They kept praying for Zhai, however, hoping that one day he would be willing to embrace his own son and mend this marriage.

Differing generational expectations with regard to child care are illustrated in the story of Xin (pseudonym, female, 26) and Yao (pseudonym, male, 27) who married relatively early among their Christian friends. They were blessed with a baby girl after two years. Hoping to breastfeed longer and care for the baby full-time, Yao decided to quit her job at a busy accounting firm. Xin's retired parents, who lived in the same city objected forcefully because they had expected to provide child care while the couple went out to work. This has become a common pattern among Chinese families with new babies—the grandparents care for the baby, giving the new parents the financial security through working full-time. Very few career women nowadays give up their jobs to care for their newborns. It is also a rising trend among young mothers not to breastfeed newborns because they fear that it will harm the beauty of their figure. Employers give up to four months of maternal leave, and most mothers either wean their babies from breastfeeding at that time or use formula milk from the beginning. In fact, breastfeeding has become so unpopular that quality infant formula has always been in short supply in most cities.

Moreover, among China's young working professionals, overwork has become a norm to secure promotions as well as to show professional commitment and success. When some international media mentions that "China is facing an epidemic of overwork," they are not exaggerating.[11] Not only has individual health been undermined, but family life of the average middle-class Chinese has also shrunk to weekend pastimes, if they can have one day off per week. Couples with young age children are not expected to be around for their children, leaving what they consider unimportant and unskilled tasks to nannies or grandparents. Young Christian couples who value quality time together as a family with young children are faced with tremendous pressure in this professional sphere. Many choose to find self-employment opportunities so that they could earn an income and care for the family at the same time.

In spite of the cultural trends, Xin and Yao believe that since God has entrusted them with the new baby, they as parents should take up the primary responsibility of caring for her. Xin's parents started to blame Yao for laying the financial burden on their only son. Two years later, Yao was pregnant again but Xin's parents urged her to abort the baby for fear of financial burdens. They also thought that having a second child went against the legal policy and would result in a huge fine. Their domineering attitudes throughout the years eventually forced the couple to decide to move to the suburbs in order to shelter their small family from these perpetual arguments.

CONCLUSION

In a country caught in frenzied transition like China, urban young people find themselves facing various challenges with regard to marriage choices. Economical concerns and practical needs win priority over true love; parental involvement tends to muddy the waters even more. Within the cultural context, first-generation urban Christians often face more complications related to marriage, such as finding a mate, planning a church wedding, or starting a family biblically. The unique demographics of the urban church,

11. Shai, "In China, 1600 People Die."

such as its reversed gender ratio, also exacerbate these challenges. Living out their faith in making marriage-related choices often brings tension between them and parents who have fully absorbed secular values and social norms. They have to fight social norms and kinship expectations. Married Christian couples also need to swim against many secular tides in bearing and rearing children. Taking Chinese society as a whole, marriage counseling has become a booming industry because marriage breakdowns are on the rise. We will discuss the challenges they face in children's education in the next chapter.

11

Education

Educating the mind without educating the heart is no education at all.

—ARISTOTLE

AFTER THE BIRTH OF their daughter, like many urban families with ample savings, Tang (pseudonym, male, 38) and his wife purchased an expensive apartment linked to an elite school district (*xuequfang*).[1] Although it was a pricy investment, they hoped that this would secure a quality education for her. Six years later, when Tang's daughter reached school age, the couple made a decision that shocked members of the extended family—they sold this apartment and started homeschooling their only child. Such a change happened all because that during the six year interval, Tang and his wife had both become Christians. Thus, the education they had previously valued now seemed too problematic. A look at what schools in China are teaching would help illuminate their choice.

RED REVIVALS IN PUBLIC SCHOOLS

In 2009, elementary schools across China put on public performances with students dressed up as Red Army soldiers singing red songs, songs loyal to the Communist regime, as a way to celebrate the founding of the Chinese

1. As evidence of how common it is for urban parents to invest their life savings in *xuequfang* property, see "Desperate Parents."

Communist Party. Participation in these presentations was mandatory. Besides public schools, universities, state-owned enterprises and neighborhood committees (*juweihui*) were also required to organize red song sing-alongs. Myths and icons of the communist founders were invoked as symbols of patriotism and loyalty.[2] More recently, the Communist Party's Central Committee reiterated the guidelines that "core socialist values" should "cover all schools and those receiving education."[3] By 2017, more than 200 public schools had been designated "Red Army Schools" that incorporate "red" content into their curriculum, according to a news article, which also quotes a school manager saying that "the Red Army spirit is a real asset for children."[4]

China's education system has been a state monopoly since 1949 because the Communist government used it as its main channel of ideological indoctrination.[5] Atheistic and socialist ideas are taught beginning in primary schools. When China further opened up its economy in the 1990s, the education market diversified to accommodate the tiered needs of an increasingly stratified society, especially the rising demand from middle-class families who could afford pricier educational commodities. Top-tier schools charge large sums of so-called "school choice fees" (*zexiaofei*) or "supportive donations" (*zanzhufei*) to families with greater economic means.[6] Various forms of bribery and rent-seeking emerged in the education sector. As a result, education inequality became more marked. Despite these changes, ideological control through curriculum design and political thought education has not loosened. In the last decade, not only did ideological indoctrination develop into ridiculous hyperboles, but cases of corruption and abuse by school teachers were also widely reported in the news.[7] In sum, even good public schools in China now enjoy the reputation of being pricy, politically stifling and staffed by demoralized teachers.

Returning to the father of our opening story, Tang is an associate professor at a city university. As a political liberal, he feels disgusted by this red revival. "It would be as absurd as hearing praises of Nazism again in today's

2. These include Maoist classics such as "The East is Red," and "Chairman Mao Is Dearest" and "Without the Communist Party There Would Be No New China."

3. Lee, "Legal Loophole Opens."

4. "Revealed: Life inside."

5. Cleverley, "Ideology and Practice," 107.

6. According to an online survey conducted by the Middle Schools and Primary Schools Education website, the average "school choice fee" among Beijing primary schools is 100 to 2000 thousand yuan (roughly twenty to thirty thousand dollars). "Top 16 Beijing Middle Schools."

7. "Chinese Schoolchildren at Risk"; "Series of Cases in China."

Germany." Tang recounts, "Since the regime never repented of its campaigns during the Cultural Revolution, it is not surprising that this red wave is coming back again." Unlike Tang, the general public has been trained to view these activities as part of their cultural heritage, and they even enjoy a nostalgic sense of the past Mao era.

In the midst of this pervasive historical amnesia, Tang is more concerned about his school-aged daughter. Numerous times Tang heard his colleagues complaining about their children's negative experiences in public elementary schools. Many activities in these schools are indoctrinating children with a political view that salutes Communism. Not only was there the requirement to join the Youth Pioneers of China (*shaoxiandui*) in first grade,[8] but children also have to practice singing "red songs" every day.[9] The symbolic pledge is a red scarf tied on the neck, and children are repeatedly taught that it was the blood of revolutionary pioneers that made this scarf red. All students in public elementary schools are required to wear this scarf at all times, and they are required to perform a ritual saluting the national flag every Monday morning. One of Tang's colleagues refuses to put this red scarf on his son, so the boy has suffered both verbal abuse from teachers and social ostracism from his peers. Despite these traumatic experiences, Tang's colleague has not withdrawn his son from this school.

Tang remembered being taught to recite "I love Beijing Tiananmen" and "There would have not been a new China without the Communist Party" in the 1970s when he was young, and he would not have his child go through this type of brainwashing as well. "It is also God's command that we should bring up the next generation in a biblical way," Tang adds.

Tang also thinks that public schools are incompetent in training children academically. The notorious driving forces are competitiveness and ruthlessness. Compared with their international counterparts, Chinese pupils have longer school days and heavier workloads. Taking cram classes in the evenings or on weekends has become the norm. Pedagogy in this system is rigid, involving mainly rote memorization and dictation. Standardization is the norm, while creativity is often discouraged. Spontaneous and curious questioning from the young is quenched early on by teachers who dismiss

8. YPC is an organization for children aged six to fourteen, run by the Communist Youth League since 1953. The mission statement of this organization is to "Be prepared, to struggle for the cause of Communism." Their pledge is: "I am a member of the Young Pioneers of China. Under the Flag of the Young Pioneers I promise that: I will love the Communist Party of China, the motherland, and the people; I will study well and keep myself fit always [lit. exercise well], and to prepare for my contributing effort to the cause of communism." Young pioneers are often referred to as "Red Scarves" as all of them are required to wear specially made red scarves around their necks.

9. Wong, "Repackaging the Revolutionary."

these questions on the grounds that "they won't be on the exam." Children were simply discouraged to think for themselves. Parental pressure and peer competition have made the path to success much narrower. The number of mental illness and even suicides has been rising among students. Moreover, from education policy-making and curriculum design to school finance and personnel management, every aspect has been tightly controlled by Communist cadres. Textbooks are designed along the Marxist line.

As a university faculty member, Tang knows well that this is a system of failures. During the past decade of his teaching career, Tang often regrets seeing the lively faces of first-year college students turning into dull, disengaged graduates. This dysfunctional and politicized machine of state-run education seems to have sucked all the life and youthful creativity out of these young people. The more Tang reflects, the more his heart feels an intense guilt from being part of this stifling system. Just as every parent desires the best for his or her own child, Tang certainly does want to see his daughter grow up in this system.

The heightened emphasis on ideology within state education since 2009 has contributed to the growth of a cohort of urban families who do not send their children to public schools.[10] Although private schools on the elementary and junior high levels are not legally allowed in China,[11] many families have made the same decision as Tang to withdraw their children from state-funded public schools entirely. Some have done so because of their Christian faith, while others simply want to protect their children from the numerous severe problems of the education system, such as exam-cramming, over-competitiveness, and the low moral standards of teachers.

DEMORALIZED TEACHERS

When the whole education system is test-driven and when student performance is linked to teachers' salaries and bonuses, public schools operate in a mechanical way, turning teachers into workers on an assembly line where old virtues such as being caring and tending gardeners are no longer rewarded. If some teachers are lenient with students, they will not be competitive in

10. Recent years saw some loosening of private education legislation, and by 2006, around 8 percent of the 197 million children aged five to fourteen years were enrolled in 77,000 non-state schools. See Mukherjee, "Private Education." Also see "China's Achilles Heel."

11. Although the state promised to legalize private education as early as in 1993, its legislation phrased ambiguous permission as "schools run by social forces (*shehui liliang banxue*)." Until today, no clearly defined laws have been made for private education. See Chen, "China Curbs Elite."

the tests. Moreover, elementary school teachers themselves are placed in the lower stratum of the educational hierarchy, making them feel relatively devalued. Some teachers use their family visitation time to find out which of their students have wealthy or resourceful parents so that they might claim personal favors in times of need. In other cases, teachers supplement their salaries by requesting paid in-home tutoring for some students. Parents not only pay teachers by the hour on evenings or weekends, they also need to prepare gifts for teachers during holidays. There is generally a low work morale among public school teachers, which is exacerbated by a corrupt educational bureaucracy and the state's recent insertion of political content into the school, not to mention the rising number of abuse cases.

Peng (pseudonym, 42, male) is a professor of engineering who spent a year abroad as a visiting scholar in the United States with his wife and six-year-old son. The boy attended kindergarten and enjoyed school in America. When they returned to China, Peng enrolled his son in a neighborhood public school for first grade. A month into the new semester, the superintendent teacher paid a home visit. The teacher asked more about both parents' jobs than about the boy. Peng felt that the teacher was expecting something, but as a teaching faculty member at the local university, he could not offer favors like private chauffeurs or influential connections. Then, the teacher offered private tutoring for the child, but Peng refused because he did not think that was necessary for first graders. They want their child to enjoy free time away from school rather than extreme test preparation at such a young age. A few months later, Peng's son told him that he missed the American school a lot because teachers there always smiled at him and treated him kindly.

In later years of Peng's interactions with this school, he has watched other parents shower teachers with favors and money. Even classroom seats are arranged to the advantage of students from wealthier and more resourceful families. This school is not even in the top tier, but a culture of bribery has been created by parents who want their children to get ahead and also by teachers who consider it legitimate to show favoritism in exchange for financial benefits. Top tier schools demand more than favors; they take bribes in the form of private donations. When this practice was banned by the state, its name was changed to something benign like "corporate sponsorships."[12]

---

12. Levin, "A Chinese Education."

PUBLIC OR PRIVATE?

Zhong (pseudonym, 38, female) became a Christian in the United States in 2009 also during a year as a visiting scholar. After her son reached the age of six, Zhong started looking for schools in her neighborhood. She hesitated about choosing public schools, so she visited most of the private elementary schools in the city. Although there are a few new private schools, each school limits enrollment to one or two hundred pupils. With the demand far exceeding the supply, every school requires interviews before making admission decisions, one with the parent and another with the prospective student. Like many anxious parents, Zhong had scheduled six to seven schools for interviews to increase the likelihood of her son to be admitted. In the midst of such frenzied demand, private schools and parents all face the rising uncertainty as to how long these schools will be allowed to exist. Although the booming private education sector has an estimated 162 thousand schools and around 45 million students from first to ninth grade, the government has not been supportive of such growth. On the contrary, since 2016, legal changes have restricted private schools for younger students because the government wonders if these schools are run "in a way supportive of socialism."[13] These changes accompanied the campaign by the Chinese state to purge the uncontrolled influence (some schools are run by foreigners) that has made its way into the education system.

Zhong's friend suggested that she could consider the more expensive international private schools in an adjacent city. The international sector of private education exists as an outlier of governmental regulation because many of them require students to hold foreign passports. Thus, most enrolled students are either children of expatriate families or of resourceful elites who have been able to secure foreign citizenship. Such is the requirement of the international school in Zhang's city. If she were to choose this route, Zhong would need to consider changing her job and moving to another city with international schools that accept Chinese nationals. But Zhong is also aware that the few international schools that do not require foreign passports are very expensive and ultra-competitive in admission. Without extra resources and connections, Zhong is likely to be put on a long waiting list. Through this difficult decision, and Zhong finds herself in dilemmas at every turn.

---

13. Chen, "China Tightens Rules for Private Schools."

CHRISTIAN OFFSPRING IN ATHEIST SCHOOLS

A fourth-generation Christian in Wenzhou, Cheng (pseudonym, female, 26) recalls that her parents acted just like other Chinese parents in her early years. They worked hard and asked Cheng's grandparents to care for her. Thus, Cheng's devout grandmother became her first Bible teacher. As Cheng recalls, "My parents deepened in their faith when I entered middle school, but before that, they acted just like other parents. They even bribed my teachers." She had always attended public schools because her parents did not see them as a problem. After Cheng started middle school, however, her parents became more committed believers. When the school began to put more pressure on testing, her parents often told her that test scores were less important than her prayer life and daily devotions. Weekend test-cramming classes could be skipped, but Sunday worship was a given. When Cheng failed her college entrance exam, her mother offered gentle comfort to her and an important reminder that she should not let test scores determine her worth and value. During this time, Cheng attended a prayer retreat with her grandmother. She felt comforted by God, and it was a turning point for her own faith too.

Even in public school, Cheng's Christian identity was never hidden, for her Chinese name meaning "holy" is conspicuous. Her classmates often pestered her with questions about her family and her Christian faith. Many of her cohorts were part of broken families with divorced parents, so her friends liked to hear her tell about how things were different in her Christian family. There was not much hostility towards her faith, since the Wenzhou region is home to an increasing number of churches.

However, when Cheng entered high school, she felt the gap between herself and her classmates widen. At home, Cheng's parents would not allow her to watch pop TV shows, listen to music or surf online. She grew quite ignorant of these cultural trends. When female classmates gathered to chat about these topics, she was often left out of the conversation. Looking back, Cheng really appreciates that her parents prevented her from indulging in such things:

> When I observe young people of my generation, I see that their life's paths have not deviated from truth because of the atheistic and communist teachings in school, but rather by fads and trends spread by the internet. Even Marxism has no grasp on them. The dangers today are secularism and materialism.

Cheng's most formative education came from her home environment. Her parents often opened their home and received preachers from other cities. To Cheng, her home is closely connected to church and service. Her parents' example of peaceful communication and devout service has shown her what is most important in life. These traits served as the anchor for her education.

Another perspective about the Chinese education system comes from the son of a Christian professor in Beijing. Mu (pseudonym, male, 28) considers himself as an atypical second-generation Christian. "I did not grow up in a Christian home," he says, "for my conversion happened shortly after my mother became a Christian in 2000, five years after my father's conversion in 1995." Mu was in a public high school when the faith of his parents also became his own. As new converts, his parents taught him very little at home about their new Christian faith. They just took Mu to church regularly and purchased Christian books for him to read. Mu recalls that his father made only one strict rule based on their faith; that is, Mu never had to enroll in test-cramming classes on weekends.

While in public school, Mu did experience a tension between his new faith and what was being taught there. At first, he dared not mention becoming a Christian at school. Once he made some casual allusions to the faith, which brought ridicule and even hostility from his classmates. This tension later became a strong motivation for Mu to consider seriously whether his faith was true. He felt the need to have a systematic understanding to undergird his faith.

> The atheism taught in public schools is also a system of thoughts. I wanted to find a systematic defense of my Christian faith as a response to atheism and materialism. It is amazing how God's Spirit has led me. To some people, this environment might have caused their faith to backslide, but for me, God used it in a different direction.

Mu seems to hold a more tolerant view of China's public schools compared to other Christians in China. When asked what kind of education he will choose for his children in the future, Mu says, "as long as Communist ideological control does not become prominent, I have no problem with sending my children into public schools." However, given the widespread red revivals, Mu also considers the difficulty. At the same time, he also has concerns about an all-Christian environment.

> I surely hope to see more and more mature Christian schools in China. But since this is a new phase of development, I worry about the hidden problems. If this is a more open and pluralistic

society where inter-faith dialogue is easier, then it will be much simpler. Unfortunately, we now live in a highly contentious society, with political campaigns masquerading as red revivals. I also don't want to see churches become more and more closed-up and self-involved in response to this.

While Mu appears to have been caught in a dilemma, he admits that the earlier a child is taught Christian values and worldview, the better; the more complete and comprehensive this Christian worldview is taught, the better. As Mu phrases it, "this worldview is crucial because it is something that, once built up, can work things out on its own."

RECLAIMING THE BATTLEFIELD

Just as unlicensed churches started in private homes since the 1980s, countless church-based schools and mini-schools are mushrooming without official recognition in China today. In the spring of 2007, Pastor Gao decided to start a school in his church in Guangzhou city. His own daughter and other five younger children of church members were reaching school age. They had discussed and debated the option of sending them to public school, but almost every family would prefer an alternative, if possible. Pastor Gao gathered two former public school teachers, two graduate students studying education and a university professor in his church to form a preparation committee. A job description of Christian teachers was circulated within the church. By summer, they were able to select three teachers and one support staff to start the first semester. The teachers wrote out course outlines for first-grade English and science curricula by referring to the ACE (Accelerated Christian Education) curriculum. By 2013, their school enrollment had increased to over 100 students.

With the rapid growth of urban churches, this trend towards Christian schooling is inevitable. However, the spontaneity and speed of such developments still caught us by surprise during our fieldwork in 2012—almost every church we visited in different cities is talking about starting its own school. Mini-schools with class sizes ranging from two students to a dozen are numerous. Parents are making sacrifices to raise funds and teach in these start-up institutions. It is difficult to estimate just how many schools there are. As a news article says, "For a country with more than 68 million Christians, a few hundred Christian schools with fewer than 60 students each is barely a drop in the Yangtze River."[14] These pioneering parents and

14. Cheng, "Off the Grid."

educators face tremendous challenges, including lack of qualified teachers and curricula, unstable facilities, financial difficulties, and fear of a complete shutdown by authorities. It is a battlefield. Despite all of these obstacles, they carried on, for as one parent succinctly says, "we have no other option but to rely on God who always provides."

Surprisingly, a national network of Christian schools does exist, largely built by a long-time educator named Liang (pseudonym, male, 42) since 2005. He said that God has called him to catch a rising tide of Christian education. The growth of urban churches made up of first-generation believers is increasingly mature soil in which Christian schools can sprout. The massive growing Christian population and their accumulated financial means are preparational conditions for an emerging Christian education sector. Liang observes:

> Today's urban church, which is estimated to have ten million or more adherents, serves as a massive baseline population. This group of believers has enough financial resources, for they come from all social status groups. More and more of these young professionals are becoming parents, so there is a huge demand for Christian education.

Interestingly, Liang's observation as an experienced educator matches our fieldwork findings. He recognizes that the year 2012 was when demand for Christian education spiked, for the number of Christian schools in his association rose to over 115 nationwide. Most of these schools are at the elementary level and consist of small classes. The demand for Christian teachers is rising as well. Many young people are considering this a worthy vocation. When college sophomore 20-year-old Jiang plans her own future career, she has an exciting vision of being a Christian educator.

> It is highly possible that another mode of education will arise in China, an unprecedented one—a systematic and Christian alternative to what we have now. This involves re-design of the whole system of subjects, objectives and class settings. This might be a total replacement of the current system, because our present education model is very unscientific.

From her own experience in public schools, Jiang has had good teachers in subjects like physics. One such teacher did not follow the textbook but had his own framework of understanding the subject. Jiang thinks that Christian teachers should do at least as well as these stimulating instructors. Since her own church has been exposed to the classical Christian education method, Jiang has been thinking about a wholly different approach to even traditional Christian schools.

The rising demand for Christian education lends itself to innovation within the given boundaries of relative freedom. Among the different models, Christian homeschooling is also gaining momentum in China. The potential of this development is unprecedented, if even a small fraction of the population chose to homeschool their children. Liang estimates that there are over ten thousand homeschooling families right now. Thousands of Christian parents are now using homeschooling curriculum in other countries, among which ABeka, Sonlight, and Veritas Press have enjoyed much popularity. Many online venders provide these curriculum resources as well as online classes, all translated into Chinese. Voluntary networks of homeschooling co-ops are being formed among homeschooling families that live in adjacent neighborhoods.

Now that elementary and even high schools are being established by Christians in China, what is the vision for post-secondary education for these children? Liang's son was homeschooled before a school took shape in his own church. According to Liang, the first cohort of Christian-school-educated students, including his own 17-year-old son, is now graduating from high school. College education, as the next step for them, will be a hard choice. Most likely Liang's son would have to prepare for the SAT to apply for studies abroad. As a long-time Christian educator, Liang says something quite shocking to us: "If sending children abroad for higher education remains the only option, then our Christian education efforts are still a failure." He is referring to the big picture of the development of Christian education. If China cannot have her own Christian colleges in place, then there will always be a ceiling effect.

REBUILDING CHRISTIAN COLLEGES

Of all the failures in China's government-funded education system, the top of the list is the *gaokao*, the National Higher Education Entrance Exam. These nine-hour tests given over two days once for all determine the fates of millions who have painfully plodded through the eighteen years in the public education system.[15] Many affluent families manage to detour this system and send their children abroad for college or even high school. In recent years, more and more Christian families with grown children have also taken this route. Some Christian colleges in the United States provide tuition waivers and scholarships for students whose parents are in ministry.

15. Gao, "The Education System."

Yet these compose only a small fraction of the increasing demand. Most middle-class families in China cannot afford the overseas option, which costs about forty thousand dollars per year.

Are Christian colleges necessary? To public-school-educated Mu whom we introduced earlier and is now in a Christian liberal arts college in the United States, the answer is "Yes." There he majored in religion and political science. Looking back, he does not consider his prior education in China's public schools being a hindrance to his Christian faith. However, for higher education, he strongly prefers a Christian college. About to start a family of his own, Mu projects this wish to his next generation:

> If I were to choose for my children in the future, I would certainly like to secure a Christian liberal arts college education for them. These colleges teach students to think hard about the purpose of education, instead of succumbing to the practical needs of finding good jobs. The Christian college I attended taught me the importance of a Christian worldview, and how a liberal arts education prepares one to engage the world. Colleges should not become just job-training centers, although some majors might require more instrumental knowledge.

Is China ready to have her own Christian colleges? Anyone familiar with China's modern history knows that Christian colleges are not a novelty in China. In fact, most existing public universities were initially founded by Western Christians before 1949 but were later confiscated and transformed by the Communist regime. Educator Liang declares that there are lessons to learn from this part of history. First, after 1907, Western Christian educators have targeted elite Chinese as the population they wanted to serve in order to impact the broader society. With this motive, Christian education strategies turned away from a gospel-centered model to a social gospel one. Ironically by 1920s, these progressive ideas contributed to the spread of indigenous Communist thoughts and later the founding of the Communist Party. Many of the earliest Communist cadres came from Christian organizations, such as the YMCA. Secondly, although many Christian colleges were founded before 1940s in China, it was Westerners who initiated and completed these projects without much participation from the indigenous Chinese. These Western Christians left their different cultural imprints and denominational marks; thus, the education system lacked coherence and sustainability. Once Western Christians were expelled from China in the early 1950s, these Christian colleges and education programs became merely empty campuses.

"Reviewing these lessons from history gives Christian educators a new perspective," says Liang. He thinks that God has prepared adequate conditions that would help current Christian colleges not to repeat this failed path. One crucial condition, as mentioned before, is massive church growth among urban Christians, who have enough financial resources for their children's education. Greater financial self-sufficiency makes it easier to pool resources, such as facilities, curricula, and paid staff. Professionalization in all walks of life also prepares these believers to address the legal issues involved. Liang describes himself as a hopeful fisherman watching the coming of an inevitable tide. He estimates that in the next four to five years, as the number high-school age children from Christian families increases, the demand for Christian colleges in mainland China will ripen this development. He thinks a slower process is more ideal. As Liang says, "Since we are building something organic in China's own soil, we need to be patient like gardeners."

CONCLUSION

Under the leadership of the Communist Party, the primary role of China's education system is to transmit Party ideology to the young. After the reform of 1978, the need for economic development became a top priority; for a time education served a slightly different goal. However, the education system remained largely "socialist," characterized by state-dominated institutions. To Christian parents, this system that propagates not only atheism and materialism but moral relativism offers more poison than nutrients to their children. The demand for Bible-based Christian education has been on the rise since the early 2000s, as the first-generation churches of young urban elite undergo the start of a "baby-boom." Christian education institutions ranging from kindergartens and elementary schools to homeschooling co-ops and high schools are sprouting all over China despite political restrictions on registration and accreditation. Never before in China's history has Christianity been able to penetrate a few generations through a theologically conservative and Bible-based education system. Given a few decades to develop, its potential is promising. Education that is distinctly Christian is a powerful trend in today's urban China due to the rising demand and empowered financial capacities of urban Christians.

12

Crosses

After over one thousand crosses were removed, if I remained silent, I would not be a pastor. . . . Believers can still gather without the crosses, but the good image of the government is gone. This is a huge disgrace to the Party and the country.

—PASTOR JOSEPH GU, CHAIRMAN OF ZHEJIANG PROVINCIAL CHRIS-
TIAN COUNCIL

OUR FINAL CHAPTER BRINGS us back to a scene from the beginning of this book. The demolition campaign to "de-Christianize the skyline of China's Jerusalem" by forcefully removing hundreds of crosses in Wenzhou within Zhejiang province has once again brought China's official Christianity into the spotlight.[1] After over fifty years of amicable relations between the Three-Self churches and the government, this crackdown marked a turning point for state-sanctioned churches. Believers who tried to shield the crosses were injured; church leaders who protested and signed petitions were silenced, removed from office or arrested;[2] lawyers who provided

1. Zylstra, "After Removing 400 Crosses." This news report quotes statistics from USCIRF Annual Report 2015. According to another news report in *The Guardian*, the number of crosses removed in this area is estimated to be over 1200 within a year and half. Also see Phillips, "China arrests Christians."

2. "A Call to 'Cry Out.'" This news report mentions an open letter signed by the bishop of the Catholic diocese of Wenzhou, together with 26 priests, calling on all Chinese citizens and Christians to speak up for their rights. Also see Wang, "Senior Pastor

legal aid to these churches were secretly arrested and forced to confess their "crimes" on TV.[3]

In neighboring cities, not only have crosses been taken down, but local Christian businessmen who had funded the building of churches found their business partners canceling deals with them.[4] By 2016, the total number of crosses that were removed is estimated to be over 1700. In line with these ongoing actions, Xi Jinping convened a "religious affairs work conference," after which he made a speech about religious policy, urging religions to "Sinicize" and "guard against overseas infiltration via religious means."[5] He explicitly required authorities to monitor religious issues on the Internet closely. In September of the same year, the State Council released a revised *Regulations on Religious Affairs*, sending a clearer signal of who is in control.[6] A long-term American missionary John (pseudonym, male, 50) told us that in January of 2017, the closing of English worship services in Beijing's registered churches serves as another example of increasing harassment by the government. In April, churches in Wenzhou, in Zhejiang Province, all received an official notice that surveillance cameras would have to be installed in their buildings.[7] A sociologist of religion Gong (pseudonym, female, 58) also told us that Jiangsu Province is likely to become the site of the next de-crossing campaign, and a few churches in that region have already been affected.

Many aspects of China's official Christianity have been remained unchanged over the past three decades. Organizationally, top leadership roles (Three Self Patriotic Movement and China Christian Council, known as the Two Councils, lianghui) are directly appointed by Communist Party officials in religious affairs, while theological seminary faculty are also selected by the government.[8] In the by-laws of the China Christian Council, it is clearly stated that the primary role of this organization is to "unite Christians across China to submit to the leadership of the Chinese Communist Party and the People's government, and to love their socialist motherland, to obey

of China." Pastor GU Yuese of Chongyi Church has served as Chairman of CCC of Zhejiang province. After being removed from his office, Pastor Gu was placed under "residential surveillance in a designated location." Quoted in Lyengar, "China has imprisoned the Pastor."

3. "US Condemns."
4. "China's Xi Warns"; Johnson, "Decapitated Churches."
5. "Xi Calls for Improved"; Campbell, "China's Leader Xi."
6. Dubois, "How will China Regulate"
7. "Surveillance Cameras Installed."
8. The three self principles are self-governance, self-support, self-propagation, all rejecting foreigners' influence on the churches.

the Constitution, laws, regulations and policies, and to actively participate in building a socialist society with Chinese characteristics."[9] Theologically, TSPM has to be consistent with the government's propaganda themes, such as "Love your country, Love Christianity; Glorify God and Benefit the People." At the local administrative level, individual congregations report basic information about believers and share accounting books with their overseers; some pay-roll-listed pastors receive paychecks from the government; and large expenditures require government approval. There is also a group of pastors who work in registered churches but do not get paid by state funds.

While acknowledging the continuity of how officially sanctioned churches operate, we also think it important to notice the changes at the local congregational level. Leadership and local political culture greatly shape how much freedom these Three-Self churches have in defying government rules. It would be erroneous to conclude that all clergy serving in these churches identify themselves with the core principle of the Three-self movement or its theology. In reality, missionary John reports that the overwhelming majority of Three-self clergy consider the official Three-self theology and administration a nuisance.

LOVE CHINA, LOVE CHRISTIANITY

China has eighteen Three-Self seminaries, all of which are state-funded. These seminaries generally have strict screening processes in addition to Bible knowledge tests; however, they tend to favor young people from Christian families. Since they usually do not receive many applicants, these seminaries normally ask local Three-Self churches to recommend young people. Many of these students have only received a middle school education. In seminary, they can earn further diplomas and bachelor's degrees. On the Jinling Union Theological Seminary website, its mission statement is clear:

> Our school is a Christian seminary in China. Our goal is to train people who politically support the leadership of the Chinese Communist Party, love the socialist motherland, persist in the "three-self" principles of the church. Our graduates are spiritually and theologically gifted, physically and mentally healthy, and they can mentor believers and lead them on the true path.

9. "By-Laws."

They are talents of the Chinese church along the principles of the Three-Self church.[10]

Chang (pseudonym, male, 38) grew up in an urban neighborhood in Shanghai that used to be the headquarters of the Three-self movement and where many pastors of Three-Self churches lived. Chang's childhood illness kept him indoors most of the time after school. Christian neighbors kindly visited him and brought him Bibles and many Christian books. During high school, Chang began to attend their church. Although he did not grow up in a Christian family, his Bible knowledge and enthusiasm for theology exceeded his peers in the church. In 1994, Chang applied into Jinling Union Theological Seminary in Nanjing, a top state-supported Three-Self seminary under the China Christian Council. With his stellar Bible knowledge, Chang scored second place in the entrance exam. To his disappointment, however, he received a rejection letter from the seminary. As Chang recalls, "the seminary said outright in its letter that my appearance did not qualify for their requirements for clergy." The real reason, he thinks, was more likely the fact that his father escaped to Hong Kong during the Cultural Revolution. This fact could have caused him to fail the political screening.

Born in 1960, Bian (pseudonym, male) is a third-generation Christian living in rural Yunan. After he graduated from high school, he worked as a contractor in the county's electricity bureau. When the Three-Self seminaries re-opened in 1984, his hometown church recommended that Bian take the entrance exam. Bian recalls that four out of two hundred applicants were selected for a second round of political background checks. After that, Bian entered Sichuan Seminary. His last semester coincided with the high waves of the Tiananmen movement. Bian then took an entrance exam in Kunming for further study at Nanjing's Jinling Seminary. After the crackdown, he was informed that someone reported him as having participated in the Tiananmen demonstration in Kunming. Bian had evidence that he was taking the test with six exam proctors watching him, but he also recalled that they did try to get a glimpse of the demonstration after the exam. Maybe that was the cause for his trouble. The seminary insisted on Bian writing a statement saying that he supported the Communist party and opposed the riot. Bian wrote down everything they asked for, but this accusation remained a source of distrust from the Three-Self seminary:

> When I was about to be ordained, I still heard negative comments about this past issue. I was known for being a dissident in the provincial Three-Self system. Even when believers supported

10. "Application Guidelines."

you and you were trusted as having no character problems, the government still looked at you with a magnifying glass.

Having served for more than two decades in his Three-Self church, Bian still considers himself a house church member, "for I have grown up in a rural house church," as he says. He thinks that by pitting Three-Self churches and unregistered churches against each other, people are making conceptual mistakes because the former is only a government-imposed category. Indeed, such a dichotomy is widely held despite the tremendous complexity of China's religious landscape since the 2000s.

Sam (pseudonym, male, 45)is an American who has served as missionary in Beijing for a decade. With good speaking skills in Chinese, he attends a Three-self church to build up relationships with local people there. Over the years, Sam has heard sermons in a few Three-self churches in the city. He recalls when the government tightened up religious policies that directly affected a local Three-self church, the pastor preached a sermon entitled "Submit to Man or Submit to God?" This message caught Sam by surprise because of its boldness in teaching that God is Christians' ultimate allegiance, not the government. "That was the only time I heard such a message in Three-self churches," says Sam. While many clergy in unregistered churches are heatedly discussing issues such as the identity of the church and its role in church and state relationships in China, there is an obviously different discourse among Three-self churches.

OVERCROWDED MEETING PLACES

Demographic changes in Three-self churches since the 1990s have also been remarkable. First, the number of attendees has been growing explosively, especially among young adults in urban centers.[11] The churches are estimated to serve 16 to 25 million believers in over 50,000 congregations across China.[12] Why such popularity? Despite TSPM's notorious past of colluding with the government to arrest church leaders and believers in the 1950s, this part of history is known only by leaders and members of unregistered churches. Most young people outside the Christian circle are unfamiliar with it. As mentioned in Chapter Four, when a new wave of foreign Christians entered China in the 1990s, Three-Self churches became safe contact points for them to meet young people who were interested in

---

11. Thomas, "Radical Revival Falls."

12. The number 16 million is quoted in Galli, "The Chinese Church's Delicate Dance." The higher estimate of 25 million is quoted in "An Interview with Gao Feng."

Christianity or Western culture. When most unregistered churches existed in semi-secrecy and joining them requires high-trust referrals, Three-Self churches were much easier to spot, both for foreigners and people interested in Christianity. They gained more visibility and popularity during annual Christmas celebrations, when many young people stepped into a church building for the first time in their lives.[13]

When Christmas Eve came in 2013, twenty-year-old Ye (pseudonym, female) wanted to spend it at a church, although she is not a Christian. She had grown tired of commercialized Christmas celebrations year by year. Her college dorm mate Lin, a second-generation Christian from Zhejiang, has been attending a nearby Three-Self church, so they planned to attend the special Christmas Eve service together. Before going there, Ye did an online search for Christian carols to get herself more prepared. They arrived twenty minutes early, but the place was already packed with many young people. The choir music sounded so sublime to Ye, unlike any celebrations she had ever been to. It felt as if her heart was washed clean. After the service, they found themselves among a crowd of over two thousand people, which caused a midnight traffic jam. It was so big that police came to the church entrance to alleviate the congestion.

Duan (pseudonym, female, 27) became a Christian while studying abroad in 2008, and when she returned to Beijing for a summer break, she made an earnest search for a church so that her mother could attend. While in the United States, Duan had heard that Three-Self churches were controlled by the government, so her first action was to ask around for a nearby house church. After having no success in locating one from her circle of friends, Duan decided to check out the Three-Self church near her home. It was the first time she ever stepped into a government-controlled church. She was prepared to hear a sermon that sounded unauthentic and political. To her surprise, when she reached the site at around nine A.M., there was a long line waiting for the second morning service. The church's first service started at 7 A.M., and the building was clearly packed with over five hundred people. She joined the line and attended the second service. The church sang traditional hymns, and the pastor gave a biblical sermon. After hearing two sisters sharing their testimonies, Duan found tears streaming down her cheeks. She was surprised by the authenticity of believers there. After the service, Duan noticed that many young people of her age were in the crowd.

Another example of growth in the Three-Self system comes from Grace Three-Self Church in Wuhan, a large city along the Yangtze River.

13. Xie, "Religion and Modernity in China," 74–93.

One day, the senior pastor Hong (pseudonym, female, 55) approached Zhao (pseudonym, male, 38), one of the biggest real estate developers in the city, to discuss a second building project. Zhao is not a believer, but his wife Qian (pseudonym, female, 36) leads an unregistered church. Many members of Qian's church are college students who were originally baptized in Grace Church but later felt the need for deeper Christian fellowship. As Qian describes, "Grace Church is very strong at outreach and evangelism, but many new believers found our church to be more family-like and stayed." Grace Church and Qian's house church had a tacit good relationship. Due to the church building project, Qian encouraged her husband Zhao to attend this Three-self church more often. Every Sunday they noticed that the building was packed, with two services of over 4000 people in total. Zhao was surprised to discover that the number was still rising, because every Sunday after the pastor makes an altar call, an average of thirty people would step forward to give their lives to God. Some shed sincere tears when saying their vows. The church baptizes 300 to 400 people each year, so the growth rate is staggering. In many ways, this Three-Self church is a new development which represented the possibility of change within the government sanctioned system. Five years later, Zhao helped Pastor Hong purchase a second building site, including a piece of land for a Christian retreat center.

THE BLURRY LINE

Whether Three-Self churches and unregistered churches exist as binary opposites depends upon the region under analysis. Considering them rivals would be an over-simplification of the local picture. The relationship between them is based more upon historical factors than theological ones. For example, in Shanghai, such polarization is more obvious, since the city has been and still is the headquarters of the Two Councils (*Lianghui*, China Christian Council and the Three-Self Patriotic Movement). In Beijing, the line is also quite clear-cut, although we observe many Three-Self trained pastors opting out and starting their own unregistered churches. In some small cities, the distinction between Three-Self and unregistered churches is non-existent because most Christians there gather in church buildings constructed by entrepreneurs on their own initiative.

Whenever ideological control tightens through mobilized campaigns, such as the red song singings, new lines of demarcation between the Three-Self churches and unregistered churches grow more solid. In cities like Chongqing and Chengdu where red revivals were once widespread, Three-Self churches became visibly idolatrous in contrast to unregistered urban congregations who rebuked them with open letters.[14] In other cities where Three-Self churches cooperate with Christians from unregistered groups, multiple factors make the line even more blurry. For instance, many believers attend and serve in more than one congregation; registered and unregistered churches share training resources; and pastors in registered churches serve as networking points for believers who are looking for nearby unregistered churches.

As we previously mentioned, Pastor Hong, a stout-looking woman in her fifties, was heading the leadership of Grace Three-Self Church in Wuhan. Her strong personality and competence brought about a series of reforms that defy the stereotypical understanding of Three-Self churches. Every Wednesday afternoon, young pastors and seminarians of this church lead different teams of believers to do street evangelism. They distribute Christian tracts and invite those they meet to church. Hong also invites foreign pastors to preach from the pulpit, often serving as an able translator herself. When Hong preaches, she often starts with a prayer asking God's forgiveness for the sins of Communist leaders in this country. Her sermons are biblical and pastoral, often boldly including the sins exposed in current social ills. Under her leadership, the church has successfully organized Chinese-English summer gospel camps for children. Altar calls for newcomers to accept Jesus Christ as their personal Savior are followed up with a unique new believers program. With the growth of membership by one thousand each year, Gong bemoans the limited pastoral care for new believers:

> I once held a meeting with other pastors and co-workers of our church all present. And I pounded the desk and asked them, 'Where are our sheep?' The statistics show that we baptize five hundred and register one thousand new believers each year, but where have they all gone?

Turnover is certainly high in this church. Typically, a new believer who came forward at an altar call would stay for one year's subsequent classes and baptism. Then many of them disappeared. Hong realizes that most new believers consider baptism as the official achievement of their Christian identity, rather than the beginning of it. To cope with this challenge, Hong pushed for neighborhood Bible study groups where seminarians and young pastors disperse into various districts of the city and spend one afternoon each with believers in that area. They often use believers' homes for such

14. An unregistered urban church in Chengdu posted a public announcement in 2010 which forbade people who were attending Three-self churches to join their Sunday services. They also discourage church members from purchasing Bibles and Christian literature at those Three-Self churches.

meetings. Given the shortage of clergy and teachers, the demand is much higher than the supply. Another option for these new believers is to find a smaller unregistered church where teachings and fellowship can go deeper.

Later, Hong collaborated with a few unregistered churches in organizing a four-day training seminar. With the help of Christian professors from a prestigious university in this city, they leased a conference room on campus and put up a sign announcing a "Sino-Western Cultural Exchange Seminar." An unregistered church leader invited a professor from Southern Baptist Theological Seminary to teach from the Old Testaments. In the classroom of forty people, over two-thirds came from unregistered churches.

While working with real estate developer Zhao on the new church building project, Pastor Hong also spent much time trying to evangelize Zhao. She thinks this man is in a strategic career, that God may use for churches in this city. Zhao is quite open about faith because his mother and wife are both good Christians who set loving examples before him. Whenever Zhao meets new friends, including government officials, he gives them Bibles as gifts. Zhao's only obstacle to the faith was scientism. After Pastor Hong gave him a set of DVDs to watch on this topic, Zhao happily confirmed that his doubts in this area were resolved.

After Pastor Hong retired and stepped down from leadership in 2012, many programs at Grace Church faded under a new leadership. Although the church still invites foreign pastors to preach, the spotlight went from exegetical sermons to miracles and healings, as churches in this city were caught in a rising tide of Pentecostalism.

There has been a steady stream of clergy who first worked with the official church and then decided to jump out of the "box." For forty-year-old Lin (pseydonym, male), the weekly preaching in a Three-self church is only part of his ministry, because he has also planted five unregistered churches. These six churches are all connected into a training network founded by Lin in 2000. When authorities approached him with questions, Lin showed them his Three-self pastor's ID (*mushizheng*) as proof that he is backed up by a recognized title. Fifty-four-year-old Pastor Jin Mingri started his own church after a decade of serving in the Three-self system. When interviewed by PBS, Jin attributes his leaving to a desire for "greater opportunities" and "openness." He unabashedly said that "We want to let our work be known."[15] Dissatisfied with the stereotypical portrayal of churches as either being underground or official, Jin advocates a third-way—emerging, independent urban churches that are out in the open. He viewed the 2008 Olympics as

15. "Extended Interview: Jin Mingri." Another interview with Jin Mingri also appeared in Spegele's article, "China's Banned Churches."

a historic opportunity for China to further open up, including her growing urban churches.

ANXIOUS CLERGY

One source of anxiety for pastors working in Three-self churches is the constant busyness from week to week simply to finish their regular tasks. Pastors who graduate from Three-self seminaries are generally not well-equipped intellectually or theologically. Once they are allocated to different clergy positions in local Three-self congregations, most of them are over-whelmed with the weekly routine as new converts keep flooding in. Take Gangwashi Church in Beijing, for example. It is famous because when former US president George Bush visited Beijing in 2005, he went for Sunday worship in this church. Since then, the Beijing local government has tacitly allowed famous foreign pastors (such as Franklin Graham) to preach there, and its membership has kept growing. Now three formally ordained pastors are leading a congregation of eight thousand people. Each year, they baptize four to five hundred new converts. Apart from these tasks, the church also supports around two hundred informal "meeting places" (*juhuidian*) for overflow gatherings. Pastors feel overloaded with the practicalities of ministry, and there is little time or interest in theological re-charging. One pastor confides to us that he barely had time to read the Bible and pray other than the time before he stepped on stage to preach. New converts look up to them for spiritual guidance, so they should always be prepared to be mentors. As Christians whose Bible knowledge is limited to the basics of the faith, however, these pastors feel the hunger for mature mentorship themselves.

Many clergy also express different degrees of anxiety working under this system especially when they have formed strong ties with house churches. At the age of 34, Xue (pseudonym, female) was ordained in a Three-Self church as its third female pastor. In her city, female pastors often make up the majority of clergy in Three-Self churches. She only had a junior high school education and since she came from a Christian family in rural Henan, Xue was recommended into a Three-self seminary at the age of twenty. Most of her classmates were children of rural Christian families. The seminary found it hard to recruit males because few young men were willing to give up their secular careers for a low-pay (sometimes no-pay) clergy job. While in seminary, Xue was discouraged by her professor to marry another seminarian because that would bring financial difficulties to the family. Before Xue met her husband, she lived on a monthly wage of 1500 *yuan* (around 250 dollars). Since the church provided a two-bedroom apartment for Xue to live in and a public canteen for clergy and staff, she lived quite well despite a meager paycheck. Although Xue did not feel financially burdened, she disliked the work because of the unreasonable demands from bossy officials who were unbelievers. As Xue says, "When spiritual people are governed by carnal people, especially on church matters, the difficulties are easy to imagine."

Xue met her husband Chen (pseudonym, 37) at a training program after Chen had graduated and returned from a seminary in the United-States. Chen was determined to start a house church, so after a year of their marriage, the couple left for Shenzhen, where Chen's friend invited them to open a new church. Chen and Xue had hoped to evangelize urban residents in the city, but most of their church members were migrant workers. Between 2012 and 2014, their church grew from seven believers to over a hundred. Then the group moved into a 600-square meter office building. With the increased visibility of this church, Chen and Xue started to receive phone calls from local authorities. Xue told them that she was a formally ordained pastor in the Three-Self system, and her pastor's permit helped them through a few interrogations. However, after the birth of their children, Xue felt increasingly strained by the double duties of childcare and ministry. Since her husband does not endorse women in the preaching position, Xue decided to quit her preaching duties except on emergency occasions.

Two years later, a new local Three-Self church invited Xue to preach there because it had no pastors with legal permits despite a growing membership. Xue had to submit to this offer, thinking that it may also provide a safe cover for her husband's ministry in their unregistered church. For two years, Xue went to preach in the Three-Self church twice a month. The church then extended a full-time offer to her, but Xue declined it because she felt hesitant to "head back on the old path." After the birth of their second daughter, she increasingly felt the need to stay home and care for her children. Xue's old worries about financial insecurity and government interrogations inevitably reemerged in her daily life.

CONCLUSION

The fact that the cross-removal campaign targeting state-sanctioned churches has lasted for more than three years makes clear the government's attitude towards the growing presence of Christianity in China. When new converts swamped Three-Self churches over the last two decades, very few of them knew the history of the Three-Self movement when it first started in the 1950s. Local leaders of these churches are confined by state policies, but many also innovate ways to grow their churches within a frenzy of economic and cultural possibilities. Only during times of red revival and in places like Zhejiang are Three-Self congregants and leaders discovering the harsh reality of what the government can do.

Apart from cross removals, government initiatives to draw a harder line for official Christianity also involve limiting theological innovations. In 2013, SARA officials announced a five-year plan to nationalize Christian theology so that it could "adapt to China's national condition and integrate with Chinese culture."[16] In May of 2014, a report from the University of International Relations and the Social Science Academic Press said that religion posed a serious threat to Chinese identity, with religious infiltration listed as one of four challenges to China's national security. In many speeches, China's president Xi Jinping has described religion, especially Christianity, as an easy tool by which foreign influence can be leveraged. In many ways, the future path of Three-Self churches is destined to be rough. Meanwhile, the Three-Self churches are experiencing an internal split between those who strive to keep their faith uncompromised and those who give in to policies that masquerade as Christian theology.[17] These policies gradually trickle down to influence the daily life of Three-Self clergy and churchgoers, as well as their relationship with unregistered churches. Moreover, pessimism about China's political climate has been growing since 2016. As *The Atlantic* recently stated in an article entitled "China's Great Leap Backward," "The China of 2016 is much more controlled and repressive than the China of five years ago, or even ten" particularly seen in "cracking down, closing up, and lashing out in ways different from its course in the previous 30-plus years."[18] Uncertainty is heightened with regard to how the political authorities will handle the churches. This is an area awaiting more research.

16. "China Plans Establishment."

17. Leaders of some county and city level councils have resigned. "Zhejiang's De-crossing Movement."

18. Fallows, "China's Great Leap Backward."

Conclusion

When the Son of Man comes, will he really find faith on the earth?

—LUKE 18:8

THE PRESENCE OF PROTESTANT Christians in China since the late nineteenth century has opened a new chapter of Chinese history, bringing it into modern times. As our title suggests, this book examines how Chinese Christians have coped with life under a hostile regime over a span of different historical periods, and how Christian churches as collective entities have been reshaped by ripples of social change. Overall, in a society where state-sponsored nationalism is rising, official corruption is rampant, social demoralization and materialism are unchecked, and where crosses are frowned upon, Christians are called to nothing but being salt and light. Following the teachings of Jesus, they must live counter-culturally.

In the zenith of the Communist revolutions of the 1950s, this meant risking imprisonment by simply professing one's faith. During the Cultural Revolution, being a Christian also brought systemic discrimination and social ostracism. In the post-1989 period, discipleship involved finding answers to life's most important questions and the formation of new religious identities. In the 1990s, being a new Christian equaled traveling a lonely spiritual journey like an orphan, with intermittently-appearing mentors and younger siblings to care for. In the early 2000s, it means living in an urban frenzy of the pursuit of wealth and consumerism. In the late 2000s and the 2010s, following Christ entails the growth of the Christian mind, with greater exposure to theological resources and engagement with social problems in urban settings. For Christians who have been used to the comfort zone of the Three-self churches, it meant waking up to more costly forms of discipleship. Over time, the Christian churches in China have been developing from unconnected individually professing believers, to loosely gathered secret meetings in homes, then to visibly present and unabashedly organized urban churches.

Even in 2017, the time of this writing, we have to admit that there is far more about churches in China that we do not know than what we know. Intriguing stories of how God works in people's hearts happen mostly unnoticed to the outside world as well as to the average Chinese. Restrictions in all of social life still limit the public witness of Chinese Christians. This realization makes the writing of this book all the more precious to us, because we see it as an effort of truth-telling and memory preservation. Chinese Christians ought to be remembered as part of Chinese history and even more broadly, as part of redemptive history.

As historian George Marsden says, "the history of Christianity reveals a perplexing mixture of divine and human factors," and a scholar's task involves "trying to identify the formative cultural elements that have either properly shaped or distorted our understanding of God and his revelation."[1] This statement captures our humble efforts in presenting this sociological portrait of Christians in mainland China—a trial effort to identify "the formative cultural elements" that have shaped our understanding of the works of both the Word and the Chinese world. It highlights the interplay between social changes and the development of Christian groups in mainland China up to the present time of Xi Jinping's leadership. Relying mainly on an oral history method for data collection, we try to allow the narratives of Chinese Christians to speak for themselves. Meanwhile, we integrate socio-historical analysis along with narrative history in order to gain a coherent understanding, allowing for the complexity of religious sentiments and experiences. This approach is helpful to resituate various historical themes and concerns into their social contexts. It is also an attempt to defy the specialization and abstraction of knowledge which tends to truncate and segment our understanding of life.

Many intersecting areas that focus on the changing Chinese society and the growth of Christianity, such as market theories in economics and economic sociology, the study of Chinese church history, and theology and Chinese society, present their findings without acknowledging their true complexity and reality because of the difference in methodological emphasis. For example, scholars of China's transition have been preoccupied with a predominantly materialistic approach, which models economic growth, social trends and political leadership. The change from an agrarian society to an urban one, or from a centrally-planned economy into a free market

---

1. Marsden, *Fundamentalism and American Culture*, 259.

economy are admittedly significant structural changes, but if one were to probe more deeply, he or she would find that real changes are about values and beliefs that give rise to social structures over a period of time. Scholars of institutionalism in social transition theories often neglect the importance of the habits of the heart on the formation of institutions and society. It is the human mind and the habits of the heart that nurture social morality when individuals engage in private or public affairs.[2]

Narrative history is about remembering. As Augustine says in the *Confessions*, memory is the mind of man, the inner self, and the formative foundation of human habits.[3] Since the 1950s, Chinese society has been characterized by the loss of memory or forgetfulness. Due to strict censorship, later generations have had no access to the history of political persecutions, the estimated death tolls during the Great Famine, the betrayals of family members during the Cultural Revolution, the cruel realities of labor camps, and the Tiananmen movement. As Louisa Lim says in her book, *The People's Republic of Amnesia*, "Chinese People are practiced at not dwelling on the past. One by one, episodes of political turmoil have been expunged from official history or simply forgotten."[4] For the Chinese, unfortunately, intentional forgetting has become a survival strategy, a habit of the heart.

Due to the loss of collective memory, the average Chinese person today is haunted by a sense of anxiety about his or her identity. When one's memory about true historical events is first erased and then re-explained by political ideologies and cultural narratives, it produces a passive dissonance and resistance in the form of nihilism or cynicism. Moreover, the loss of memory also leads to a post-Communist nostalgia. Thus, younger generations, who have not experienced the same political persecutions as their parents or grandparents endured, evince a utopian imagination and self-identification about Maoism and the Communist era. Even those who have lived through the harsh Communist years also tend to forget the past violence, injustice and lack of freedom; yet they need to remember in order to regain a sense of rootedness in the Chinese society. What lies behind the moral problems of today's Chinese society is its inability to deal with past wounds and memories. People fear political pressure and withdraw from talking about these painful recollections. Because the forming of the human mind has a social dimension, the lack of honest sociality inhibits people from forming a healthy habit of the heart.[5]

2. Bellah et al., *Habits of the Heart*, 275–96.
3. Augustine, *The Confessions*, 192, 196.
4. Lim, *The People's Republic of Amnesia*, 5.
5. Augustine, *The City of God against the Pagans*, 917–18.

Memory, especially personal confessions by Christian believers who are able to recall past events and people honestly, serve as a shared social identification in relieving identify anxiety in a transitional society like contemporary China. The Christian theology provides two axes for viewing past injustice and cruelty: human depravity and God's sovereignty. With the axis of God's sovereignty in place, the Chinese Christian can look back upon past wrongs and injustice and still find goodness and purpose. This perspective grants the moral courage to recall and remember but to do so without holding onto bitterness. During the social transition in South Africa after *apartheid*, the slogan "Without Truth, No Reconciliation" encouraged people to recall past wounds in order to heal and move on. In comparison, today's China still lacks the freedom to discuss publicly past wounds, making individuals unable to become accountable entities and thus also unable to confess their past individual wrongs done to others. True reconciliation between social classes and ethnicities is indeed impossible without open discussion and personal confession. According to Augustine's theology of memory, man must face the true past and truth itself in order not to fall into a state of alienation. Through remembering, one has to face his or her own self, and such a sober awareness of selfhood enables the individual to shoulder responsibilities for truth and for others. This is something most needed in Chinese society. Based on this foundation, reconciliation between individuals and classes can be achieved.

If the voices of Chinese Christians have the power to inspire people today, it is because of their genuine belief and their persistent clinging to God. They have experienced many sorrows and troubles along their pilgrimage, but even in the midst of imprisonment, poverty, social isolation, social prejudice and marginalization, and materialistic temptations, they have persevered and never lost faith in the goodness of God. At the same time, it ought to amaze readers that the centuries-old Christian message can still take root and produce life-changing effects in a society like Communist China.

Appendix 1

A Qualitative Comparative Analysis
of Church-Level Data in Two Cities

To MAKE THINGS CLEAR, we use the following set of parameters appropriate to the Chinese context for a qualitative assessment of church organizational openness: church naming, publicity, leadership, Sunday closure and financial accountability. (They will be further explained, in turn.) In general, we define church groups whose practices deny access to the general public, or that are characterized by a high degree of underground, informal and secretive features as "closed." Groups that are open to the public are considered "open." A semi-closed type lies somewhere in the middle of this spectrum, tending towards the closed end, while a semi-open type tends towards the open end. These qualitative definitions, while relative, are straightforward to use.

Church naming: Church groups that do not explicitly name themselves or have ambiguous and unidentifiable names (such as "uncle Wang's home") show a certain closed bearing to the public. In contrast, intentional use of identifiable church names marks a first step towards openness.

Publicity: Church groups that circulate their meeting times and locations exclusively among believing members show features of a closed organization. In these groups, any change of time or location is communicated only through closely-knit networks. Usually they do not print or distribute Sunday service programs either. The names and identities of preachers or speakers are kept confidential among the group. So, in comparison, the practices of making meeting locations, schedules and contact information accessible to the general public, and printing and distributing Sunday service programs indicate a high degree of openness.

Leadership structure: Pastoral teams led by a "leading brother" (an often-used title for leadership) with founding credentials and higher seniority, followed by a secondary hierarchy of "co-workers" (a title for secondary leadership) chosen by the top leaders is another characteristic of a closed fellowship. Church offices are often created and designated by the top leadership, and formal ordination is intentionally avoided. Church by-laws are informal codes known only to the core members. In comparison, pastoral teams that seek formal ordination, install church offices through open procedures and set up formal by-laws known to the public are considered open.

Sunday service closure: Church groups that set up a probationary period for new believers and those who transfer from other churches before they are qualified to participate in Sunday services are closed in outlook. Visitors are not included in their Sunday services either. In comparison, churches that welcome members of the public are considered open.

Financial accountability: Church groups that keep financial records only for the use of top and secondary leadership are considered closed. The leadership team can discuss among itself how to spend any funds, but such information is not shared with other members, not to mention the general public. In comparison, churches that regularly publicize their budgets and spending to members and the general public are open.

In Table 1 we give a summary of 17 church groups we studied according to the five openness parameters. It shows that compared to nameless groups before the 1990s, most churches now have distinct names to set their church identity apart from other groups. A few groups that have opened up their Sunday services to the public belong to the charismatic and fundamentalist backgrounds. The majority of self-proclaimed evangelical churches still implement a "three-month" probation period for new members and those who transfer from other churches. Our interviews with believers who changed jobs from Beijing or Chengdu to Shanghai confirmed this experience; they reported that the probation rule alienated them from unofficial churches. One of them finally decided to attend the Three-Self church. Most groups we studied in Shanghai, are still characterized by a closed posture through their publicity, leadership, Sunday service and financial accountability.

Table 1. A Qualitative Assessment of 17 Unofficial Churches in Shanghai

Church	Theological background*	Naming	Publicity	Leadership	Sunday closure	Financial
UY	L	C	C	C	C	C
GL	E	O	SC	C	C	C
PC	E	O	C	C	C	C
UC	E	O	C	C	C	C
GU	F	O	O	O	O	O
GS	C	O	SO	C	O	C
PL	L	O	C	C	C	C
CF	E	O	C	O	SC	SO
LS	E	O	C	C	C	C
MZ	E	O	SC	C	SO	C
LC	E	C	C	C	C	C
HL	E	O	C	C	C	C
WB	C	O	O	C	O	O
BC	C	O	C	C	C	C
BB	E	O	SC	C	O	C
SJ	F	C	C	C	O	C
DC	E	O	C	C	C	C
%		82.4	11.8	11.8	29.4	11.8

O=Open, C=Closed, SC=Semi-closed, SO=Semi-open
*L=Little Flock, E=Evangelical, F=Fundamentalist, C=Charismatic

In Table 2 we give a summary of 12 church groups we studied according to the five openness parameters. It shows that currently most churches have developed openness in naming, publicity and Sunday services. Especially where the opening up of Sunday services to the public is concerned, Chengdu churches generally do not keep visitors and new believers out. It is important to mention that an increasing number of churches bought their own properties during our three years of fieldwork. Given the fact that real estate prices in Chengdu are considerably lower than those of Shanghai, such a trend is not surprising. Overall, openness characterizes the organizational forms of most churches we investigated in Chengdu. The churches that are pushing for openness in all five parameters claim to have a reformed theological background.

Table 2. A Qualitative Assessment of Twelve Unofficial Churches in Chengdu

Church	Theological background	Naming	Publicity	Leadership	Sunday closure	Financial
GB	R	O	O	O	O	O
LWC	R	O	O	O	O	O
SL	F	C	C	C	SO	C
LG	E	O	O	O	O	O
SA	C	O	O	C	O	C
TC	P	O	O	C	O	C
SL	E	O	O	SC	O	SO
PX	E	C	SC	C	O	C
HP	E	O	O	SC	O	SC
VC	C	O	O	C	O	C
GB	P	O	O	SC	O	O
CSC	R	O	O	O	O	O
%		83.3	83.3	33.3	91.7	41.7

O=Open, C=Closed, SC=Semi-closed, SO=Semi-open
*R=Reformed, E=Evangelical, F=Fundamentalist, C=Charismatic, P=Pentecostal

Based on the five qualitative parameters, Tables 1 and 2 show that on every indicator, churches in Shanghai show a more closed pattern from those in Chengdu. Again, we do not claim this to be a random sampling, but at least it allows us to gain a better understanding of these churches' organizational features, given the insurmountable difficulties in conducting a random sampling survey of these semi-hidden networks. Among these, publicity and Sunday service closure show the strongest contrast. Only 11.8 percent of Shanghai churches we studied made their information accessible to the public, compared to 83.3 percent in Chengdu.Furthermore, only 29.4 percent of Shanghai churches open up their Sunday services to the public, compared to 91.7 percent in Chengdu.

Appendix 2
A full translation of a CCP document

If Party Members' Religious Conversions Went On Unchecked,
There Would Be Dire Consequences

Source: *China Discipline and Inspection News*, May 25, 2015

RECENTLY THE WENZHOU MUNICIPAL Party Committee of Zhejiang province claimed during an inspection that problems involving a small number of party members who converted to religion need to be solved. Inspections in this city started in education, public health and higher education systems, and a new investigation on who among the party members have converted to religions had been carried out. Those with no Communist ideals and viewpoints are considered as unqualified to be party members, and their memberships should be nullified.

These measures are quite representative of Wenzhou in dismissing those whose thoughts are not with the CCP. It has become an important project of strict party governance through strengthening the party's ideology and the ideology of being a party member. Since last year, the central inspection group has made it clear from their second inspection feedback that a few local party members are converting to religions and participating in religious activities. This shows that this minority of party members has turned away from the Party's dialectic materialistic worldview into religions. This has caused heightened attention, and it has been included in the area of disciplining.

The Marxist worldview is a dialectic materialistic one. The worldviews of religions are idealistic ones without exception. Philosophically speaking, there is a fundamental distinction between materialism and idealism, and they are not compatible either to any individual or any political party. Marx himself stated directly that "communism, in essence, starts with atheism." Communist Party members cannot believe in any kind of religion, and this has been an important thought principle as well as an important organizing principle of our Party from its founding days. There is no question about it.

According to our Constitution, Chinese citizens have freedom of religious beliefs. But party members are not common citizens; they are pioneering fighters in the vanguard for a communist consciousness; they are firm Marxists and also atheists. Therefore, our Party has stipulated many times that party members are not allowed to believe in religions, nor must they participate in religious activities.

Landslides in thought are the most series diseases. In reality, some Party members no longer believe in Marxism-Leninism; their interests are not with their work or career; but they busy themselves with religious activities and turn themselves into religious believers. Especially some cadres and leaders who took the lead to convert into religions or worship gods or buddhas and participate in superstitious things are to blame in this respect. If this slide in morale goes unchecked, it will certainly confuse the thoughts of party members and loosen our party organization. The ultimate consequences are unthinkable.

Currently, a special education project "Three Strict and Three Solid" is being carried out. One of its main goals is to solve the thought problems of party members, such as wavering in their beliefs, being lost in their spirits or weak in ideology, etc. When faced with this problem of a small number of party members being converted to religions, on the one hand, we should strengthen thought education and let the majority of party members imprint the Party as their surname into the deepest part of their thoughts; on the other hand, we should also strengthen the organization of our party members. That is, we should strictly expel any party member whose thoughts have corrupted and whose actions have strayed, in order to purify the Party and to fortify a strong fortress.

Appendix 3
Translation of an Interview with Gao Feng

NOTE: ON NOVEMBER 2 of 2015, a Hong Kong-based network Phoenix Satellite Television published an interview with the top leader of China's official Three-self churches, Gao Feng, who is currently the chairman of China Christian Council and president of the Jinling Seminary. In this article commemorating the 100th birthday of Bishop Ding Guang Xun, first president of China's Christian Three-self Patriotic Movement Committee, Gao comments on the emergence of unregistered denominations in China, particularly the Calvinist churches.

Original article: http://dxw.ifeng.com/shilu/dingguangxun/1.shtml

Phoenix TV: Bishop Ding used to defend home-gathering Christians before the Nineteenth Document. In later years, he even suggested forming the Two Councils to express goodwill to Christians who do not espouse the Three-self movement. What do you think Bishop Ding's opinions were regarding house churches?

Gao Feng: Actually, in the 1980s, Bishop Ding talked about this issue a lot. He used to follow the Anglican tradition, which had a high view of itself and stressed education. On the one hand, the Anglicans nurtured many religious leaders for China; on the other hand, they did not think highly about other denominations. But Bishop Ding had an open heart. He mentioned China's house churches when giving speeches in other countries, but what he meant by house churches differs from what people today think of them. Today house churches are a conceptualization by people who claim that there are two churches in China, the Three-self and the house church. By naming some as Three-self, they refer to churches that cooperate with the government, and thus all churches that stand against the government are considered house churches. Such a distinction is made by some hostile foreign forces. I would rather call them "house meetings." Bishop Ding also mentioned the developments of these house meetings. We had a limited number of church buildings when Christianity entered into a fast-growing phase. Strictly speaking, those so-called house churches are unregistered Christian groups who pose a great challenge to both the state and our legal church. This group grows very fast and their make-up is quite complicated. Now we have legal churches and organizations, but these tend to be restricted by policies. Unregistered illegal churches, on the contrary, have larger room to develop. For example, when our legal churches plan to send people overseas for training, we have to go through a long process of recommendations, reports and political screening. But illegal churches can easily send out people overseas. The same is true with how churches work. Legal churches have very strict rules. But illegal gatherings are not bound by that many rules. As long as they do not engage in criminal activities, even the Public Security departments leave them alone. This means that they exist in a vacuum of state policy, a grey area. This is a contributing factor to why illegal churches have been growing so fast.

Phoenix TV: Despite different conceptualization of what house churches are, Professor Yang Fenggang in Purdue University recently had an online chat with Pastor Wang Yi of a house church. They suggested that some "Alliance of House Churches" be established in China to connect today's house churches. What do you think of this?

Gao Feng: Anti-China forces have proposed to use Calvinist theology, thoughts and institutions to consolidate illegal house churches in China. . . . This actually shows that illegal assemblies in China have grown to a sizeable scale. It used to be that house churches were disconnected from each other, and that they do not submit to one another's authority. But suppose some international forces join them to form a solidarity, then that would be a big problem.

Phoenix TV: Do you think the plan to set up an Alliance of House Churches in China would succeed? What do you mean by a big problem?

Gao Feng: They try to unite domestic and overseas resources and consolidate all illegal unregistered churches under one umbrella. This is nearly impossible, because house churches themselves are rent by disunity. In reality, many of them are opinionated, unwilling to submit to one other and domineering. But this appears to be the direction they are trying to move in. By proposing this plan, it shows that they have been thinking about it, and this might challenge our legal bottom-line.

Phoenix TV: What do you mean by "thinking about it" and "legal bottom-line"?

Gao Feng: Take registration, for example. Now there are two important processes to legally register as religious groups: one is through the civil administration departments, and the other is through religious bureaus. In the future, they (house churches) might claim that every Chinese citizen has freedom of religion according to the Constitution. If the government does not find any faults with them in terms of doctrines or rules, then their registration would be granted. This will undermine our bottom-line, and it would make our government very passive.

Bibliography

Allen-Ebrahimian, Bethany. "Meet China's Pro-Life Christians (and Buddhists)." *Foreign Policy* (August 5, 2015). http://foreignpolicy.com/2015/08/05/china-abortion-pro-life-planned-parenthood-video-christian/

————. "The Making of a Chinese Nationalist Internet User." *Foreign Policy* (August 10, 2015).http://foreignpolicy.com/2015/08/10/the-making-of-a-chinese-nationalist-internet-user/

Aikman, David. *Jesus in Beijing: How Christianity is Transforming China and Changing the Global Balance of Power*. Washington DC: Regnery, 2003.

Anderlini, Jamil. "'Western Values' Forbidden in Chinese Universities." *Financial Times* (January 30, 2015). http://www.ft.com/intl/cms/s/0/95f3f866-a87e-11e4-bd17-00144feab7de.html/.

"An Interview with GAO Feng." Hong Kong Chinese Phoenix TV (November 2, 2015). http://dxw.ifeng.com/shilu/dingguangxun/1.shtml/.

Andew, Jacobs. "Chinese Professor Who Advocated Free Speech Is Fired." *The New York Times* (December 10, 2013). http://www.nytimes.com/2013/12/11/world/asia/chinese-professor-who-advocated-free-speech-is-fired.html/.

"Application Guidelines." Jinling Union Theological Seminary website. http://www.njuts.cn/wen.asp/.

Augustine. *The Confessions*. Translated by Maria Boulding. New York: New City, 1997.

————. *The City of God, against the Pagans*. Edited by R. W. Dyson. Cambridge: Cambridge University Press, 1998.

Bauman, Zygmunt. *Modernity and the Holocaust*. Ithaca, NY: Cornell University Press, 1989.

Bays, Daniel. "Chinese Protestant Christianity Today." *The China Quarterly* 174 (2003) 488.

————. "From Foreign Mission to Chinese Church." *Christian History Institute*, Issue 98. Christianity Today, 2008. http://www.christianitytoday.com/history/issues/issue-98/from-foreign-mission-to-chinese-church.html/.

————. "Christianity in China 1900–1950: The History that Shaped the Present"; "From Foreign Mission to Chinese Church." *Christian History and Biography* 98 (Spring 2008) 6–13.

————. *A New History of Christianity in China*. Vol. 7. Hoboken, NJ: John Wiley & Sons, 2011.

Bellah, Robert N. et al. *Habits of the Heart: Individualism and Commitment in American Life*. New York: Harper & Row, 1985.

Benjamin Carlson. "The World according to Xi Jinping." *The Atlantic* (September 21, 2015), 6. https://www.theatlantic.com/international/archive/2015/09/xi-jinping-china-book-chinese-dream/406387.

Bentley, Julia G. "The Role of International Support for Civil Society Organizations in China." *Harvard Asia Quarterly* (Winter 2003) 11–20.

Bian, Yanjie, Xiaoling Shu, and John R. Logan. "Communist Party membership and regime dynamics in China." *Social Forces* 79 (2001) 805–41.

Bonhoeffer, Dietrich. *Letters and Papers from Prison.* Minneapolis: Fortress, 2010.

Brown, Andrew. "Chinese Calvinism Flourishes." *The Guardian*, May 27, 2009. http://www.theguardian.com/commentisfree/andrewbrown/2009/may/27/china-calvin-christianity/.

Buckley, Chris. "Uncertainty Over New Chinese Law Rattles Foreign Nonprofits." *The New York Times*, December 29, 2016. https://www.nytimes.com/2016/12/29/world/asia/china-foreign-ngo.html.

"By-Laws." the Two Christian Councils of China website. http://www.ccctspm.org/quanguolianghui/zhangcheng_jixie.html/.

Cai, R. et al. "Systems of Prevention against Religious Infiltration into Universities." *Thought Education Research* 7 (2010) 62–64.

Calabresi, Massimo. "China Expands Student Spying Network, Says CIA." *Time* (Jan 24, 2011). http://swampland.time.com/2011/01/24/china-expands-student-spying-network-says-cia/.

"Calvinism on the Ground in China." a *China Source* blog article, October 28, 2014. http://www.chinasource.org/blog/posts/calvinism-on-the-ground-in-china/.

"A Call to 'Cry Out' against Cross Removals in China." *The New York Times* (August 7, 2015). https://mobile.nytimes.com/blogs/sinosphere/2015/08/07/a-call-to-cry-out-against-cross-removals-in-china/

Campbell, Charlie. "China's Leader Xi Jinping Reminds Party Members to Be Unyielding Marxist Atheists." *Time* Magazine, April 25, 2016. http://time.com/4306179/china-religion-freedom-xi-jinping-muslim-christian-xinjiang-buddhist-tibet/.

Cao, Nanlai. *Constructing China's Jerusalem: Christians, Power, and Place in Contemporary Wenzhou.* Stanford: Stanford University Press, 2010.

Cao, Siqi. "Zhejiang CPC Bans Religious Beliefs among Applicants." *Global Times* (February 1, 2015). http://www.globaltimes.cn/content/905305.shtml/.

Chai, Ling. "Tiananmen 10 Years On." *New Perspectives Quarterly* 16.4 (1999) 25–26.

———. *A Heart for Freedom: The Remarkable Journey of a Young Dissident, Her Daring Escape, and Her Quest to Free China's Daughters.* Carol Stream, IL: Tyndale House, 2011.

Chan, Cheris Shun-ching. "The Falun Gong in China: A Sociological Perspective." *The China Quarterly* 179 (2004) 665–83.

Chan, Stephen and Sun Yi, ed., *John Calvin and Sino-Christian Theology (Jiaerwen yu hanyu shenxue).* Hong Kong: Logos & Pneuma, 2010.

Chen Jie, "The NGO Community in China." *China Perspectives*, Vol.68 | November-December 2006. http://chinaperspectives.revues.org/3083/.

Chen, Te-Ping. "China Curbs Elite Education Programs." *The Wall Street Journal*, December 20, 2015. https://www.wsj.com/articles/china-curbs-elite-education-programs-1450665387/.

————. "China Tightens Rules for Private Schools." *The Wall Street Journal*, November 11, 2016. https://www.wsj.com/articles/china-tightens-rules-for-private-schools-1478868356/.

Chen, Zemin. "Drops of Theological Thought in the Chinese Church." *Jingfeng* 68 (1981) 28.

Chen, Zhigang. "Structural Changes in CCP Membership." *Tansuo Journal* 6 (2010): 7.

Cheng, Tiejun, and Mark Selden. "The Origins and Social Consequences of China's *Hukou* system." *The China Quarterly* 139 (1994) 644–68.

Cheng, June. "Off the grid," *World* Magazine (August 21, 2015). https://world.wng.org/2015/08/off_the_grid

Cheng, Nien. *Life and Death in Shanghai*. New York: Grove, 2010.

Chin, Josh and Yang Jie. "China Gets Its Claus Out for Christmas." *The Wall Street Journal*, December 25, 2014. http://blogs.wsj.com/chinarealtime/2014/12/25/china-gets-its-claus-out-for-christmas/.

"China Bans Establishment of Christian Theology." *China Daily*, August 7, 2014. http://en.people.cn/n/2014/0807/c90882–8766262.html/.

China Education Ministry. "On Cultivating and Implementing Socialist Core Values and the Morality Education in Elementary and Secondary Schools." *China Education Ministry Foundations*, No. 4, 2014.

"China Plans Establishment of Christian Theology." *China Daily*, August 7, 2014. http://europe.chinadaily.com.cn/china/2014–08/07/content_18262928.htm/.

"China to 'Regulate' Foreign NGOs with New Law." *Reuters*, December 22, 2014. http://www.reuters.com/article/us-china-politics-ngos-idUSKBN0K00NX20141222/.

"China's Achilles Heel: Education System." *Forbes*, Dec 1, 2012. https://www.forbes.com/sites/junhli/2012/12/01/chinas-achilles-heel-education-system/#188d7f02926a

"China's Future: Xi Jinping and the Chinese Dream." *The Economist*, May 4, 2013. http://www.economist.com/news/leaders/21577070-vision-chinas-new-president-should-serve-his-people-not-nationalist-state-xi-jinping/.

China's National Civil Servants Exam Website. http://www.chinagwy.org/html/xwsz/zyxw/201109/21_31985.html/.

"China's Xi Warns Against Religious Infiltration from Abroad." *Associated Press*, April 24, 2016. http://bigstory.ap.org/article/0181dc9eb62b4c91ae76818b97c17eb0/chinas-xi-warns-against-religious-infiltration-abroad/.

"Chinese Schoolchildren at Risk of Sexual Abuse." *News China Magazine*, April 2013. http://www.newschinamag.com/magazine/chinese-schoolchildren-at-risk-of-sexual-abuse/.

"Chinese Grads Still Eager to Nab Government Jobs." *Washington Street Journal blog*, Nov. 27, 2013. http://blogs.wsj.com/chinarealtime/2013/11/27/chinese-grads-still-eager-to-nab-government-jobs/

"Chinese Professor Sacked after Criticizing Mao Online." *Reuters*, Jan 10, 2017. http://www.reuters.com/article/us-china-mao-idUSKBN14U0EG?il=0/.

Chow, Alexander. "Calvinist Public Theology in Urban China Today." *International Journal of Public Theology* 8.2 (2014) 158–75.

"Christians Held in Shanghai." *Radio Free Asia* (November 30, 2009). http://www.rfa.org/english/news/china/christians-detained-11302009095909.html/.

"Christian Church Shut Down by Hundreds of Police and Armed Thugs." *Daily Mail* (December 11, 2009). http://www.dailymail.co.uk/news/article-1235065/Christian-church-China-shut-hundreds-police-armed-thugs.html/.

"Civil-service Exams, the Golden Rice-Bowl: Young Graduates, Once Risk-takers, Now Want to Work for the Government Again." *The Economist*, Nov. 24, 2012. http://www.economist.com/news/china/21567124-young-graduates-once-risk-takers-now-want-work-government-again-golden-rice-bowl/.

Cleverley, John. "Ideology and Practice: A Decade of Change and Continuity in Contemporary Chinese Education." *Comparative Education* 20.1 (1984) 107–16.

Cook, Richard R., and David W. Pao. *After Imperialism: Christian Identity in China and the Global Evangelical Movement*. Studies in Chinese Christianity. Eugene, OR: Pickwick Publications, 2011.

Cohen, Paul A. *China and Christianity: The Missionary Movement and the Growth of Chinese Anti-Foreignism, 1860–1870*. Cambridge: Harvard University Press, 1963.

Dai, Qing. *My Imprisonment*. Hong Kong: Mingbao, 1990.

De Tocqueville, Alexis. *Democracy in America*. Washington, DC: Regnery, 2013.

Dickson, Bruce J. "Integrating Wealth and Power in China: the Communist Party's Embrace of the Private Sector." *The China Quarterly* 192 (2007) 827–54.

Ding Guangxun. "The Cosmic Christ." *Jinling Theological Journal* 14–15 (1991) 2–4.

———. "The Church in China—Speech Given at the Retreat of the World Baptist Alliance." *Jinling Theological Journal* 21 (1994) 8–9.

———. "Looking Back along the Road" (April 24, 1995). In *Collected Essays of Ding Guangxun*, Nanjing: Yilin, 1998.

"Desperate Parents Are Driving Up Shanghai's Property Prices." *Global Times* (September 6, 2015). http://www.globaltimes.cn/content/940819.shtml/.

Doyle, G. Wright. "Gender Imbalance in Chinese Churches." *Christianity in China*, Global China Center. http://www.globalchinacenter.org/analysis/christianity-in-china/gender-imbalance-in-the-chinese-church-causes-consequences-and-possible-cures.php/.

Duara, Prasenjit. *Rescuing History from the Nation: Questioning Narratives of Modern China*. Chicago: University of Chicago Press, 1995.

Dubois, Thomas. "How Will China Regulate Religion?" *East Asia Forum* (September 2016). http://www.eastasiaforum.org/2016/09/21/how-will-china-regulate-religion/.

Esherick, Joseph. *The Origins of the Boxer Uprising*. Berkeley: University of California Press, 1987.

"Enter the Chinese NGO." *The Economist*, Apr 12, 2014. http://www.economist.com/news/leaders/21600683-communist-party-giving-more-freedom-revolutionary-idea-enter-chinese-ngo/.

"Expansion of Christian Church in the Birthplace of Confucius Creates Controversy in China." *Time*, January 28, 2016. http://time.com/4197803/christian-church-qufu-confucius/.

"Experiencing Chinese Christians during the Sichuan Earthquake," a *Sina* blog article, January 1, 2009. http://blog.sina.com.cn/s/blog_5d226e3d0100bnka.html/.

"Extended Interview: Jin Mingri." *Frontline World, PBS*. Online: http://www.pbs.org/frontlineworld/stories/china_705/interview/extended.html/.

Fairbank, John K. *The Great Chinese Revolution 1800–1985*. New York: Harper & Row, 1986.

Fällman, Fredrik. "Chinese Christianity Is More than Calvin." *The Guardian*, 6 June 2009. http://www.theguardian.com/commentisfree/belief/2009/jun/05/religion/.

———. "Calvin, Culture and Christ? Developing of Faith among Chinese Intellectuals." In *Christianity in Contemporary China: Socio-cultural Perspectives*, edited by Francis Khek Gee Lim. London: Routledge, 2013.

Faries, Nathan. *The "Inscrutably Chinese" Church: How Narratives and Nationalism Continue to Divide Christianity*. Lanham, MD: Lexington, 2010.

Falkenstine, Mike. *Chinese Puzzle: Putting the Pieces Together for a Deeper Understanding of China and Her Church*. Longwood, FL: Xulon, 2008.

Feng, X. "Methods, Features of Religious Infiltration into University Campuses and Prevention Strategies." *Lanzhou Academic Journal* 2 (2007) 114–116.

France-Presse, Agence. "China Begins Demolition of 'Oversized' Church." *The Guardian*, April 28, 2014. http://www.theguardian.com/world/2014/apr/28/china-demolition-oversized-church-sanjiang/.

Fu, Bob, and Nancy French. *God's Double Agent: The True Story of a Chinese Christian's Fight for Freedom*. Grand Rapids: Baker, 2013.

Fulton, Brent. *China's Urban Christians: A Light That Cannot Be Hidden*. Studies in Chinese Christianity. Eugene, OR: Pickwick Publications, 2015.

Galli, Mark. "The Chinese Church's Delicate Dance." *Christianity Today*, November 1, 2004. http://www.christianitytoday.com/ct/2004/november/30.68.html/.

Gao, Ertai. *In Search of Home* (*Xunzhao jiayuan* in Chinese), Guangzhou: Huacheng, 2004.

Gao, Helen. "The Education System that Pulled China Up May Now Be Holding It Back." *The Atlantic*, June 25, 2012. https://www.theatlantic.com/international/archive/2012/06/the-education-system-that-pulled-china-up-may-now-be-holding-it-back/258787/

Gao, Shining and He Guanghu. "Main Problems of Today's Chinese Christianity." *Christian Times*, April 11, 2011. http://www.christiantimes.cn/news/2369/.

Gan, Nectar. "Ban on Religion Is 'Unshakeable' Principle of Communist Party, Cadres Are Warned." *South China Morning Post*, November 14, 2014. http://www.scmp.com/news/china/article/1639754/ban-religion-unshakeable-principle-communist-party-cadres-are-warned/.

Glock, C. Y. "The Role of Deprivation in the Origin and Evolution of Religious Groups." In *Religion and Social Conflict*, edited by Robert Lee and Martin E. Marty. New York: Oxford University Press, 1964.

Gong, Xiantian, ed. *Cultivation of Thoughts and Morality and Basics of Law*. Beijing: China Legal Institution, 2004.

Greenhalgh, Susan. *Cultivating Global Citizens: Population in the Rise of China*. Cambridge,: Harvard University Press, 2010.

Greif, Avner. "Cultural Beliefs and the Organization of Society: A Historical and Theoretical Reflection on Collectivist and Individualist Societies." *Journal of Political Economy* (1994) 912–50.

Griffiths, Michael B. *Consumers and Individuals in China: Standing Out, Fitting In*. London: Routledge, 2013.

"Guidance for Establishing a Party Branch." *Chinese Communist Party News*, June 30, 2014. http://dangjian.people.com.cn/GB/17388322.html/.

Han, Hongyun. "Trends in Educational Assortative Marriage in China from 1970 to 2000." *Demographic Research* 22 (2010) 733–70.

Havel, Vaclav. *The Power of the Powerless: Citizens against the State in Central-Eastern Europe*. London: Hutchinson, 1985.

————. *Open Letters: Selected Writings, 1965–1990*. New York: Vintage, 1992.

He, S. "Religious Infiltration into Universities and Preventative Measures." *Shenyang Normal University Newspaper: Social Sciences* 32.3 (2008) 109–111.

Hu, Jie. *Searching for Lin Zhao's Soul*, an online documentary circulated since 2004. http://www.chinasuntv.com/pro/ct3122.html/.

Hu, Ping. "Cynicism: A Spiritual Crisis in Today's China." *Beijng Spring* (November 2011). https://beijingspring.com/bj2/2010/280/20111121152948.htm

Hunter, Alan, and Kim-Kwong Chan. *Protestantism in Contemporary China*. Cambridge: Cambridge University Press, 1993.

Hunter, Jane. *The Gospel of Gentility*. New Haven: Yale University Press, 1984.

Hume, Tim. "Chinese Court Sentences Cuit Members to Death over McDonald's Killing." *CNN News*, Oct 13, 2014. http://www.cnn.com/2014/10/13/world/asia/china-eastern-lightning-death-sentence/.

Hsu, Immanuel C. Y. *The Rise of Modern China*. New York: Oxford University Press, 1975.

Hsu, Promise. "Why Beijing's Largest House Church Refuses to Stop Meeting Outdoors." *Christianity Today*, April 26, 2011. http://www.christianitytoday.com/ct/2011/aprilweb-only/beijinghousechurch.html/.

"If Party Members' Religious Conversions Went on Unchecked, There Would be Dire Consequences." *China Discipline and Inspection News* (*Zhongguo jijian jiancha bao*) (May 25, 2015). http://csr.mos.gov.cn/content/2016–04/30/content_33295.htm/.

James Fallows. "China's Great Leap Backward." *The Atlantic*, December 2016. https://www.theatlantic.com/magazine/archive/2016/12/chinas-great-leap-backward/505817/

James, William. *The Varieties of Religious Experience*. Cambridge: Harvard University Press, 1985.

Jason Kindopp. "Fragmented yet Defiant: Protestant Resilience under Chinese Communist Party Rule." In *God and Caesar in China: Policy Implications of Church-State Tensions*, edited by Jason Kindopp and Carol Lee Hamrin. Washington, DC: Brookings Institution, 2004.

Jin, Qiu. *The Culture of Power: the Lin Biao Incident in the Cultural Revolution*. Stanford: Stanford University Press, 1999.

Johnson, Ian. "Church-State Clash in China Coalesces Around a Toppled Spire." *New York Times*, May 29, 2014. http://www.nytimes.com/2014/05/30/world/asia/church-state-clash-in-china-coalesces-around-a-toppled-spire.html/.

————. "Decapitated Churches in China's Christian Heartland." *New York Times*, May 21, 2016. https://www.nytimes.com/2016/05/22/world/asia/china-christians-zhejiang.html

Keck, Zachary. "Why Is China Nationalizing Christianity?" *The Diplomat*, August 12, 2014. http://thediplomat.com/2014/08/why-is-china-nationalizing-christianity/.

Kleinman, Arthur. *What Really Matters: Living a Moral Life amidst Uncertainty and Danger*. New York: Oxford University Press, 2006.

Kong, W., and L. Zhang. "New Situations of Religious Infiltration into Universities." *Chongqing Socialist Academy Newspaper* 1 (2010) 59–61.

Kuyper, Abraham. *Lectures on Calvinism*. Peabody, MA: Hendrickson, 2008.

Lake, Roseann. "All the *Shengnu* (leftover) Ladies." *Salon*, March 1, 2012. http://www.salon.com/2012/03/12/all_the_shengnu_ladies/.

Lawrence, Susan V. "The Lions in the Communist Den." *Far Eastern Economic Review*, August 22, 2002, 24–27.

Lee, Joseph Tse-Hei. "Watchman Nee and the Little Flock Movement in Maoist China." *Church History* 74.1 (2005) 68–96.

Lee, Karen. "Legal Loophole Opens Up Chance for Homeschooling." *South China Morning Post* (Jan 7, 2014). http://www.scmp.com/news/hong-kong/article/1399191/legal-loophole-opens-chance-homeschooling/.

Leese, Daniel. *Mao Cult: Rhetoric and Ritual in China's Cultural Revolution*. New York: Cambridge University Press, 2013.

Leung, Ka-lun. *The Rural Churches of Mainland China since 1978*. Hong Kong: Alliance Bible Seminary, 1999.

Lewis, C.S. "Is Theology Poetry?" In *The Weight of Glory and Other Addresses*, 140. New York: MacMillan, 1965.

Levin, Dan. "A Chinese Education, for A Price." *The New York Times*, Nov 21, 2012. http://www.nytimes.com/2012/11/22/world/asia/in-china-schools-a-culture-of-bribery-spreads.html/.

Li, Jin and Li Ma. "The Belhar Confession and Social Transition in South Africa." *Caijing*, August 8, 2014. Online: http://magazine.caijing.com.cn/20140804/3670734.shtml/.

Li, Jingkang. *A Journey of Salvation* (*Mengen licheng*, in Chinese) An online Christian library. http://www.jidujiao.com/shuku/files/article/html/0/675/index.html/.

Li, Yi. "Changes in the Dating Market." *Sociological Study* 4 (2011) 122–36.

Lim, Louisa. *The People's Republic of Amnesia: Tiananmen Revisited*. New York: Oxford University Press, 2014.

Li, Zoe. "China Denies Church Demolition is Persecution of Christians." *CNN News*, May 2, 2014. http://www.cnn.com/2014/05/01/world/asia/china-church-demolished/.

Linz, Juan J. "Totalitarian and Authoritarian Regimes." In *The Handbook of Political Science*. Vol. 3, *Macropolitical Theory*, edited by Fred I. Greenstein and Nelson W. Polsby. Cambridge, MA: Addison-Wesley, 1975.

Liu, B., C. Hui, J. Hu, W. Yang, and X. Yu. "How Well Can Public Service Motivation Connect with Occupational Intention?" *International Review of Administrative Science* 77.1 (2011) 191–211.

Liu, Tongsu and Wang Yi. *Observing China's Urban House Churches* (*Guankan zhongguo chengshi jiating jiaohui*, in Chinese). Taipei: Christian Arts, 2012.

Liu, Xiaobo. "The Nobility of the Common People in the 1989 Movement." A Chinese overseas website *Boxun*. http://blog.boxun.com/hero/liuxb/156_1.shtml/.

Lodge, Carey. "Mega-church Demolished in China; Government Says Building Was Illegal." *Christianity Today*, April 29, 2014. http://www.christiantoday.com/article/government.demolishes.chinese.church/37093.htm.

Lu, Jiangyong, and Zhigang Tao. "Determinants of Entrepreneurial Activities in China." *Journal of Business Venturing* 25.3 (2010) 261–73.

Lu, Si. *Pragmatic Strategies and Power Relations in Disagreement: Chinese Culture in Higher Education*. Boca Raton: Universal, 2004.

Lutz, Jessie G. (ed.), *Christian Missions in China, Evangelists of What?* Boston: Heath, 1965.

Lyengar, Rishi. "China Has Imprisoned the Pastor of Its Largest Official Church." *Time*, January 31, 2016. http://time.com/4201870/china-hangzhou-pastor-gu-yuese-detained-crosses/.

Ma, Li and Jin Li, "Remaking the Civic Space: the Rise of Unregistered Protestantism and Civic Engagement in Urban China." In *Christianity in Chinese Public Life: Religion, Society, and the Rule of Law*, edited by Joel Carpenter and Kevin den Dulk. Palgrave Studies in Religion, Politics, and Policy. London: Palgrave Mac-Millan, 2014.

MacFarquhar, Roderick, John K. Fairbank, and Denis Crispin Twitchett. *The Cambridge History of China*. Cambridge: Cambridge University Press, 1978.

———. *The Origins of the Cultural Revolution*. Oxford: Oxford University Press, 1997.

Marquand, Robert. "In 'China's Jerusalem,' Party Members Must Now Profess Atheism." *Christian Science Monitor*, February 4, 2015. http://www.csmonitor.com/World/Asia-Pacific/2015/0204/In-China-s-Jerusalem-party-members-must-now-profess-atheism/.

Marsden, George M. *Fundamentalism and American Culture*. New York: Oxford University Press, 2006.

Mao, Zedong. *Collected Works*. Vol. 5 (in Chinese). Beijing: People's Publishing House, 1977.

McGrath, Alister. *A Life of John Calvin*, Chinese translation. Beijing: China Social Sciences, 2009.

The Middle Schools and Primary Schools Education Bureau. "Top 16 Beijing Middle Schools with Highest School Choice Fees." January 9, 2012. http://www.g12e.com/new/201201/yu2012010914450183095517.shtml/.

Miles, James A. R. *The Legacy of Tiananmen: China in Disarray*. Ann Arbor: University of Michigan Press, 1997.

Ministry of Education. "Implementing the China Dream." *Sina News*, September 16, 2013. http://news.sina.com.cn/c/2013-09-16/124128228334.shtml

Mukherjee, Andy. "Private Education in China is at Cusp of a Boom." *Bloomberg Press* news, March 13, 2007. http://www.sddt.com/News/article.cfm/.

Mullaney, Thomas. "Seeing for the State: The Role of Social Scientists in China's Ethnic Classification Project." *Asian Ethnicity* 11 (2010: 325–42.

Murong, Xuecun, "China's Television War on Japan." *New York Times*, Feb. 9, 2014. http://www.nytimes.com/2014/02/10/opinion/murong-chinas-television-war-on-japan.html/.

———. "Beijing's Propaganda Crisis," The Opinion Pages. *New York Times*, March 17, 2014. http://www.nytimes.com/2014/03/18/opinion/murong-beijings-propaganda-crisis.html/.

"National Postgraduate Entrance Exam of 2011 (2011 *Yanjiusheng Kaoshi*)." A Chinese test preparation website. http://kaoyan.eol.cn/zhengzhi_3978/20110214/t20110214_576351.shtml/.

National Workers' Union. "Strictly Guard against Infiltrations into Migrant Workers." *New Beijing News* (Xinjingbao), February 18, 2009. http://news.sina.com.cn/c/2009-02-18/024517234816.shtml/.

Nee, Victor, and Peng Lian. "Sleeping with the Enemy: A Dynamic Model of Declining Political Commitment in State Socialism." *Theory and Society* 23 (1994) 253–296.

"New Signs that China is Scrutinizing Foreign NGOs." *New York Times*, June 27, 2014. https://sinosphere.blogs.nytimes.com/2014/06/27/new-signs-that-china-is-scrutinizing-foreign-ngos/

"New Rules Harden Communist Party's Control over Religions." *UCA News*, September 25, 2015. http://www.ucanews.com/news/in-china-new-rules-harden-communist-partys-control-over-religions/74324/.

Qi, Yaqiang and Jianlin Niu. "Dating and Marriage in China: Trends and Changes since 1949." *Sociological Study* 1 (2012) 106–29.

Oster,Shai. "In China, 1600 People Die Every Day from Working Too Hard." *Bloomberg News*, July 3, 2014. https://www.bloomberg.com/news/articles/2014-07-03/in-china-white-collar-workers-are-dying-from-overwork

Ostergaard, Clemens Stubbe. "Governance and the Political Challenge of the Falun Gong." *Governance in China* (2004) 207–25.

"Painless Abortion Advertisements Misled Teenage Abortions." *Xinhua News*, March 1, 2014. http://www.chinanews.com/sh/2014/03-01/5898762.shtml/.

"Parent Meddling Makes for Unmerry Marriages in China: Report." *The Wall Street Journal* blog article, February 11, 2015. https://blogs.wsj.com/chinarealtime/2015/02/11/new-study-casts-skeptical-eye-on-parental-matchmaking-in-china/

Pew Research Center. "Religion and Public Life Project: Religion in China on the Eve of the 2008 Beijing Olympics." http://www.pewforum.org/2008/05/01/religion-in-china-on-the-eve-of-the-2008-beijing-olympics/.

Philips, Tom. "China Accused of Anti-Christian Campaign as Church Demolition Begins." *The Telegraph*, April 28, 2014. http://www.telegraph.co.uk/news/worldnews/asia/china/10792386/China-accused-of-anti-Christian-campaign-as-church-demolition-begins.html/.

———. "Thousand Christians Forced from Church as Demolition Campaign Spreads." *The Telegraph*, May 19, 2014. http://www.telegraph.co.uk/news/worldnews/asia/china/10841738/Thousand-Christians-forced-from-church-as-demolition-campaign-spreads.html/.

———. "China Arrests Christians Who Opposed Removals of Crosses." *The Guardian*, August 27, 2015. https://www.theguardian.com/world/2015/aug/27/china-arrests-christians-opposed-cross-removals-zhejiang

———. "China Universities Must Become Communist Party 'Strongholds,' Says Xi Jinping." *The Guardian*, Dec. 9, 2016. https://www.theguardian.com/world/2016/dec/09/china-universities-must-become-communist-party-strongholds-says-xi-jinping

"Potential of the Chinese Dream." *China Daily*, March 26, 2014. http://usa.chinadaily.com.cn/opinion/2014–03/26/content_17378648.htm/.

"Pummelling the Little Platoons: The Communist Party Wants to Squeeze Civil Society. That Would Be Unwise as well as Unjust." *The Economist*, August 22, 2015. http://www.economist.com/news/leaders/21661665-communist-party-wants-squeeze-civil-society-would-be-unwise-well/.

"Public Petition on the Anti-Constitutional Nature of the Demonstration Law." *Human Rights in China Biweekly*, January 22, 2014. http://biweekly.hrichina.org/article/14100/.

Pye, Lucian W. *The Spirit of Chinese Politics*. Cambridge: Harvard University Press, 1992.

———. "Civility, Social Capital, and Civil Society: three powerful concepts for explaining Asia." *Journal of Interdisciplinary History* 29 (1999) 766–69.

Reed, Gay Garland. "Moral/Political Education in the People's Republic of China: Learning through Role Models." *Journal of Moral Education* 24.2 (1995) 99–111.

"Revealed: Life Inside China's 'Red Army' Schools." *South China Morning Post*, February 13, 2017. http://www.scmp.com/news/china/society/article/2070357/revealed-life-inside-chinas-red-army-schools/.

Searle-White, Joshua. *The Psychology of Nationalism*. New York: Palgrave MacMillan, 2001.

"Series of Cases in China Bring School Sex Abuse Out of Shadows." *Los Angeles Times*, June 1, 2013. http://articles.latimes.com/2013/jun/01/world/la-fg-china-child-sex-abuse-20130602/.

Schurmann, Franz. *Ideology and Organization in Communist China*. Berkeley: University of California Press, 1966.

Schwarzmantel, John. "Nationalism and Fragmentation since 1989." In *The Blackwell Companion to Political Sociology*, edited by Kate Nash and Alan Scott. Hoboken, NJ: Wiley, 2008.

Scott, James C. *Weapons of the Weak: Everyday Forms of Peasant Resistance*. New Haven: Yale University Press, 2008.

Shen, Ying. "So Unexpected to See More Chinese Believe in Christianity Now." *Southern Weekly*, July 10, 2009.

Simmel, Georg. "Fundamental Problems of Sociology." In *The Sociology of Georg Simmel*, edited by K. H. Wolff. Glencoe, IL: Free, 1964.

Skocpol, Theda. *States and Social Revolutions: A Comparative Analysis of France, Russia, and China*. Cambridge: Cambridge University Press, 1979.

Solomon, Richard H. *Mao's Revolution and the Chinese Political Culture*. Berkeley: University of California Press, 1971.

Song, Tian Zhen. *A Recovered Diary: Extract of a Song in Shangjie's Diary*. Hong Kong: Xuandao, 2006.

Southam, Hazel. "Converted after China's Earthquake," *Times*, April 20, 2013. http://www.thetimes.co.uk/tto/faith/article3744141.ece?CMP=OTH-gnws-standard-2013_04_19/.

"Sons of Heaven: Inside China's Fast-growing NGO." *The Economist*, Oct. 2, 2008. http://www.economist.com/node/12342509/.

Spegele, Brian. "China's Banned Churches Defy Regime." *The Wall Street Journal*, July 28, 2011. https://www.wsj.com/articles/SB10001424052702304567604576451913744126214

Smith, James K.A. *Letters to a Young Calvinist*. Grand Rapids: Brazos. 2010.

Smith, Steve A. "Talking Toads and Chinless Ghosts: The Politics of 'Superstitious' Rumors in the PRC, 1961–1965." *The American Historical Review* 111 (2006) 405–27.

Spence, Jonathan D. *The Search for Modern China*. New York: Norton, 1991.

Stanley, Brian. "Introduction: Christianity and the End of Empire." In *Missions, Nationalism and the End of Empire*, edited by Brian Stanley and Alaine M. Low. Grand Rapids: Eerdmans, 2003.

Stark, Rodney. *The Rise of Christianity: A Sociologist Reconsiders History*. Princeton: Princeton University Press, 1996.

Stevens, Stuart. *Night Train to Turkistan: Modern Adventures along China's Ancient Silk Road.* New York: Atlantic Monthly, 1988.

Strand, David. "Protest in Beijing: Civil Society and Public Sphere in China." *Problems of Communism* 39 (1990) 1–19.

"Surveillance Cameras Installed in Churches." *China Digital Times*, April 2017. http://chinadigitaltimes.net/2017/04/churches-zhejiang-required-install-surveillance-cameras/.

Teets, Jessica C. and Marta Jagusztyn. "The Evolution of a Collaborative Governance Model." In *NGO Governance and Management in China*, edited by Reza Hasmath and Jennifer Y. J. Hsu. Vol. 48. London: Routledge, 2015.

Tilly, Charles. *Identities, Boundaries, and Social ties.* Boulder: Paradigm, 2007.

Tracy, Kate. "China Lifts High the Cross (Right off Dozens of Churches)." *Christianity Today*, May 30, 2014. http://www.christianitytoday.com/gleanings/2014/may/china-lifts-high-cross-right-off-dozens-churches-zhejiang.html/.

Thompson, Mark R. "To Shoot or not to Shoot: Post-totalitarianism in China and Eastern Europe." *Comparative Politics* 34 (2001) 63–83.

Thomas, George. "Radical Revival Falls on China's State-Controlled Churches." *CBN News*, February 11, 2016. http://www1.cbn.com/cbnnews/world/2016/February/An-Unexpected-Move-of-God-in-Communist-Controlled-China/.

"Uncivil Society: A New Draft Law Spooks Foreign Not-For-Profit Groups Working in China." *The Economist* (August 22, 2015). http://www.economist.com/news/china/21661819-new-draft-law-spooks-foreign-not-profit-groups-working-china-uncivil-society/.

"US Condemns Zhang Kai's Forced 'Confession' on Chinese State TV." *BBC News*, February 27, 2016. http://www.bbc.com/news/world-asia-china-35676223/.

Vala, Carsten T. and Kevin J. O'Brien. "Attraction without Networks: Recruiting Strangers to Unregistered Protestantism in China." *Mobilization: An International Quarterly* 12 (2007) 79–94.

Van Sant, Shannon. "Church Demolition Highlights China's Religion Policy." *Voice of America*, May 13, 2014. http://www.voanews.com/content/church-demolition-highlights-chinas-religion-policy-/1913487.html/.

Veg, Sebastian. "China's Political Spectrum under Xi Jinping." *The Diplomat*, August 11, 2014. http://thediplomat.com/2014/08/chinas-political-spectrum-under-xi-jinping/.

Wacker, Gudrun. "Beijing is Haunted by the Olympic Ghosts." *SWP Comments*, April 9, 2008, 1.

Walder, Andrew George. "The Party Elite and China's Trajectory of Change." *China: An International Journal* 2 (2004) 189–209.

Wang, Alice. "Senior Pastor of China's First Mega-Church Removed, Official Announced." *China Christian Daily*, January 22, 2016. http://chinachristiandaily.com/2016-01-22/church/senior-pastor-of-china-s-first-mega-church-removed-from-from-office_450.html/.

Wang, Shaoguang. *Failure of Charisma: The Cultural Revolution in Wuhan.* New York: Oxford University Press, 1995.

"Warning over Religious Believers in Chinese Communist Party Ranks." *Radio Free Asia*, May 25, 2015. http://www.rfa.org/english/news/china/china-religion-05252015112309.html/.

Watts, Jonathan. "Violence Flares as the Chinese Rage at Japan." *The Guardian*, April 16, 2005. https://www.theguardian.com/world/2005/apr/17/china.japan

Weber, Max. *Economy and Society*. Edited by Guenther Roth and Claus Wittich. Berkeley: University of California Press, 1978.

Wielander, Gerda. *Christian Values in Communist China*. London: Routledge, 2013.

Whyte, Martin K. and William Parish. *Urban Life in Contemporary China*. Chicago: University of Chicago Press, 1984.

Woodberry, Robert D. "The Missionary Roots of Liberal Democracy." *American Political Science Review* 106 (2012) 244–74.

Wong, Edward. "Repackaging the Revolutionary Classics of China." *New York Times*, June 29, 2011. http://www.nytimes.com/2011/06/30/world/asia/30redsong.html/.

Wong, Edward. "Clampdown in China Restricts 7000 Foreign Organizations." *New York Times*, April 28, 2016. https://www.nytimes.com/2016/04/29/world/asia/china-foreign-ngo-law.html

Wu, Yuwen. "The Abuse of China's 'Left-behind' Children." *BBC News*, August 12, 2013. http://www.bbc.com/news/world-asia-china-23628090/.

Wright, Teresa, and Teresa Zimmerman-Liu. "Atheist Political Activists Turned Protestants: Religious Conversion among Chinese Dissidents." *Journal of Church and State* 57 (2015) 268–88.

"Xi Calls for Improved Religious Work." *Xinhua News*, April 23, 2016. http://news.xinhuanet.com/english/2016-04/23/c_135306092.htm/.

Xie, Xiaheng. "Religion and Modernity in China: Who Is Joining the Three-Self Church and Why." *Journal of Church and State* 52 (2010) 74–93.

Xu, Dingxin. "The Key to Making a Success of Jinling is to Maintain a Correct Educational Policy and Theological Direction." *Jinling Theological Journal* 1 (1999) 24–25.

Yan, Yunxiang. *Private Life under Socialism: Love, Intimacy, and Family Change in a Chinese Village, 1949–1999*. Stanford: Stanford University Press, 2003.

Yang, Ching-Kun. *Religion in Chinese Society*. Berkeley: University of California Press, 1961.

Yang, Mingdao. "Dragon Leaders or Older Sons." A *China Partnership* blog article. http://www.chinapartnership.org/blog/2017/5/dragon-leaders-or-older-sons-how-the-doctrine-of-grace-alone-impacts-chinese-pastors/.

Yang, Fenggang. "Lost in the Market, Saved at McDonald's: Conversion to Christianity in Urban China." *Journal for the Scientific Study of Religion* 44 (2005) 424.

———. "Differentiating Religion, Superstition and Cults." *Gong Shi Online* (a Chinese academic website). http://www.21ccom.net/articles/zgyj/ggzhc/article_20140627108481.html/.

Yang, Kelly. "How the New SAT Test will Instill Values into Impressionable Young Chinese Minds." *South China Morning Post*, August 19, 2014. http://www.scmp.com/comment/article/1576794/how-new-sat-test-will-instil-us-values-impressionable-young-chinese-minds.

Yang, Rae. *Spider Eaters: A Memoir*. Berkeley: University of California Press, 2013.

Yang, Xiaokai. "On Christianity and Democracy." http://blog.boxun.com/hero/yangxk/40_1.shtml/.

———. *My Second Testimony*. http://www.cclw.net/withess/5–05/jybrssd.htm/.

Yang, Xiaokai, and Susan McFadden. *Captive Spirits: Prisoners of the Cultural Revolution*. Oxford: Oxford University Press, 1997.

Yang, Xianhui. *Jiabiangou Memories (Jiabiangou Jishi* in Chinese). Guangzhou: Huacheng, 2008.

Yuan, Zhiming. "The 'June Fourth' Generation Today." *Word & World* 17 (1997) 192–95.

Yuen, Lotus. "Communist Party Membership Is Still the Ultimate Resume Booster: How China Maintains Interest in Its Ruling Party, Even as Communism Itself Fades Away." *The Atlantic*, May 29, 2013. http://www.theatlantic.com/china/archive/2013/05/communist-party-membership-is-still-the-ultimate-resume-booster/276347/.

Zhao, Dingxin. "An Angle on Nationalism in China Today: Attitudes among Beijing Students after Belgrade 1999." *The China Quarterly* 172 (2002) 885–905.

Zhao, Suisheng. "A State-led Nationalism: The Patriotic Education Campaign in Post-Tiananmen China." *Communist and Post-Communist Studies* 31 (1998) 287–302.

Zhao, Suisheng. "The Olympics and Chinese Nationalism." *China Security* 4.3 (2008) 48–57.

Zhao, Tianen and Wanfang Zhuang. *A Contemporary History of Christianity in China: 1949–1997*. Taipei: Zhongfu, 2010.

Zhao, Xiao. "Market Economies with Churches." A Chinese business website. http://www.danwei.org/business/churches_and_the_market_econom.php/.

"Zhejiang's De-crossing Movement Is Splitting the Three-Self Church." *Mingjing News* (August 25, 2014). http://mingjingnews.com/MIB/news/news.aspx/

Zhou, Jiacai, Zhao Kuangwei & Wei Xiaolei. "Encourage and Support Protestantism in Strengthening the Construction of Theological Thinking." *Explorations in Religious Work* (2008) 75.

Zhou, Wei. "Liberalism and China's Churches." *China Source Quarterly* 17.2 (2015) 5–7.

Zhu, Weiqun. "Communist Members Should Not Convert into Religions." *Qiushi* (Dec. 16, 2011). http://21ccom.net/articles/zgyj/xzmj/article_2011121750497.html/.

Zhu, Weiqun. "CCP Members Should Not Believe in Religions." *Chinese Communist Party News*, Dec. 16, 2011. http://theory.people.com.cn/GB/16625667.html/.

Zuo, Jiping. 1991. "Political Religion: The Case of the Cultural Revolution in China." *Sociology of Religion* 52 (1991) 99–110.

Zylstra, Sarah. "After Removing 400 Crosses, China Proposes Where Churches Can Put Them Instead." *Christianity Today*, May 7, 2015. http://www.christianitytoday.com/gleanings/2015/may/after-removing-400-crosses-china-proposes-zhejiang-wenzhou.html/.

———. "Young, Restless, and Reformed in China." *The Gospel Coalition*, March 27, 2017. https://www.thegospelcoalition.org/article/young-restless-and-reformed-in-china/.

Index

Abortion, 44, 136, 140, 145, 146
Aikman, David, 98, 136
Anti-Christian movement, 94
Anti-western, 100
Atheism, 26, 49, 87, 90, 111, 157, 162,
184
Augustine, 105, 122, 177, 178
Arminianism, Arminian, 121, 126,
132

Back to God Ministries International,
52
Bays, Daniel, ix, 51, 77
Back to Jerusalem, 103
Bellah, Robert, xvi, 177
Beijing, xv, 5, 7–8, 11–12, 34, 41, 70,
72–73, 76, 90, 96, 101, 104, 110,
120, 122–24, 138, 152, 157, 164,
167–69, 172, 180
Beijing Olympics, 96, 104
Bible, xv, 1, 8–11, 16, 22–24, 27, 43,
45–46, 50–56, 59–60, 62, 64, 66,
71–72, 77, 79, 85, 97, 111–13,
116, 118, 121, 128, 131, 136, 141,
156, 162, 165–66, 171–72
Buddhism, 68, 111, 125
Business as mission, 52

Calvinism, 119–27, 129–34
Campus Crusade for Christ, 54, 56,
140
Campus fellowship, 55, 57, 82, 90, 141
Catholic, xii, 2, 5–6, 67, 113
CCTV (China Central Television), 38,
97–98, 102,

Censorship, xiii, xiv, 33, 48, 61, 96–98,
110, 177
Civil society, xii, 4, 36, 80, 81, 109,
125
Chao, Charles, 122
China Inland Mission, 5, 24, 67
CCP, (Chinese Communist Party), 4,
32, 34, 82–95, 99–100, 104, 184
Chengdu, xv, 65–69, 71–72, 74,
76–78, 80–81, 102, 115–17, 120,
145, 169, 180–82
Chow, Alexander, 125
Christian education, xvii, 127, 158–62
Christian identity, xii, 50–51, 57, 59,
85, 88, 156, 170
Church openness, 73–74, 76
Church switching, 76
College Entrance Exam (Gaokao), 40,
99, 113, 156, 160, 166
Communist Youth League, 25, 135
Confucianism, Confucian, Confucius,
47, 96, 131, 134
Congregation, xi, 60, 64, 68, 72, 78,
122, 128, 130, 133, 136, 142, 165,
167, 170, 172
Consumerism, 136, 175
Conversion, 2, 9, 13, 16, 18, 19,
23–25, 29, 32, 33, 35, 37, 39–40,
43, 47, 49, 54–55, 61, 66, 69, 85,
89, 102, 107, 109, 111, 124–25,
128–29, 142–43, 157, 183
Corruption, 28, 35, 44, 91, 97, 151,
175
Counter-revolutionary, 7–8, 16–17,
19, 38, 44

Cultural Christians, 122
Cultural Revolution, xvi, 8, 10, 16, 20, 24–26, 33–36, 38, 40, 46, 51, 121, 152, 166, 175, 177

Danwei, 8, 17, 24, 66, 91, 95, 137
Denominationalism, denominational, denomination, 64, 67, 79, 120–21, 133, 161, 185
Demographic, 68, 130, 136, 148, 167
Demolition, xi, 31, 44, 163
Demonstration, 40, 47, 95–96, 101, 102, 105, 166
Demoralized, demoralization, 32, 43, 151, 153, 175
Detention, 7, 11–12
Ding, Guangxun, 87
Disillusionment, 32–35, 38–40, 43–44, 48, 105, 111, 117, 125
Doyle, Wright, 131, 136

Ecclesiology, 74, 78, 125
Education, 1, 4–6, 21, 29, 33, 38, 41, 47–48, 61, 69, 78, 84, 88–89, 91, 93, 95, 99, 102–5, 110, 115, 117, 127, 134, 137, 149–51, 153–62, 165, 172, 183, 185
Evangelism, 3, 5, 57–58, 63, 80, 110, 112, 116, 169–70
Ethics, 87, 101, 136, 145

Falungong, 99
Fanqiang (to circumvent Internet censorship), 98
Foreign Christians, 1, 4–5, 10, 13, 27, 50, 52, 54, 56, 63, 67, 105, 121, 167
Fulton, Brent, x, 134
Fudaoyuan (Party Counselor), 82

Globalization, 95
Greif, Avner, 79
Guangming Ribao (Light Daily), 84

Havel, Vaclav, 15, 17
House church, xiii, 27–28, 39, 42–43, 49, 56–58, 62–63, 65–66, 72–73, 75–76, 79–80, 85, 98, 103, 107, 111, 119, 129–30, 143, 167–69, 172–73, 185–87
Hukou, 4

Imperialism, imperialist, 4, 26, 51, 94, 100
Imprisoned, imprisonment, 1–3, 5–6, 8–11, 13, 17–19, 24, 26–27, 36, 42, 67, 77, 84, 175, 178
Infiltration, 4, 88, 94, 100, 164, 174
Informants, 45, 56–57, 90
Ideology, 1, 3, 10, 16–17, 20–21, 29, 32–33, 35, 39, 48–49, 86, 88, 91, 94–95, 99, 111, 125, 153, 162, 183–84
Intellectuals, 2, 22, 35–36, 61, 63, 70, 122–23, 125–27, 129, 139
Internet, xi, 48, 50, 61, 66, 96–98, 156, 164

Jen, Isaac, 52
Jerusalem of China, x, 163
Jiabiangou (a notorious labor camp), 21–22, 24
Jinling Union Theological Seminary, 113, 165–66, 187
Korea, Korean, 56
Korean War, 4, 94
Kuomingtang (KMT), 4, 19
Kung, Pin-mei, 6
Kuyper, Abraham, 119–20, 124–25

Labor camp, 6–7, 10, 17, 21–22, 24, 177
Lenin, Leninism, 9, 84, 184
Liberalism, 55, 125–26, 129, 134
Lin, Zhao, 2
Little Flock (Chinese Local Assembly or *Xiaoqun*), 5–6, 8–9, 67, 77, 127, 129, 181
Liu, Xiaofeng, 60

Mao, Maoist, Maoism, xii, 2–3, 5, 9, 19–20, 22, 25, 33–34, 82, 84, 91, 95, 119, 137, 141, 152, 177
Marriage, 7, 17, 21, 25, 103, 110–11, 135–39, 141, 143, 147–49, 173

Marx, Marxism, 9, 18, 30, 38, 44, 84, 89–91, 95, 100, 153, 156, 183–84
Mass conversion, 24, 32, 40, 124
Materialism, 33, 117, 156–57, 162, 175, 183
Media, 5, 11, 35–36, 61, 66, 84, 88, 93, 96–98, 100, 102–5, 111, 148
Migrants, migrant workers, 67–68, 107, 110–11, 118, 145, 173
Migration, 16, 69, 110
Miracle, 22–23, 146, 171
Mission, missionary, missional, 3, 50–51, 54, 56, 58, 62–63, 67–68, 77, 87, 103, 107, 110, 112–13, 115–16, 118, 121, 124, 131, 134, 143, 164–65, 167

Nanjing, 102, 166
Nationalism, 94–95, 99, 103–5, 175
Navigators, 54, 56
Nee, Watchman, 3, 5–6, 121
Neighborhood committee (*Juweihui*), 151
Netizen, x, 87
Networks, 4–5, 9, 14, 24, 52, 57, 67–68, 71–72, 75, 80, 97, 105, 109, 159–60, 170–71, 179, 182
Nobel Prize, 2, 36
NGO, 69, 71, 107–15, 116–18

One-child policy, 136, 144–45
Open Doors, 27, 52
Opportunism, 44, 49, 86, 110
Outdoor worship, 12, 72, 74
Overseas, 10, 37, 39, 57, 85, 90, 94, 139, 143, 161, 164, 186

Party-state, xii, 17, 27, 29–30, 33, 35, 37, 87
Patriotism, 41, 93, 95–96, 98, 101–2, 105, 151
Pentecostalism, 171
Persecution, 1, 9, 13, 18, 23–24, 26, 28–30, 33, 51, 63, 66, 68, 76, 80–81, 98, 121, 124, 129–30, 177
Personnel dossier (*dang'an*), 84

Pietist theology, Pietism, 5, 63, 77, 80, 116, 121, 124, 127, 130–31
Professionalization, 162
Propaganda, 5–6, 17, 19–20, 24, 26, 32, 34, 38, 49, 67, 84, 96–99, 103–5, 165
Property, 16, 34, 178
Public Security Bureau, 7
Public school, 150–59, 161
Publishing, 12, 60–61

Qi Gong (Life Energy Cultivation), 32

Red Army, 150–51
Red Guard, 1, 10, 20, 34
Reformed, 78–79, 120, 122, 124, 126–28, 130, 132–34, 181
Regulations, 66, 69, 80, 164–65
Relocation, 73, 75
Rural church, 10, 27, 97, 117

Secular, secularization, 29, 62, 102, 112, 116, 124, 134, 137–38, 149, 156, 172
Sent-down youth movement, 9, 34–35
Shanghai, 5–7, 9, 16, 55, 57, 65–81, 99, 101, 113, 133, 138–39, 166, 169, 180–82
Shenzhen, 173
Shouwang Church, 11–13, 72, 76
Sichuan earthquake, 68, 71, 74, 106–7
Small group, 35, 53, 56, 73
Social order, 4–5
Social hostility, xii, 28, 92, 96, 101, 156–57
Socio-historical analysis, xvi, 176
Spence, Jonathan, 4–5
Spring Festival (*chunjie*), 97, 138–39, 141
State Administration of Religions Affairs (SARA), 61, 174
State-owned, 12, 85, 89, 98, 151
Sung, John, or John Song, 3, 121

Totalitarian, totalitarianism, post-totalitarian, xii, 17–18, 24, 28–29

Theology, theological, 3, 5, 37, 43, 49, 59–61, 63–64, 72, 76–81, 87, 94, 103, 105, 112, 116, 118–34, 162, 164–65, 169, 171–72, 174–78, 181–82, 186
Three-self churches, Three-self Patriotic Movement, 5, 9, 18, 22, 26–28, 37, 50, 53–56, 62–63, 67–68, 87, 94, 96, 98, 100, 123, 141, 143, 163, 165–74, 180, 185
Thought work, 17, 25
Tiananmen, 31–37, 40–45, 47–49, 83–83, 126, 129, 152, 166, 177
Tong, Stephen, 122
Two Councils (*Lianghui*), 164, 169

United Front, 26–27, 90
United States, 29, 57, 59, 90, 100, 139, 143, 154, 155, 160–61, 168, 173
Urban church, 60–63, 66, 79, 89, 98, 106, 112, 117–18, 120, 123, 129–30, 132, 136–37, 139–40, 147–48, 158–59, 171–72, 176

Urbanization, urbanized, urbanism, 66, 68, 106, 124

Wang, Mingdao, 3
Weber, Max, 20, 121, 133
Wenzhou, 67, 70, 90–91, 120–21, 133, 156, 163–64, 183
Worldview, 2, 15–19, 22, 29–30, 60, 77, 124, 126, 158, 161, 183
Woodberry, Robert, 61
Wuhan, 102, 168, 170

Xi, Jinping, x, 82, 89–90, 93, 102, 108, 164, 174, 176
Xiaomin, 104
Xu, Ben, 61

Yang, Fenggang, x, 57, 186
Yang, Xiaokai, 1–2
Yi Guan Dao (Way of Basic Unity Society), 5

Zhejiang, x, 163–64, 168, 174, 183